D1518398

ARMY, STATE AND SOCIETY IN ITALY, 1870–1915

Army, State and Society in Italy, 1870–1915

John Gooch

Reader in History
University of Lancaster

St. Martin's Press   New York

First published in the United States of America in 1989

Printed in China

ISBN 0-312-02523-8

LIBRARY OF CONGRESS
Library of Congress Cataloging-in-Publication Data
Gooch, John.
Army, state and society in Italy, 1870-1915/John Gooch.
      p.   cm.
Bibliography: p.
Includes index.
ISBN 0-312-02523-8 -$35.00 (est.)
1. Italy—History, Military.   2. Italy—History—1870-1915.
3. Italy. Esercito—History.   I. Title.
DG484.G66 1989   88-23368
945.09—dc19   CIP

For Ann

Contents

Foreword

I am grateful to the following institutions for financing the research on which this book is based: The British Academy, which appointed me one of its founding Wolfson Fellows; the British Academy Small Grants Fund; the William Waldorf Astor Foundation; the Wolfson Foundation; and the Senate Research Fund of the University of Lancaster.

I am especially indebted to general Rinaldo Cruccu, *cap'ufficio* of the Ufficio Storico dello Stato Maggiore dell'Esercito when I arrived on the doorstep of that institution in 1976, for his help and warm friendship. He and his successors, General Oreste Bovio and General Pierluigi Bertinaria, have patiently answered my many requests – in person and by post. The staff of the Ufficio Storico have been unfailingly courteous; and I am particularly grateful to Major Alfredo Terrone and Major Ferdinando Frattolillo who offered assistance, sympathy and cups of espresso coffee – all of which were gratefully received.

I also wish to acknowledge the help and assistance of the Director and staff of the Ufficio Storico della Marina; the Director and Staff of the Archivio Centrale di Stato; Professoressa Emilia Morelli, Dr Alberto Maria Arpino and the staff of the Istituto per la Storia del Risorgimento; and the staffs of the Biblioteca Nazionale Centrale, the Biblioteca Militare Centrale (Ministero della Difesa), and the Biblioteca dell'Istituto per la Storia Moderna e Contemporanea. In England, the staff of the Public Record Office showed their customary efficiency.

In Rome, my domestic path was smoothed by the late Aldo Mariotti and Carol Mariotti; Michael and June Morgan; Guido and Margherita Renzi; dottoressa Alessandra Rinelli; and Dr and Mrs David Whitehouse.

This book is built on a foundation of Italian scholarship. I have benefitted greatly from the works of Professor Giorgio Rochat, Professor Massimo Mazzetti, Professor Lucio Ceva, Professor Fortunato Minnitti and Professor Piero Del Negro. An earlier version of this manuscript was read and reviewed by Professor Brian Sullivan of Yale University, Professor MacGregor Knox of the University of Rochester and Professor Paul Halpern of Florida State University. It was immeasurably improved as a consequence. I am also grateful to Mr Richard Oliver Collin and Dr Nicola Labanca for providing information and help. Successive drafts were typed with great skill and stamina by Mrs Rosemary Fenton, Mrs Barbara Atkins, and Mrs Linda Persson.

A large part of this book was written while I was a Secretary of the Navy Senior Research Fellow at the US Naval War College, Newport, RI.

John Gooch
Ellel, 1987

Introduction

'I am lucky, and under me, even in Africa, everything must go well.'
General Oreste Baratieri, 1895
'Let us dare, but let us dare quickly.'
General Alberto Pollio, 1911
'When the cannons begin to sound, everything will fall into place.'
Marshall Rodolfo Graziani, 1940

Modern Italy has a low military reputation. Defeated twice in 1848–49, saved by the French in 1859, defeated again in 1866 but saved by Prussia, smashed in Abyssinia in 1896 and unable to conquer Libya in 1911–12, her entry into the World War in 1915 looks doomed by track-record alone. After two years of war she came to the brink of military collapse in October 1917 and only began to score victories in the dying days of November 1918. Twenty-five years later, in September 1943, after an inglorious and incompetently managed war, she collapsed entirely. Only the Ethiopian war of 1935–36 and the Spanish Civil War stand on the credit side of the balance – and they are not shining laurels.

Along with military inadequacy has gone a diplomatic acquisitiveness which generally outran Italy's military capabilities. Bismarck remarked disparagingly that Italy had a 'large appetite and rotten teeth', and, when an Italian delegation turned up in Berlin in 1878 hoping for territorial gain, he asked sarcastically, 'What, have they lost another battle?' Italian diplomats were well-enough aware of their country's military deficiencies not to gamble with force in Europe between 1866 and 1915. They did gamble in Africa, and their soldiers failed them. In examining Italian military policy between 1870 and 1915, I have partly sought to explain those failures. In so doing I have had an eye to the longer story, so that this analysis also looks beyond cause and effect as explanations of particular events and towards the defining characteristics of the army as an Italian institution. In less grand terminology, this book is a Bismarckian dental examination.

To date little has been published in English on the Italian army during these years, so that narrative is necessary before analysis means much.[1] The Italian literature has only recently moved from establishing facts to making analytical propositions. In keeping with the need to dress the Italian monarchy in robes of martial splendour, much pre-1914 writing concentrated on glorifying the role of the crown and concealing military or diplomatic incompetence. During the Fascist years a number of important memoirs and the first reliable factual narratives appeared. Much of this military history was officially sponsored by the war ministry and written by serving or retired officers. Naturally enough, they abstained from dissecting the inner workings of the army and instead criticised individual soldiers and blamed the politicians.

After the Second World War a group of historians led by Piero Pieri wrote the authoritative military history of the Risorgimento. Their narratives are models of professional scholarship; but, inhibited by temperament and political persuasion and uninfluenced by the social sciences, they too forebore to attempt an institutional analysis of the Italian army. Such an analysis has appeared over the last twenty-five years, mostly from the pen of the Marxist historian Giorgio Rochat. For Rochat it is axiomatic that the Italian army was devised and operated as an instrument of domestic repression. In Liberal Italy its task was to maintain social equilibrium and political order by defending the state against its internal enemies – the democratic left, popular revolt and Catholic reaction. This mission determined Italy's military structure, producing a system of national conscription inspired by fears of popular insurrection and by the need to control a country whose unification was not yet fully assured.[2] The army, Rochat suggests, accepted this task with alacrity and pleasure: thus, as a repressive force, it conducted government policy in 1898 'with enthusiasm'.[3] Reality, however, was not quite so clear cut.

Interpreting the function of the Italian army in this way can, of itself, explain professional incompetence. At one level, a system of conscription driven by social necessity was, by the same token, militarily grossly inefficient. At another, since the defence of Italy against external foes was very much a secondary consideration the army tackled the problem half-heartedly. Rochat and his collaborator, Giulio Massobrio, have indeed suggested that the army viewed its task as no more than defending Italy against France long enough to allow British or German intervention, thereafter hoping to gain a political solution.[4] This view, as we shall see, reflects only a partial truth.

While analyses of the social role of the army dominate recent Italian military history, its inner workings have been much less studied. Historians of both Left and Right agree that, despite its vicissitudes, the Italian officer corps on the eve of the First World War was notably compact and dedicated, its morale high and its command-capacity good.[5] This happy circumstance was in part due to Italy's having hoisted herself towards the pinnacle of German 'scientific' soldiering after 1882, when she created the post of chief of the general staff. Thereafter successive ministers of war – who were almost always generals – gradually relinquished their powers to intervene on technical and operational issues, allowing the chief of staff ever greater autonomy as they turned to managing the military budget.[6] This invites the supposition that there was nothing very much structurally wrong with the army by 1914 and, therefore, that mistakes and misfortunes can be explained by unique and unfortunate combinations of circumstances. Again, this view is open to doubt.

Any historian must first map his ground before he can interpret its contours. In this case establishing the facts is particularly difficult. The absence of any of the records of the Italian war ministry, save for a handful of random documents at the Archivio Centrale di Stato, makes the reconstruction of military policy an awkward task. Assessing the role of the crown in any detail is harder still. The only available documents – those of the Ministry of the Royal Household – are strikingly discreet, so that any propositions about royal influence must be especially tentative. Fortunately a variety of other sources make up for these lacunae.

In looking for broader trends as well as explaining particular events I have found the literature of civil–military relations useful in framing questions, but remarkably unhelpful in providing answers. For one thing, as William Fuller has rightly noted, much of it is devoted to trying to explain why soldiers do or do not intervene to control national politics.[7] As the Italian case shows, armies can live active political lives on a number of levels without ever trying to change governments. For another, classic civil-military theory seems to confirm the historian's sense of the uniqueness of his subject. Liberal Italy, at least until the end of the nineteenth century, was characterised by a conservative ideology, low military professionalism and a degree of military power which, whether labelled 'low' or 'high', makes it, according to Samuel Huntington, a type of civil-military relations 'unlikely to occur except in the most unusual circumstances'.[8]

There is some benefit in following up the proposition that the character of the state determines the character of the military. Italy at Unification was a poor and backward country. The bulk of the population was made up of landless or tied peasants who lived in abject poverty and ignorance: a survey in 1864 suggested that of a population of 26 000 000 only 12 per cent were literate. Education was always a privilege of the minority: not until 1877 were children legally obliged to go to school until the age of nine, and at the turn of the century fewer than five in every thousand attended a secondary school. Loyalties were local or regional, not national, and in the south the peasantry distrusted anyone or anything outside the family.[9] Nor were the lower classes unique in possessing characteristics which weakened the state. Liberal Italy, in the words of Gaetano Salvemini, 'was supported by a weak judicial and moral conscience, both in the rulers and in the ruled'.[10] To a degree, Italian military policy reflected the context in which it was made.

As well as providing a chronological history of that policy, I have tried to keep in focus three broad and overlapping thematic interests: politics, professionalism and planning. In each case the broad questions suggest themselves. How 'politicised' was the army, and with what consequences? How cohesive and corporate was the officer corps, and how professional in its concern to improve its intellectual level? How seriously did the soldiers take war-planning, and what considerations shaped their proposed solutions? In this way I have tried both to explain the particular and to identify the general, for it seems to me that in many respects the army of Fascist Italy was strikingly like its Liberal forebear.

1 The Army and the Risorgimento

When Rome fell in 1870 the long-standing desire of the princes of Savoy 'to consume Italy like an artichoke, leaf by leaf' seemed well-nigh satisfied. Soon the wars of the Risorgimento became encrusted with legends of the fiery military patriotism of Victor Emmanuel II and of the virtues of the Piedmontese Army. 'The Piedmontese', wrote Emilio De Bono, later one of the Mussolini's marshals, 'were soldiers from their heads to the tips of their toes: rich in fine military traditions, faithful to the monarchy, with strong sentiments of duty and honour'.[1] The image of military Italy which was created during the Risorgimento was politically necessary: Piedmont's right to the leadership of a united Italy, and the right of the house of Savoy to assume the honours and privileges of Italian monarchs, rested heavily on the fact that they had been earned by force of arms. In reality, those wars were marked for Italy by the pursuit of objectives defined with undue caution or excessive optimism, by royal leadership which was often hesitant and confused, and by military failure.

The wars of the Risorgimento established a pattern of civil-military relations and forged a military structure which lasted until 1915 and beyond. The army was thrust into the political arena by the crown. Soliders became members of both the senate and the chamber of deputies; there they protected the ideals of a conservative monarchy. They also entered cabinets as ministers of war. In consequence the high command became politicised: the opportunity of office allowed generals to pursue individual schemes of reform and the requirement of a general in cabinet forced every prime minister to select between them. This practice divided the high command as individuals. Regional rivalries divided it into cliques.

Political and social considerations defined the structure of the army. A mass army of short-term conscripts carried with it the necessity to admit – or force – larger numbers of the middle class into the officer corps. More broadly, such a popular army would legitimise the demands of the Left to widen the political nation. This the crown did not wish to see. Political imperatives therefore acted to define the nation's relationship to its army in a way which institutionalised suspicion, mistrust and hostility on both sides.

1

One further outcome of the wars of the Risorgimento is worth noting. Although the army and its leaders performed poorly on the field of battle, they were not forced to pay the price of failure. That price might have been exacted in one of two ways. Either the army would have had to overhaul its officer corps and revise its manpower structure in order to improve efficiency; or Piedmont Savoy would have had to modify its territorial ambitions and settle for very much less than rule over the whole Italian peninsula. The chance configurations of European international relations permitted Italy to avoid either option and find a third way: by accepting first French and then Prussian assistance she was able to retain her inefficient military structure and yet gain almost all her objectives. Later, when Italy's grandiose appetites so manifestly outran her inadequate military resources and expertise, the wars of the Risorgimento seemed to justify ambition.

In 1820 the Piedmontese officer corps was dominated by the nobility; twenty years later almost half were middle class.[2] However, shrinking numbers of aristocratic candidates and a larger entry from the *borghesia* represented a compromise which was strictly limited to the regular officer corps, where a long-term process of socialisation could ensure the maintenance of conservative monarchist ideals. Reserve officers, who spent most of their lives outside the barrack-gates, were a doubtful quantity and in 1839 they were virtually eliminated from the army, thereby removing a source of extra officers in wartime.[3] Attempts to build a reserve army likewise succumbed to social pressures. Partial conscription was introduced in 1815, but an attempt to integrate reserves with the regular army by enforcing short periods of service in barracks collapsed in 1821 amidst complaints that peasants had become indoctrinated with subversive ideas whilst in the cities and were spreading the vices of regular soldiers into the countryside.[4] France set a pattern in 1824, abandoning a reserve in favour of a regular army in which recruits served eight years, and in Prussia the conscript system was drastically watered down to lessen the burden on citizenry and treasury alike. In 1832 Piedmont followed suit. A regular core of 16 000 professional soldiers served alongside a levy of 8000 *provinciali* who did one year's active service followed by seven years in the reserve and eight in the territorials. The annual class was selected by lot. One-third were called into the army while the remainder escaped scot-free; the unlucky ones could evade their obligation by hiring a substitute or paying a tax. This system emphasised the divisions in Piedmontese society: money could buy exemption, and in any case the

525 000 inhabitants of the island of Sardinia were wholly free from any military obligations.

The tiny Piedmontese army, unprepared for war against a major power, was put to the test in 1848. On 18 March Milan rose against its Austrian masters, and the next day it sought Piedmont's aid. When Marshal Radetzky retired from the city, Charles Albert announced his intervention in the name of national liberation. Determined to take command himself, the king appointed General Antonio Franzini as 'war minister in the field' and 'quarter-master general' and then entangled the army irrevocably in the coils of conflicting authority by appointing a separate chief of staff, General Carlo Salasco. Charles Albert's habit of calling his corps commanders together for councils of war further weakened any centralised command.[5] With political aims focussed more clearly on Lombardy than on Austria, and with no clear military objectives at all, Charles Albert led his unfortunate army into 'the war of lost opportunities'.[6]

Crossing the Ticino, the Piedmontese army marched cautiously towards the Quadrilateral whilst the king, who reached Pavia on 29 March, debated what to do. A daring plan to lay siege to Legnago, cutting Radetzky off from reinforcements, was eventually rejected in favour of cautiously stringing the army out along the right bank of the Mincio to deny the enemy access to food supplies in Lombardy. On 26 April, a month after the war had begun, the Piedmontese began lining up between Lake Garda and Villafranca. After fighting a pointless battle at Santa Lucia on 6 May and capturing Peschiera, Charles Albert sank back into his accustomed lethargy. Radetzky seized his chance quickly and efficiently, switching 30 000 troops east to take Vicenza.[7]

By mid-June Charles Albert was becoming aware that his army, through no fault of its own, did not match his ambitions:

> Our forces have been designed with the aim of sustaining a war of independence inside our own country infinitely more than with a view to foreign expeditions . . .[8]

The king was now running out of men. When the war began 38 battalions had been formed out of the first three classes of the reserve, but they were chronically short of officers. This same deficiency made it impossible to call up the remaining five classes. In desperation the untrained class of 1828 was called up, but a proposal to mobilise 50 battalions of national guards was blocked on the grounds that they would be dangerously bourgeois in character and that, in any case, there was no equipment for them. Finally Piedmont scraped together twenty-four reserve battalions and packed them off to the front. They were too few to affect the course of the war.[9]

During June Charles Albert awaited the results of a plebiscite in Lombardy which voted overwhelmingly for union with Piedmont. Having secured popular backing, he was willing to settle for most of Lombardy and the duchies of Parma and Modena, secured by English intercession rather than by force of arms; but his government would accept nothing less than the expulsion of Austrian troops from Italy. Then, on 25 July, Radetzky overwhelmed the Piedmontese at Custoza. An armistice was announced by the king on 10 August. For the first time, but not the last, Piedmont's ambition outstripped her military capacity.

As 1848 moved to a close, Anglo-French attempts at mediation collapsed, and a democratic administration came to power in Piedmont prepared to continue the war sooner than surrender. Charles Albert wanted to restore the prestige of the monarchy and was happy to fall in with secret arrangements to become effective head of the army in a new campaign. A nominal commander was found in the Polish General Chrzanowski, a veteran of the Napoleonic war. Chrzanowski's mental rigidity and defensive-mindedness, and his lack of energy and initiative, rendered him entirely unsuitable for his post.[10] La Marmora and Dabormida had worked wonders in the army, sacking incompetent commanders and improving supply and medical services, but the twin problems of a shortage of officers and a lack of trained reserves persisted. Weariness and uncertainty generated an atmosphere of resignation and scepticism in the ranks which boded ill for the future.[11]

Political considerations again played a predominant part in strategic planning, and Chrzanowski had to bend to Charles Albert's wish to re-enter Milan as a triumphal liberator. Chrzanowski was prepared to take aggressive action, but only if the Austrians retreated behind the Mincio or the Adda as they had done in 1848. There was no likelihood that they would do so, for they were not now in need of reinforcements and had no insurrections at their back as had been the case a year earlier. The king's plan for attack, and Chrzanowski's for defence, both dictated a concentration on Novara, and the preferred alternative of the majority of the generals – to advance on Piacenza, Cremona and Mantua – was ruled out.

On 20 March 1849 Piedmontese troops crossed the Ticino in a reconnaissance in force towards Magenta. Struck by the coolness of their reception, the king immediately ordered them back again. Three days later the battle of Novara sealed Charles Albert's fate. A single

Austrian corps under D'Aspre attacked the Piedmontese at eleven in the morning and fought alone for five hours before reinforcements came up. Paralysed by indecision, Chrzanowski delayed his counter-offensive until it was too late. The casualty lists were more-or-less equal but the outcome was decisive. On the night of the battle Charles Albert abdicated in favour of his son, Victor Emmanuel II, and an armistice was concluded three days later.

The first war of the Risorgimento was lost partly through inept political leadership. However, Charles Albert also owed his defeat to his unwillingness to mobilise popular support for fear of the contamination of republicanism. Middle-class volunteers were greeted with a marked lack of enthusiasm, and although the 'year of the revolution' threw up no fewer than 139 militias across Italy the king resolutely refused to allow any of them to participate in his royal conquest of Lombardy.[12] Peasant agitation, the consequence of crushing Austrian taxation and the steady erosion of communal rights, was even less welcome and no significant use was ever made of it.[13]

Peasant activism posed no great problems for the future: it could simply be disregarded. The mobilisation of the middle classes in defence of Milan, Venice and Rome raised issues about the social composition of the army of unification which were more difficult to ignore. The gallant struggles of the Venetian republic under Manin, which finally surrendered to Austria on 24 August 1849, and the Roman republic led by Mazzini and Garibaldi, which fell to French troops on 2 July 1849, underwrote the claims of the middle class to participate in future military action to reunify Italy. Patriotic enthusiasm could be tapped to remedy the deficiencies of the small, dynastic Piedmontese army; but while popular armies offered the attraction of numbers, they also carried the germs of republicanism.

The relationship between the Piedmontese army and its monarch was significantly redefined by Victor Emmanuel's acceptance of the constitution introduced by his predecessor on the eve of the revolt in Milan. Whereas before 1848 the soldiers had sworn an oath to God and the king, they now swore loyalty to the king and bound themselves to observe the constitution and the laws of the state, 'for the inseparable good of the King and the Patria'. Article five of the *Statuto* gave the king command of the army, but he was now bound to treat the military as partners in his royal crusade or risk their intervention in politics on the side of the government. The role assigned to soldiers in the political arena is evidence of the importance the crown placed upon the partnership. In 1849 12 per cent of the chamber of deputies and almost one-third of the senate were soldiers.[14] General Quaglia's remark in 1850 that 'the interests of the people and their sovereign are identical' reveals that the army leadership was well aware of its political role and accepted the royal bargain.[15]

Reform of the Piedmontese army was imperative, and a major need was for more and better officers. The middle class was the most obvious reservoir to tap, but the military conservatives were totally opposed to such a step. In order to fill the gap a law of 13 November 1853 reserved one-third of all promotions to the rank of second lieutenant for former non-commissioned officers; it remained in force until 1896, when the proportion was reduced to a quarter. A similar measure had been enacted in France in 1818 and had helped produce an officer corps which, though politically quiescent, was also routine-ridden and stood in exaggerated respect for regulations. In much the same way, Piedmont purchased military acquiescence at the cost of accepting a professionally limited junior corps of officers.

With the military service law of 20 March 1854 Alfonso La Marmora sought to create a French-style professional army which could challenge Austria when the time came. Every adult male was in theory liable for military service at the age of 21. In practice a small fraction served for eight years; the remainder were divided by lot into two categories. The first category served for five years in the active army followed by six years in the reserves, whilst the second category served five years in the reserves alone, receiving a total of 40 days' training. Of the annual class of 50 000 only a quarter did any form of service, while the remainder were either exempted or invalidated for health reasons.[16] Those unfortunate enough to be caught in the first category could escape service on payment of a tax of 3000 lire – then equivalent to the annual salary of a professor at the University of Turin.

Selective service entailed exemptions and medical grounds for exclusion, and a comprehensive list formed part of the law.[17] The many categories of exemption, and the discrimination which the law encouraged, led the Piedmontese to try to avoid a burden which legislation encouraged them to think of as bad luck rather than as one of the obligations of citizenship. A duel began between individual and state, for almost all the causes of rejection could be simulated. Soap was used to produce foaming at the mouth and apparent epilepsy; stammering, deafness, eczema, ulcers and haemorrhoids were also commonly simulated; and symptoms of cardiac arrest were produced by holding pepper or tobacco in the anus.[18] Each symptom had its appropriate official countermeasure; and anyone found guilty of seeking to evade military service faced imprisonment for up to a year and a heavy fine. The military treated those who came before the medical examinations as potential if not actual malingerers, and the lengths to which they went to test physical ailments were as a consequence sometimes gruesome.

The apparent convergence of military professionalism with mass participation seemed to be reinforced by the passing of the 'Blood Law' in 1857 under which all those previously exempted from call-up were to become second-category reservists. However, this was little more than a cosmetic gesture, for when the state already spent 28 per cent of its budget on the military there was little opportunity to train larger numbers. Of 18 000 selected for the *leva* in 1859, 5000 served for the five-year term, 4000 did 40 days, and the remainder were sent home. Financial and political considerations combined to create the impression that Piedmont did not greatly value popular participation in the military adventures which were about to befall her. Nevertheless, as a second round with Austria grew imminent some 20 000 volunteers swarmed into Piedmont from Lombardy, Modena, Tuscany, the Romagna and elsewhere. La Marmora cared for them not one bit. Eventually, in March 1859 it was agreed that they should form a special corps, the *Cacciatori delle Alpi*, under Garibaldi's command.[19]

Political calculations underlay the conduct of the second war of the Risorgimento no less than the first. This time, however, they reflected the presence of a dominant ally. Napoleon III was prepared to assist in the creation of a kingdom of upper Italy; he was not prepared to see central Italy fall under the sway of Victor Emmanuel II. These limited aims underpinned the military convention signed by France on 26 January 1859. A 'non-revolutionary' pretext for war was to be provided by manoeuvring Austria into issuing an ultimatum to Piedmont. Austria obliged on 23 April, demanding that Piedmont put her troops back on a peacetime footing and disband the mass of volunteers sheltering under her protection. The war which broke out three days later had a curiously Janus-like character. On the Italian side it was taken in varying degrees as a war of national liberation; but as far as France was concerned it resembled an eighteenth-century cabinet-war designed to achieve limited territorial adjustments. The tensions inherent in this contradiction mounted until they finally determined when, and how, the war ended.

Italy's military contribution confirmed her status as junior partner. La Marmora's system fielded a force of some 60 000 men. To it were added 200 000 French troops, and it was reinforced in the field in June and July with 10 000 volunteers and 23 000 second-category reservists.[20]

Despite reforms in the artillery, engineers and transport services during the previous decade, the army took the field lacking horses, maps of Lombardy, bridging equipment and siege artillery. Victor Emmanuel took supreme command but held it for only eighteen days before Napoleon III took over on 14 May.

After some hesitation, Napoleon decided to turn the right flank of the Austrian positions defending Milan at Novara. Accordingly, the bulk of the French troops crossed the Ticino and fought a costly encounter-battle with the Austrians at Magenta on 4 June. Italian participation was limited to one battalion of *bersaglieri*. Afterwards, Napoleon III paused, allowing the Austrians to clear Milan and retire east. As the emperor and the king entered the city on 8 June Garibaldi demonstrated the effectiveness of popular war by moving north and east of Milan to capture Brescia and Salò. While the French hesitated Franz Joseph reorganised the Austrian forces, taking supreme command himself. The Austrian army at first retired behind the Mincio but then recrossed it, and on 24 June the battles of Solferino and San Martino ended the war. The day was won by the French and the Piedmontese, but at a high price: 2431 dead and 12 152 wounded, slightly more than the enemy's losses.[21]

Napoleon's enthusiasm for the war now evaporated. Manpower costs had been high, and unexpected nationalist fervour was breaking out in central Italy. Accordingly the emperor unilaterally proposed an armistice on 5 July and, three days later, Franz Joseph accepted it. Contrary to later legends, Victor Emmanuel and his military entourage were more than ready for an armistice. Sardinian headquarters were pessimistic about the future development of the campaign and feared that further reverses would mean the acceptance of worse terms than were currently available. In any case the conservative nobility which dominated the upper reaches of the army had only been persuaded with difficulty to take part in a campaign conducted under liberal-nationalist principles and were becoming ever more alarmed at the growth of republicanism, as personified in Garibaldi and his men. The high command was also faced with the intractable problem of making up losses in action. A peace which gained Lombardy – a traditional objective of the house of Savoy – would free them from the dominance of the French which they disliked, and at the same time offer the opportunity to cleanse the revolutionary forces.[22]

The second war of the Risorgimento did nothing to resolve the conflict between the regular army and the volunteers. Enthusiastic nationalists in Massa and Carrara had been instructed in no uncertain terms that local revolution was but a small and unimportant cog in the

Franco–Piedmontese war-machine, but volunteers had played their part on the field of battle under Garibaldi's leadership. They were to do so to an even greater degree during the ensuing 16 months, as Garibaldi and his famous 'Thousand' first landed in Sicily and then conquered the mainland kingdom of Naples before handing over the captured territory to Victor Emmanuel at Teano on 26 October 1860. At the same time, a painful and difficult process of expansion took place as the Piedmontese army swelled to accommodate large numbers of new recruits before finally emerging as the Italian Army on 4 May 1861.

First, during the second half of 1859, came 41 000 Lombards. Then, early the following year, the 50 000 men of the Tuscan and Emilian army were added to the growing north Italian forces. The problem they posed was complicated by the structure of their officer corps. With only some 200 officers available their commander, General Manfredo Fanti, resorted to a series of rapid promotions between May 1859 and March 1860 which caused the Sardinian army considerable alarm as it watched Tuscans overtaking more experienced Piedmontese officers in rank, and the lower levels of the officer corps being filled with promoted non-commissioned officers and volunteers.[23]

To maintain control over the new units, the Piedmontese officer corps was expanded between January 1859 and February 1860 from 3195 to 5224; only half of the newcomers had attended a military academy or served in the ranks. On 25 March 1860, the swollen Sardinian army was formally united with the army of Central Italy. To 4990 Sardinian officers were added 1294 from Emilia and 1062 from Tuscany.[24] A political practice which adversely affected the functional competence of the army was about to begin:

> Many officers who, in the Sardinian army, had not been thought worthy of advancement beyond the lowest ranks were quickly advanced two or three steps in the new Italian army, so that they came to exercise functions for which they were not adequately prepared.[25]

The officer corps was becoming a body which lacked homogeneity, common traditions and even, in some cases, military experience.

The task of welding together an Italian army was confided to Fanti, who became minister of war on 22 January 1860. A Modenese and a former Mazzinian who was now a convinced monarchist, Fanti saw in Turin's army the only model for military expansion. His unique background and status made him a powerful political figure.[26] Fanti first altered the structure of the thirteen divisions for which he was now responsible. Where La Marmora's regiments had comprised four battalions each of four companies, he introduced a new organisation of three battalions, each containing six companies. This increased the need for junior officers whilst lowering the requirement for senior ones. Fanti coped with this, and carried forward the process of 'Piedmontisation', by adding to the officer corps another 2265 second lieutenants, all drawn from the Piedmontese officer-schools or from the ranks. In the process of adding new infantry, cavalry and field-artillery units to the army, Fanti also began the practice of making up units by drawing recruits from two geographical regions. This was designed to speed the creation of an Italian nation by fostering a sense of *Italianità* and by countering regional loyalties.

Fanti had also to engineer the absorption into the army of the Bourbon forces of Naples and Garibaldi's volunteers. As far as the 97 000 rank-and-file of the Bourbon army was concerned, the issue was the extent to which political unification was to be matched by military merger. La Marmora wanted to have nothing to do with them; to him they were 'rabble . . . who would corrupt our soldiers if put in amongst them'.[27] Cavour also believed they should be left out of the national army. Finally the four youngest classes in the army were recalled and general conscription was introduced in the south. By 30 September 1861 there were 57 968 former soldiers of the army of the Two Sicilies serving in the new *Esercito italiano*, of whom some 48 000 had been retrieved from the countryside. A further 41 000 ex-Bourbon troops remained at large. The 3600 Bourbon officers were winnowed by an examining commission, and 1086 entered active-service units.[28]

The Garibaldini posed a much greater problem. By the time the campaign of 1860 ended Garibaldi commanded 7343 officers and 45 496 troops; the combined armies of Sardinia, Tuscany and Emilia had only three more officers, though they comprised four times as many men. Garibaldi's officers threatened to swamp the already far from homogeneous officer corps of the new army. His men, coming largely from the *piccola borghesia*, did not share the peasant background of the rest of the rank-and-file; their incorporation into the army might widen the socio–political base of the Risorgimento and lead to demands for a greater degree of popular political involvement.[29]

Victor Emmanuel, carried away by the excitement of riding into Naples at the head of a victorious army in which the Garibaldini had done most of the fighting, rashly promised that the volunteers would be preserved on equal footing with the regular army.[30] But Fanti threatened to resign if the Garibaldini were admitted into the army, and without him there could be no national army at all. On 16 November 1860 they were disbanded. Half the Garibaldini officer corps was quickly weeded-out by special commissions, and it soon became clear that volunteer officers who aspired to make permanent careers begun under the cloak of enthusiasm rather than the mantle of sober professionalism were not going to have an easy passage. A small but fortunate minority used the fact that they had previously held regular commissions to transfer into the regular army. The remaining 2949 were ordered to present themselves at depots in Piedmont by 15 February 1861 if they wished to be considered for regular commissions. All but 183 did so. Their enthusiasm availed them little, for two months later almost all of them were told that a decision was in abeyance. In March 1862, under pressure to find more officers, the government admitted 1997 former Garibaldini into the army at the rank they had previously held, but with seniority from the date of the decree. They were matched by a further 1199 newly promoted Piedmontese second lieutenants, bringing the total officer corps to 16 051.[31]

Fanti's reforms aroused the wrath of two vociferous opponents, and in the spring and summer of 1861 a storm broke over the heads of the war minister and the premier as debate raged about the future shape of the army. La Marmora, in a speech to parliament on 23 March 1861 which bristled with unsuppressed hostility, launched a detailed attack on the new large infantry regiments which Fanti had created. La Marmora's argument was too narrowly technical for the deputies to follow and in any case Fanti plainly enjoyed the full support of Cavour; he needed to do little in reply other than suggest that he admired the military system of France whereas his predecessor found inspiration in the army of Frederick the Great.

Garibaldi's challenge was more serious. His claim for a place for his volunteers challenged Fanti's concept of a regular army based on the Piedmontese officer corps and limited conscription. A military system founded on popular enthusiasm might also lead to pressures to expand the electorate – currently only 2 per cent of the population. The parliamentary battle was fierce, and the outcome shaped military Italy for the next half-century.

Fanti saw no place for volunteers. They were averse to higher authority, to discipline and to anything which ran counter to their own wishes; they were intolerant of delay and of privation; they obeyed the man and not the rank; they valued innovation above all else. 'This can be valuable in some circumstances,' he admittted, 'but it becomes annoying and very expensive when the guns have ceased their fire'.[32] He was prepared to offer the Garibaldini a term of two years' service, in which case they would have to pay for their own weapons and uniforms; otherwise they would have to return home.

Garibaldi responded bitterly. It was evident, he said, that 'the minister of war always intended to dissolve the army of the south, with all the cunning imaginable'. He asked why Italy was prepared to accept the southern provinces but not the armies which had done so much to free them, and called for the reorganisation of the armies of the south as an act of justice and a measure of safety.[33]

Cavour faced a dilemma. He did not want the Garibaldini inside the army lest they infect it with republicanism; yet he could not afford to let them exist outside it lest they move against Rome independently, thereby precipitating a war against France and Austria. Backing Fanti, he offered the Garibaldini employment in a voluntary national guard for use in wartime. He was not prepared to accept Garibaldi's proposal for a permanent 20 000-man force. Garibaldi stuck to his guns but, with Fanti immovable, with former Garibaldini officers confirming the indiscipline of the volunteers, and with Enrico Cialdini thundering in the columns of the press, 'We don't want the Garibaldini in the army of Victor Emmanuel', any reconciliation was impossible. Cavour made the vote one of confidence in the government and carried the day by 194 to 79, with five abstentions.

Garibaldi vainly continued his struggle. As a sop, a parliamentary commission was set up to examine proposals by him for compulsory service in a national guard. The aim of this, Garibaldi openly admitted to Cavour, was to supersede the standing army.[34] On 15 June 1861 the parliamentary commission produced its report and buried the chances of Garibaldi's mass army. All citizens over 21 and not proletarians would have the right to join a national guard, but there was to be no obligation to do so; and organisation was to be up to battalion level but no higher. Class antagonism was readily apparent in the recommendations, and the commissioners made it patently clear that they did not trust the loyalty of all Italians. The idea of a nation-in-arms was temporarily dead. It would be revived nine years later, after the first battles of the Franco-Prussian war had demonstrated the utility of mass citizen armies.

The first task facing the Italian army was to repress the brigandage which ravaged the south from 1861 to 1866. Discontent at the introduction of conscription was fuelled by the government's failure to meet its own deadlines for sharing-out lands, and by the non-materialisation of promised public-works programmes. By the summer of 1861 brigands were occupying and sacking entire towns. Fearing a general Bourbon uprising the authorities instructed General Cialdini to quell the disturbances. He and his successor, La Marmora, made effective use of mobile tactics backed with extensive legal powers. The campaign against the brigands required a substantial military commitment: by 1863 120 000 troops were tied down by the campaign and almost three-quarters of the infantry had served in the south. Official figures after the war's end, in December 1865, listed 5212 brigands killed and 5044 arrested; but total civilian deaths may have numbered tens of thousands. Military casualties were few.

Fighting a guerrilla war tested the capacities of the junior officers commanding the small detachments which combed the hills for *renitenti* evading conscription; but senior officers were not called upon to manoeuvre large formations against a trained and disciplined enemy armed with heavy weapons. One undesirable consequence was that the bulk of the army came to regard southerners as at best unreliable and at worst downright hostile. Senior officers did their duty, apparently without many qualms; Govone was one of the few who openly denounced the corruption of the Neapolitan ruling class on whose side the army was ranged.[35]

The war against brigandage drove the new Italian state yet further into debt at a time when the military budget was carrying large amounts of extraordinary expenditure for barrack-building, artillery and special equipment. In 1862 military spending represented 40 per cent of total expenditure and 80 per cent of actual financial receipts; three years later these figures had shrunk to 26 per cent and 37 per cent respectively. Total military expenditure during the years 1861–65 amounted to 1 296 693 463 lire, almost one-third of overall state expenditure. Though public revenue was increasing during these years its rate of growth was far from sufficient to sustain the appetite of the army. Thus, between 1862 and 1866 the Italian public debt increased by a massive 80 per cent.[36]

Just as politics determined the social structure of the army, it also dictated the introduction of national conscription in 1863. Those selected for service in category I served five years in the ranks, whilst category II served only 40 days and then went straight into the reserve. Selection was by lottery, and exemptions and substitution were preserved. In the first year 11.5 per cent of those legally obliged to present themselves failed to appear, but after that absenteeism settled down to an average annual figure of four per cent.[37] The 'leisured' classes were somewhat less patriotic. In 1864–5 just under 1 per cent escaped service by paying a tax of 3 200 lire, and less than one-third of 1 per cent hired substitutes to serve in their stead. This figure increased steadily during the decade until in 1869 – the year of the great bourgeois 'escape' – 7 per cent of the contingent removed their names from the lists by means of substitution, exchange or payment.[38] At the same time the numbers entering the first category shrank from 60 000 in 1863 and averaged 40 000 by the end of the decade.

The new Italian army was soon put to the test. The war of 1866, by which Italy gained control of the last Austrian enclave in the peninsula when it received Venetia, was a diplomatic triumph but a military humiliation. Many years later, Cosenz remarked pungently, 'That campaign demonstrated all our defects in conducting war'.[39] Confusion over who was to command the army was a bad omen. Victor Emmanuel was determined to take a leading role but recognised the need for an experienced chief of staff. There were four candidates: La Marmora, Cialdini, Della Rocca and Petitti. The king first suggested Della Rocca, who was an accomplished courtier, then appointed Petitti when no one else would concur, and was finally forced to accept La Marmora, who had been prime minister since 1864 and who only succeeded in handing over the government to Ricasoli three days before war was declared on 20 June. La Marmora thought himself superior to everyone else; Cialdini, who could not be denied a command, was notoriously independent and self-willed; everyone was nervous about the king's overestimation of his own military capacity. The loyalty of some of the non-Piedmontese generals, notably Pianell and Sirtori, was doubted, and everyone suspected everyone else of treason or overweening personal ambition. Ricasoli noted gloomily in his diary on 3 June, 'The army and the navy are riven with jealousy and rival cliques'.[40]

The Italians disregarded a suggestion from Berlin that they drive on the Isonzo and the heart of the empire in concert with the Prussian campaign in Bohemia. Instead it was decided to go straight for the Quadrilateral, La Marmora's army of twelve divisions attacking across the Mincio while Cialdini's force of eight divisions crossed the Po. A council of war held at Bologna on 17 June sowed the seeds of disaster when it failed to determine which of the two armies was to launch the main attack and left both to operate independently. There was agreement on one thing: Garibaldi's volunteers, who were to attack the Trento from Brescia, should have as restricted a role as possible.

On 23 June La Marmora's force of 100 000 men crossed the Mincio and began to advance on Villafranca. Their commander believed the Austrians to be on the far side of the Adige, but they were not. Archduke Albert had concentrated his 75 000 troops south of Lake Garda, ready to fall on the Italian left flank. The battle of Custoza, which took place the following day, was a disaster of such magnitude that Alberto Pollio, writing of it 37 years later, said that it still weighed on the army 'like a leaden cloak'.[41] The Austrians attacked first in what became an encounter-battle, composed of a series of small local engagements in which the Italians were usually outnumbered. La Marmora soon lost control of the battle, and then made the grave error of trying to regain his grip on it by galloping about looking for individual commanders. All hopes of central direction at once evaporated. Disorganisation degen- erated into chaos and then into panic and at nightfall the army of the Mincio retreated, leaving 714 dead on the field, 456 fewer than the Austrians. What turned a setback into a defeat was a combination of psychological collapse and a lack of support from Cialdini.

During the next ten days complete chaos reigned at the summit of the army. La Marmora resigned. Cialdini, the king's preferred candidate, refused to take over unless the king left the field, and, since the house of Savoy was unwilling to demonstrate that its military capacity was inferior to that of its Hohenzollern ally, La Marmora got his job back. Then, on 3 July, the Prussian army crushed the Austrians at Königgrätz. Mediation began the following day but, despite an offer of the immediate cession of the Veneto, the Italians decided to press on in the hope of greater gains. At a grand council of war held at Ferrara on 14 July, Cialdini was given 150 000 men and ordered to advance on the Isonzo and Trieste; La Marmora was instructed to take Venice and help the Garibaldini in the Trentino; and Admiral Persano was told to put to sea and worst the Austrian navy.

On 20 July the Italian navy was routed at Lissa, and the following day, while Garibaldi's troops were defeating the Austrians at Bezzecca, Bismarck accepted the Austrian offer of a truce without consulting Italy. With Austrian troops pouring south and Napoleon III putting pressure on Turin Italy had to give up hopes of the Trentino. The king, Ricasoli and Cialdini all wanted to continue the struggle, but La Marmora recognised that further fighting could lead to little but disaster, and on 12 August he signed an armistice with the Austrians.

Divisions and rivalries within the high command undoubtedly contributed to Italy's unhappy military experiences, and the king's interventions may have played a significant role in creating the conditions for disaster. But a search for individual scapegoats conceals important deficiencies in the military instrument which the king and the generals had sought to utilise: the state of the army goes some way towards explaining the whole sorry episode.

The army of 1866 was very much less homogeneous than that of 1859:

40 per cent of it had been enrolled from the northern provinces after 1860, and a further 31 per cent from Umbria, the Marches and the South after 1861. As De Bono later wrote:

> The army was Italian in little more than name, because it was still an amalgam, or perhaps a mosaic, of the various elements – often disparate – with which it had been put together.[42]

Its poor cohesion and lack of morale were manifest off the battlefield as well as on it: 12 269 soldiers deserted in 1866, whereas in the first eighteen months after unification only 4633 had done so.[43] The officer corps was deeply divided: in 1866 half were former rankers, while 43 per cent came from the officer schools. Piedmontese dominated both groups, so that the lower ranks of the officer corps had some homogeneity of origin, though not of background or, perhaps, of expertise. In the middle ranks, there was a balance between Piedmontese and others which made for mutual antipathies and mistrust; and many had, for reasons already explained, enjoyed rapid promotion which had elevated them beyond their capacities. The squabbles at the top were but the tip of an iceberg.

The army also suffered from cuts in the military budget after 1861. Della Rocca made no secret of his bitterness at the poor state in which it went to war, complaining that false economies had produced 'an army of tatterdemalions'.[44] Finally, poor military judgement had swept the army to defeat. Enrico Cosenz, later the first chief of the Italian general staff, held that the high command had committed three fatal errors. It had gone to war with improvised formations; it had scattered its forces instead of concentrating on objectives one-by-one; and La Marmora had failed to give adequate direction to the army.[45] Lack of cohesion, resources incommensurate with ambitions, and low professional competence remained characteristic of the Italian army over the next half-century.

The Prussian victories of 1864 and 1866 cast doubt on the military value of the French-style army which Italy now possessed. La Marmora led the party which ascribed Prussian success to the needle-gun. Others pointed out that the value of trained reserves fighting alongside the regular army was now incontestable. A commission was appointed to propose a new organisation for the army bearing in mind financial exigencies, the need to defend the frontiers and the maintenance of public order. The proposal finally presented by General Thaon Di Revel in April 1867 chopped off three classes of category I troops and two of category II to form a third-line garrison-militia similar to the Prussian *Landwehr*.

The generals began openly expressing dissatisfaction at the confusion and flux in military affairs; Paola Caselli wrote in 1867, 'We are advancing towards the disorganisation of an army which is not yet even organised, so that if we wish to put the army into action we shall find ourselves even less well prepared than in the past'.[46] Their worries proved temporarily groundless, since Thaon's scheme was not even discussed. The chamber was preoccupied with the need to make economies, and instead disbanded eight regiments of infantry, delayed the call-up of the class of 1846 and suppressed some higher commands. The same fate met proposals by the next minister of war, Bertolè-Viale, to reduce the length of service from five years to four and call up a larger number of men in category I to compensate, a scheme which collapsed with the fall of the Menabrea government in 1869.

By the late 1860s a national army had been patterned to conform with the political and social goals of Piedmont's grandees. Division, lack of cohesion, and mistrust were institutionalised within it; and its relationship with the Italian people was founded on suspicion. The process of creating a national army had produced an officer corps fractured by professional, social and regional differences. The high command was united in its loyalty to the crown but divided by personal rivalry and ambition. The roots of later disasters lie here.

The pattern of civil–military relations established during the Risorgimento was disastrous for the army. It stood between crown and parliament, but it faced the throne. Its political recruitment may have been useful in safeguarding the crown, but divided the high command when it came to serving the government. To take or retain power, every administration had to find a general who would accept whatever financial limitations the budgetary situation currently demanded. A unified high command might have used its power to refuse office as a lever against the civilians, as the Japanese army did in the 1920s; but the Italian high command was not unified. Instead, the opportunity of office made generals into politicians, and the need for royal favour made them into courtiers. It would be hard to find a better recipe for division and dissent.

2 A Policy for Defence

Rome had been proclaimed the capital of Italy in March 1861, but the opportunity to incorporate it into the new state did not occur until August 1870, when war broke out between France and Prussia. The king and some of his more conservative generals were certain that France would win and wanted to intervene on her side to extract Rome from a grateful neighbour. The early battles indicated that things might not work out as they supposed; then, on 1 September, the armies of Napoleon III were crushed at Sedan. On 4 September came news of the birth of the Third Republic and the next day General Raffaele Cadorna was authorised to take Rome.[1] Slowly, and with considerable difficulty, he assembled an army. The artillery opened fire on the walls of the city at 5.15 a.m. on the morning of 20 September. The battle was brief and almost bloodless, for after a breach had been battered at Porta Pia the papal forces surrrendered. The last of the wars of the Risorgimento was over by 10.10 a.m.[2]

Unified Italy's fragility and vulnerability posed problems for her soldiers and her statesmen. An anti-clerical regime faced the threat of a 'black' reaction inside Italy and intervention by Catholic powers on the Pope's behalf. The ruling conservative Right also had to contend with the forces of republicanism, personified inside Italy by Garibaldi and posted outside in the shape of the Spanish and French republics. Repressive internal fiscal policies helped spark riots which emphasised the lack of domestic unity and provided an immediate purpose for the army: alarm that parties 'opposed to the existing political state of Italy' might stir up trouble led the war minister to issue orders in August 1871 preparing the regional military commands to support public order.[3] Although these alarms were short-lived, strikes in 1872 and 1874 bore clear witness to the volatility of the Italian social order. And from Rome politicians of every stripe watched nervously as property taxes in the south tripled between 1860 and 1877. The army's role as a tool of domestic order had a high priority for politicians.

The Right chose to seek security not by force but through an unassertive foreign policy. 'We are not rich', foreign minister Visconti Venosta remarked in 1872, 'we are not strong'; and Nigra, Italy's ambassador to France, spoke for many when he remarked three years later that 'a war, whatever its outcome, would be for newly-created Italy a disaster'.[4] When, in 1876, the Left came to power it brought with it an urgent desire that Italy count for something more among the great powers. The army's role changed accordingly.

In the debates of the 1870s all parties agreed that a ready and effective military force was essential 'if not to gain, then at least to conserve and hold Italy's position among the powers of Europe'.[5] The Franco-Prussian war challenged Piedmont's traditional manpower policy by suggesting that quantity was more important than quality. In resolving this question, the Italian high command united to block a reformist war minister from the Right. Military conservatism, and an innate lack of confidence in their soldiery, also led the military to adopt a defence policy which hinged on extensive – and expensive – fortification. Even so, the soldiers expected their enemy to break into Italy across the land frontier; the most favourable outcome they could envisage was victory in a great defensive battle in the Po Valley.

The French defeat in 1870 raised the central issue of whether the newly united nation should stick to the Piedmontese model or look to Prussia for its example. There was no easy consensus on what had brought the Prussians victory. Liberal reformists and the Left explained success in terms of the effectiveness of the *levée-en-masse* and the value of popular energy, properly harnessed; conservatives highlighted the principles of obedience which were characteristic of the semi-feudal Prussian state; soldiers emphasised the importance of Prussian organisation and pointed to the influence of the general staff. Issues which had previously gone undiscussed, such as the abolition of substitution, now forced their way on to the political agenda as politicians and soldiers reassessed the value of the Piedmontese model.

It fell to Cesare Francesco Ricotti-Magnani to oversee reform. Born in Novara on 3 June 1822, Ricotti had spent his cadet years at the military academy in Turin and had then joined the artillery. He had taken part in all the wars of the Risorgimento from 1848 onwards, as well as fighting with the Piedmontese contingent in the Crimea, and had done his first stint at the war ministry in 1864. Though not the first choice as minister – the king would have preferred Bertolè-Viale – he was to prove energetic and far-sighted during his six years in office.

Ricotti faced a situation in which category II recruits were rarely called out for military training, and those in category I were often called to the colours late or sent home early. This was a direct consequence of the pressure to balance the budget, which for the army had shrunk from 250 million lire a year between 1861 and 1865 to 160 million between 1867 and 1872. Faced with severe financial limitations and considerable international pressures, Ricotti saw his task as three-fold: to produce a first-line army of 300 000 without any increase in costs; to provide some 120 000 reserves with which to make good wastage in time of war; and to create a second-line army for territorial defence, thereby freeing the permanent army for active military operations.[6] In so doing, Ricotti reversed traditional Piedmontese priorities and gave quantity preference over quality. To do this, he sought to reduce the period of military service from five years to three, while increasing the size of the annual class to 60 000, to abolish substitution and payment to evade service altogether, to introduce one-year volunteers on Prussian lines with the aim of creating a reserve of potential officers from among the educated *borghesia*, and to institute a new reserve in the form of a provincial militia.

The arguments put up in support of Ricotti in the chamber of deputies revealed social as well as military motivations for reform. Domenico Farini, an arch-conservative, pointed out that the abolition of all exemptions prevented arms being left only in the hands of the common people who

> after having done military service, do not return to the fields and the workshops but remain in the cities, unused to work, accustomed to discipline, knowing their own strength and often driven by hunger, the most ready, the most effective and most easily assembled instrument for anyone whose mind had turned to sedition.[7]

Clemente Corte, a general and a member of the moderate Left, raised the issue of social justice, pointing out that from the moment the grain tax had been introduced it became an inevitable corollary that military service should also fall on the leisured classes.

The law passed on 19 September 1871 embodied most of what Ricotti sought. Substitution was abolished, as was payment to evade service completely. One-year volunteers, who had opted for that status before the ballot, postponed their entry into the ranks until the age of twenty-four, undertook to meet their own expenses for uniform and equipment and paid a fee of 2000 lire to the state. Between 1871 and 1915 an average of 1500 recruits a year undertook this form of military service; it perpetuated social inequality without ever producing compensating military advantages. Low educational standards were set and volunteers failed to achieve expectations: a parliamentary commission of inquiry reported in 1907 that whereas they were supposed to attain the rank of sergeant on leaving, more than 40 per cent of the one-year volunteers were exiting as mere corporals. In one respect, however, the innovation was a success: Ricotti afterwards claimed that he had only expected to get some 500 volunteers a year.[8]

The law of 1871 reduced the period of military service to four years, and in 1875 Ricotti shortened it to three. He also attempted in 1874 to introduce a tax on all those exempted from military service, but failed. Exemptions continued almost unabated: between 1863 and 1875 an average of 25 per cent of those liable to serve were excused from doing so, two-fifths of them on the grounds that they were the only male child. More questionable was the discretion exercised by the examining commissions in deciding who to exonerate on medical grounds: the most common reasons given were 'constitutional weakness' and deficient chest development, and they were most commonly found among the leisured classes.

To maximise the potential of the regular army and the mobile militia Ricotti presented a bill to the chamber in December 1875 creating a territorial militia. It was, he pointed out, less a creation than a reform since it sought to improve the state of the national guard, which had been inaugurated in August 1861 but of which 'there is no trace whatever'.[9] Cadres for 300 battalions, amounting when fully-manned to a million men, were to be formed; in wartime their main task was to be to garrison the interior and certain portions of the coast, freeing trained forces to take the field. This third tier of the Italian military structure came into formal existence as a result of a law passed by Ricotti's successor on 30 June 1876, but lacked real substance.

Ricotti also strove to speed up Italian mobilisation. He wanted an army like that of Prussia, where it was enough to send a telegram for the troops to move on to a war footing, instead of having to begin by sacking or promoting thousands of officers.[10] La Marmora, ever an obstruction to reform, denied that military science had yet been reduced – as he termed it – to moving faster than an adversary and with more men, but Farini reminded him that time had become a much more important factor in warfare now that railway engines had speeded up the movement of armies. It was, he added, of special importance to Italy given her shape and her need to concentrate her armies in the north, for if an enemy caught her before her forces had been properly deployed the result would be certain disaster.[11]

Much the best way to ensure speedy mobilisation was to base the army on territorial recruitment, but almost everyone agreed that in this respect the Prussian example could not be followed. The army was primarily an instrument of reunification; Niccola Marselli likened it to 'the great crucible within which all provincial elements submerge themselves in Italian unity',[12] Also provincial armies might pose a threat to the security of the state – a problem currently preoccupying Thiers in France. However desirable militarily, regional recruitment was politically impossible.

Regional military districts were the next best thing, and Ricotti set up 45 of them in November 1870, adding another eight within a year. In peacetime their function was to receive category I recruits from the surrounding region and give them preliminary training before sending them off to their regiments elsewhere, and to do all the training of category II recruits; in wartime they received and armed local reservists before sending them straight to their regiments at the points of strategic deployment, thus cutting out the intermediary stage of travelling to the regimental depot which might well be at the other end of the country. As a consequence of this reconstruction, it was claimed that the active army could be mobilised in eight days and the provincial army in 15.

The seal of approval was given to Ricotti's ideas by Niccola Marselli. Born in Naples in 1832, Marselli had been trained in the Bourbon army of the Two Sicilies; by the time that reform came to be the issue of the day in 1870 he had become Italy's leading military intellectual. In a study of the Franco-Prussian war published in 1872 he urged that Italy apply the substance of the Prussian system but not its secondary form, stressing the importance of military instruction and patriotic sentiment, but admitting that differences in social and political structure did not permit Italy to apply a system of universal military service. Marselli argued that the real triumph of Prussia was due less to her military system than to her civilisation: 'Without the reform of men, that of institutions is in vain'.[13] For Marselli, the reforms of von Moltke and von Roon had put the barracks at the service of civilised society, and he welcomed the shift away from democratic concepts of military service and towards patriotic ideals, which were somewhat less unruly.[14]

Ricotti's quest for efficiency prompted him to divide the army into ten corps, each of two divisions, to which wartime commanders were allocated. In 1872 the Alpini were created: locally recruited units specialising in mountain-warfare, whose role was to hinder an invader attempting to cross the Alps. Bronze breech-loading artillery pieces were introduced, and in 1875 Ricotti proposed to buy 400 8.7cm steel guns from Krupps – significantly, Italy herself did not have the foundries to make them. The 130 generals on active service were collectively given the title 'General Staff' and a committee of the general staff was established under Cialdini to advise the government on strategic questions. Though potentially highly influential, the committee had little more than a paper existence since Cialdini lacked any power to take practical measures to put his recommendations into effect. Such power was carefully conserved within the war ministry and belonged from December 1873 to its newly created general staff division.

Ricotti also took a lively interest in educational matters, introducing new training manuals and regulations and improving the education offered in the military schools. In the latter activity, he had to contend with a steady decline in applications which he was incapable of reversing. He also initiated the practice of brigade camps, though until 1874 there were only a limited number of fixed locales in which troops manoeuvred, and almost every year the exercise was held in the same place. Not until 1903 were German-style manoeuvres introduced in which only the opening scenario was set and events allowed to unfold in their own way instead of new situations being set every day.[15]

Just as Ricotti had to reshape a disorganised army to face the task of war in the modern world, so he also had to systematise the defence of a kingdom which was highly vulnerable before 1866 and to which the addition of the Veneto had added a new and nightmarish dimension. On 2 August 1871 Ricotti presented a general plan for the defence of Italy. For continental Italy there was to be a 'systematic' defence, for peninsular Italy a series of strong-points. The lengthy process of mobilisation was to be protected by a string of mountain fortifications which would preserve it from disruption. Three lines of defence would protect the north: a series of block-works would defend the Alpine passes; then, if the old Quadrilateral fell, the army would retreat to the Po Valley and hold the bridgeheads for an eventual counter-offensive; if this too failed, the final defensive line would lie along the Appennines, centred on Bologna. The strong-points in the peninsula would comprise the forts of Ancona and Lucera, large fortified camps at Rome and Capua and fortified ports which would include Livorno, Civitavecchia and Gaeta. The full plan called for the construction of 97 *piazze di guerra* at a cost of 306 million lire, a 'reduced' version for 77 *piazze* costing 146 million lire.[16] It was wholly defensive, and its lack of a single focus was a reflection of Italy's general strategic vulnerability. When it was presented to parliament in December 1871 it was cut in half and then lost to view for eighteen months as it underwent detailed scrutiny by a parliamentary commission under Depretis.

While Depretis's commission deliberated behind closed doors, Italy watched anxiously as France began an unexpectedly rapid military revival. Details of her military laws and her railway building programmes were public knowledge. The war ministry also received reports from Paris in the spring of 1873 that military circles favoured using French naval superiority to land troops beyond the Alpine barrier in the event of war. The list of possible targets was worryingly long: it included Genoa, Savona, the Ligurian and Tuscan coastlines, Rome and Naples.[17] Fear of France was all-pervasive, and the British ambassador reported 'a disagreeable feeling of uneasiness as to the future pervading the public mind, which induces people to think that the sooner such military preparations as can be made are made the better'.[18] Then, on 5 June 1873 Depretis's commission published its final report. Its grand design was for an offensive bastion resting on Genoa, Piacenza, Mantua and Venice and, if this were lost, on Bologna. Ricotti was bitterly opposed to any such 'internal redoubt', which he felt embodied defensive and defeatist attitudes.

As parliament debated its policy for defence, a detailed examination of the threats against which Italy must protect herself began. In June 1873 a special commission on coastal defence conceded that the navy was not merely necessary but essential, since it protected the army's flanks and rear, and called for more funds for naval expansion. The soldiers were prepared to back this recommendation: Cosenz opposed spreading out divisions to aid in coastal defence as this would deprive the army of much-needed muscle and the artillery representative, General Longo, admitted that neither the heavy artillery already in existence, nor that under development, was capable of defending the coast.[19]

A detailed study of war against France completed the following month stressed French naval supremacy and the vulnerability of Italy's lengthy coastline. In the main theatre the lack of defensive works would make it easy for France to reach the plain of Lombardy; therefore the Italian army would have to confront an invasion by land at the valley openings before the enemy could concentrate his attacking columns. The planners felt that it would be possible to launch an attack into France, taking the fort of Briançon as a preliminary move in a thrust through the old province of Savoy, but acknowledged difficulties of communications and supply. A somewhat defensive conclusion called for a fleet powerful enough to defend the extended coastline and recommended barring the Alpine and Appennine passes and improving the defended harbours and coastal and interior forts. If these conditions were not fulfilled Italy would have to give up all ideas of an offensive and 'allow a part of our territory to be invaded, the better to be able to concentrate our forces in order to confront the enemy with larger forces than his'.[20] Since Italy lacked the means to fulfill these requirements, defence was her only strategic option.

Although Italy was vulnerable, the planners did not think she was about to find herself at war. In current circumstances a single-handed war against France was regarded as very unlikely. An Italo-German war against France was more probable, in which case Italy might have to take the offensive. She could either attack from the Alps in combination with a German attack from the Moselle and the Vosges, joining up with the German army towards Besançon or Langres; or she could move against Lyons and the heart of France, dividing the enemy's forces and securing the German left flank. A single-handed war against Austria was thought improbable; if it did occur, Italy would be forced to stand on the defensive unless Hungary rebelled against Vienna. An Italo-German war against Austria was extremely unlikely and one against France and Austria merely 'possible'.[21]

Military co-operation with Germany now began to obtrude into Italian military planning. In February 1873 Rome had learned that von Moltke was drawing up plans for war against France or Russia or both. At that time Berlin was contemplating Italian assistance only against both enemies combined, in which case, if she chose to intervene, Italy would have the task of penetrating the Rhone valley and finding a way to join up with German forces advancing from Alsace.[22] A year later von Moltke's interest was a more active one. He quizzed the Italian military attaché on how long it would take Italy to concentrate 200 000 men in Piedmont, and was told of the plans to deploy in the Po Valley and of the vision of Bologna as a general redoubt. His reaction was that Italy would do better to spend her money on improving the active army with a view to taking the offensive and entering France if war broke out.

Vous seriez sûrs de nous y trouver he said, lingering on the phrase, then he repeated, you are wrong to spend so much on fortifying your coasts. Attack; that is the best way to defend yourself and to force the French fleet to put back into Toulon.[23]

In March 1874, as the military began to work on its war scenarios, the chamber of deputies locked horns over the reduced general defence plan proposed by Depretis – still an expensive option at 79 700 000 lire. Corti sounded the first note of caution. A study of history had convinced him that fortifications were of decreasing importance. Wars were won by giving battle, and battles were won by transporting large numbers of soldiers rapidly to where they were needed. He was also alarmed lest mediocre generals be influenced in their strategy by the existence of particular forts, and preached the virtues of a decisive battle in the Po Valley: 'If the army wins, then all is well, but if is beaten there is no fortification in the world which will save us'.[24]

Some deputies opposed the scheme on the grounds of economy. Others supported it, believing that alliances were won only by those powers which showed themselves strong and that the weak were sought by no one – a theme which would be heard increasingly in debates on Italian defence policy. Di Gaeta probably spoke for many in doubting the effectiveness of large and expensive fortifications in general but recognising that certain places, such as the western Alpine passes, were so vulnerable as to need them.[25]

Bertolè-Viale gave the key speech in the debate. Answering the varied criticisms, he suggested that fortifications were only the complementary part of a state's defences 'but a very necessary complement and, I would say, an indispensable one'. He revealed that the great encounters by which Italy would be defended would take place in the Po Valley, but did not accept the view that Italy would be finished if they were lost; she could fall back on the natural defensive line of the Po and the Appennines, defend it and then gradually take the offensive. In wartime, it followed that the mass of the army was necessarily going to be concentrated in the Po Valley, which meant that other places must be defended – most notably Rome.[26]

The debate about where and how to defend Italy was conducted against a backdrop of acute financial stringency. Italy's wealth was much less than that of the other great powers, and her military expenditure was absolutely and proportionately smaller than theirs: in 1874 Russia spent 28.7 per cent of her budget on her army; Germany 21.6 per cent; France 27.7 per cent; Austria 16.2 per cent; and Italy only 14.7 per cent.[27] The army had also to compete with other claimants on the public purse, of which the cuckoo in the nest was the public debt, the servicing of which took almost one-third of Liberal Italy's available monies. Ricotti successfully held the military budget at one-fifth of state expenditure, less than the previous decade but still a great drain.[28] There was little prospect of more money: the country remained in the down-swing of an economic cycle until 1879, when there was a ten-year upswing followed by another crisis.

Confronted with this situation, the government took to asking for money for parts of programmes rather than for whole packages. The chamber of deputies had agreed to spend 78 million lire re-equipping the artillery, completing clothing and mobilisation equipment stores, improving the railways and introducing the new Vetterli breech-loading rifle. It was now asked to vote a further 79 million lire, leaving a balance of some 150 million for later approval. It agreed to the requested sum for the 'revised' scheme of fortification, recognising that it could not provide the Po Valley with defences out of the money available. The plan was subsequently withdrawn on the eve of its approval by the senate because of pressing financial complications.

While the deputies wrestled with the financial dilemma, the general staff committee turned its attention to converting the hypotheses of war framed during the previous winter into detailed studies of Italy's military options. The problem of war with France dominated its work. If she took the offensive her main lines of operation would be along the converging valleys of five rivers north and west of Turin and south of Alessandria. It was estimated that she would be able to launch fourteen army corps across the frontier twelve days after mobilisation began. To dictate peace she would have to defeat Italian troops on the Po, chase them out of strong positions on the Appennines and defeat the last detachments in the valleys of the Arno and the Tiber.[29] The convergent topography of the area dictated Italy's strategic response. Light troops would delay the enemy on the mountain crests; a more solid defence would be put up at the mouths of the valleys to gain time; and the main manoeuvre would 'profit from the Alpine obstacle which will hold the attacker's columns apart from one another [allowing one] to throw oneself against one or other of them with possibly preponderant force'.[30] Forward Alpine defensive zones were suggested to counter faster French mobilisation.[31]

If the French attacked along the southern route by way of Nice, eight corps were to be deployed around Alessandria. This plan counted on at least twenty-five days and up to a month in which to deploy; if there were a delay in mobilisation for any reason, or if part of the force had to be detached from the main theatre of the Po Valley, there would not be enough time to perform this manoeuvre.[32] The possibility that France might also try a coastal landing to pin down or distract the Italians did not perturb the planners: they would take four days to land and unite two army corps, while two Italian army corps could be on the spot in three days and would probably have won a victory even before all the enemy troops had combined.[33]

The essence of Italian defensive strategy was 'to wait the arrival of the enemy columns on the plain between the mouths of the Alpine valleys and seek to mass against them and defeat them individually'. The problem was that the French were assumed to be capable of getting to the plains before the Italian army had completed its deployment.[34]

Obviously the enemy had to be slowed down during his passage of the Alpine zone, and since it was poorly defended this would mean finding extra manpower without weakening the main force more than was strictly necessary. The need to forge a policy for the Alpine zone was strengthened by the fact that the frontier would be vulnerable to surprise attacks to gain possession of the hilltops and ease the crossing. An enemy would encounter obstacles at Ventimiglia, Savona and Genoa; likewise the Val d'Aosta was defended. However, the valleys immediately west of Turin which lacked advanced defences lay in the central line of a triple French thrust.

The question of Italy's capacity to mount an offensive into France had already been raised in 1873–74. It was also exercising von Moltke. 'Italy is indefensible' he was reported as having concluded; 'the preoccupation with the peninsula will weigh too heavily in the balance – Italy defends herself in France'.[35] Italian minds had already turned to this possibility and a series of studies was drawn up to weigh the chances of a successful offensive. Italy's planners began by questioning the widespread belief that the strategic offensive was the first element of victory. Of two equal forces, the winner would be the one most quickly in order and most ably directed; therefore to balance out the enemy forces was the first requirement.

> No-one, we think, can deny the fact that in the greater number of instances the safest and easiest way to gain this objective is the defensive.[36]

Taking the offensive was also difficult, due to the geography of the frontier and the weakness of Italian forces.

Seven possible lines of advance existed, but geography and French fortifications ruled out five of them. The best was that of the Upper Isère by way of the Lesser St Bernard pass: there were no forts blocking it until Albertville, which the French had begun to fortify in the summer of 1874. If Italian forces had to link up with those of Germany, it would be best to strike by this route towards Langres and Lyons. However, although two army corps could be fed across the frontier at both the Lesser St Bernard and Moncenisio passes at least five would be needed, and it was by no means clear how the fifth corps could be deployed quickly and effectively.[37] The passage of an Italian invading force would be greatly eased by the construction of a railway line in the Val d'Aosta but Ricotti ruled it out because the provinces concerned could not contribute to its construction, the state could not afford it and it would lack the commercial utility to sustain itself.[38]

By the summer of 1876 planning for an offensive war against France presumed an alliance with Germany as its only practical basis. If Germany attacked through Lorraine there appeared little prospect of effecting a junction between the two armies. An attack from Alsace would require the German left to extend south via the Doubs Valley to meet advancing Italian forces which would take at least 40 days to reach the plain of Lyons. Because of the problems of time and distance, the planners could see no way in which to unite German and Italian forces except by breaking Swiss neutrality to make use of the Sempione, Gottard and Spluga passes. If Swiss neutrality were respected, '*there is no plan of campaign which presents conditions favourable to the junction of the Italian and German armies*'.[39] Acting in the dark as regarding German intentions, the planners then drew up a scheme in which five Italian corps would advance by way of the Lesser St Bernard and Moncenisio passes, and three corps by way of Argentiera and Monginevra; their objective would be Albertville-Grenoble, from which point they would either move on Lyons or swing north to meet the Germans.

The defence policy drawn up in the first half of the 1870s reflected the extent of Italy's strategic vulnerability. It also contained at least as many problems as solutions. One was that of local attacks designed to hinder Italian mobilisation and deployment; to guard against interruption from the sea two Italian corps were withdrawn from Genoa and Savona to guard Alessandria. On the issue of defending the Alpine zone the war minister and the general staff committee disagreed. Ricotti approved of the idea proposed by the commanding general at Turin for an active forward defence, seizing some twelve passes at the moment that war broke out.[40] Bertolè-Viale and his committee saw Alpine defence as merely the prelude to the main act of any defensive war and criticised the local commander for committing too many men to the forward zone.[41] Nor was France the only threat. Some attention was given to the problems posed by war against Italy's other powerful neighbour, Austria-Hungary, and a preliminary defence plan existed by the end of 1875. It consisted of little more than a sketch in which six corps were strung out along the Po between Verona and Padua with three more in reserve at Bologna.[42]

For a variety of reasons, much of the Italian planning was still hypothetical. No clear foreign policy input determined with whom and in what circumstances Italy might be allied. No mechanism existed to mobilise and deploy the Italian army in execution of the schemes, although Ricotti had several times pointed out the need for one; nor would the first mobilisation instructions appear until after his successor had come to the war ministry. A transport section was only created in the general staff in 1875; its first movement-tables were devised during the course of the year, but were very unsophisticated. And the planners had always to reckon with Italy's parlous transport position. Lines were few and mostly single-track: only one line ran from the valley of the Arno to the Po, and because of the inclines it had only half a normal line's efficiency. The length of the Italian peninsula, and its mountainous nature, meant that lines had to be built almost on the shore, and as French naval strength mounted the vulnerability of such lines to interdiction became pressingly apparent. The railway system in the north was not even under national control, being run by the South Austrian railway company until July 1878 when Italy took it back and a commission was set up to inquire into its future.

A full fortification policy, however desirable, threatened to be prohibitively expensive, and Ricotti was determined to give priority to soldiers not masonry. So necessity and preference combined to produce the idea of fortifying only a few peripheral points. In January 1875 a plan was presented requiring 20 million lire for fortifications, with a further 3 500 000 for armaments and 10 million for stores, to be spent in the quinquennium 1875–79. This was a considerable reduction on the schemes of 1871, but to balance the budget it was cut even further to 20 million, of which 13 million was to go on fortifications for land defence. Rome was notably absent from the list, and an attempt by the secretary general of the war ministry, Veroggio, to force the government's hand by demanding that it be made the politico–moral centre of the nation and the final defensive redoubt resulted in his being sacked by Ricotti and replaced by Domenico Primerano.[43] Shortly after this a change of government produced a new direction in military affairs.

In March 1876 the Left finally gained power in Italy and Depretis formed his first ministry, with Luigi Mezzacapo as war minister. Then aged 61, Mezzacapo was the first southerner to hold the office, and the first non-Piedmontese since Fanti in 1861. Educated in the Bourbon army, he had fought for the Venetian Republic in 1848–49 and then gone into exile on Malta, moving to Turin in 1853. He had played an important part in the Tuscan campaign in 1859, and became a lieutenant-general the following year. He was made inspector of military education in 1864, and nominated senator six years later. Described by the British ambassador as 'a scientific rather than a practical soldier', he had served on most of the important military commissions and was very experienced.[44]

One of Mezzacapo's first acts in office was to compile an inventory of his inheritance. As an indictment of his Piedmontese predecessors it made dismal reading. There were 240 000 infantry but only 210 000 Vetterlì rifles. There was also a chronic shortage of ammunition: 25 million rounds where there should be 69 million. Apart from a shortage of ammunition limbers, the field artillery was in good state; its 12cm muzzle-loaders were being phased out and 400 new guns were due from Krupps by September. Heavy artillery was in a much more parlous condition: only one 32cm cannon existed, with no ammunition, though a further four were under construction. The Italian inventory also contained 82 24cm cannon and 206 22cm howitzers.

As far as fortification went, many new works had been built in the western Alps. However, Genoa was in virtually the same state as it had been in 1861 and so were Civitavecchia, Gaeta, Messina, Ancona and Venice. The coasts of Sardinia and Sicily and the ports of Livorno, Naples, Brindisi, Palermo and Taranto were quite undefended; and even if they were fortified there was no artillery to put in them. Many of the inland *piazze* were weak, particularly Piacenza and Bologna, and in Mezzacapo's view were in a worse state than they had been in 1866. On mobilisation, Mezzacapo saw 'some delay and confusion' as unavoidable, and he believed that the heavy tasks of the district depots would add to this.[45] A shortage of officers meant that the mobile militia was capable only of garrisoning forts in the interior. Wartime staffs were non-existent and wartime commanders for reserve divisions had not been appointed. All in all, Italy was clearly far from being ready for war.

Mezzacapo's policy was to improve the quality of the troops at the cost of quantity. Thirty-six thousand category II troops were left untrained, and the money saved was used to hold 12 000 category I troops for an extra four months. He also took a decisive step towards resuscitating the policy of heavy fortifications against which Ricotti had battled when, in May 1877, he diverted 5 million of the 13 million lire set aside for Alpine defence to fortify Rome. Over the succeeding five years a string of fifteen forts was constructed around the capital, three kilometres outside the walls and generally two kilometres apart, forming a polygon 40 kilometres in circumference. They cost a total of 23 million lire.[46] Many of the forts still stand, inhabited now not by soldiers but by gypsies.

As a southerner, Mezzacapo was viewed with mistrust in many quarters. The divisions in the Italian high command, which had been papered over after 1866, opened up with a vengeance when he unleashed the so-called 'revenge of the Nunziatella' – named after the Bourbon military academy at Naples which he had attended. Ricotti had been concerned about the incapacity of the officer corps and had introduced a law empowering him to retire those no longer fit for active service. Mezzacapo now took that policy somewhat further. A royal decree, signed on 18 May 1877, put a dozen generals on the retired list. Among the Piedmontese generals who fell victim to Mezzacapo were Raffaele Cadorna, who had taken Rome in 1870, and Petitti di Roreto, twice minister of war.

The manner in which the sackings were carried out was certainly unfortunate: Petitti apparently learned of his dismissal while reading a newspaper at his barber's.[47] Political considerations were thought to lie behind them, either in terms of a general revenge exacted on the lords of the Turin military academy by their Bourbon opposite numbers for the defeat sixteen years earlier, or because some generals had voted the wrong way on the abuse of the clergy bill. However, Mezzacapo was much exercised by command competence. Even the ultra-conservative Cialdini, who at first talked of resigning, was 'obliged to admit that many of those who have been retired are indeed past good service'; and the king wanted two more generals sacked.[48]

Mezzacapo also earned the wrath of the conservative military establishment by challenging the sacred principle of seniority which had governed promotion in the upper reaches of the officer corps. As well as sacking twelve lieutenant-generals – the highest rank in the peacetime army – he had promoted 14 major-generals and 31 colonels, all chosen by selection, over the heads of senior colleagues. In so doing he had reinterpreted an 1853 law on promotion which had in theory allowed for choice but in practice made seniority the most important factor. Ricotti had been moving in the same direction, having used a law of 1871 and a royal decree of 1874 to block the promotion of the lazy or the unfit beyond the rank of major, but had operated on the basis of seniority higher up the scale. Mezzacapo believed that if good men were to be attracted into the officer corps and used to best advantage, selection was essential in order to offer the more able the prospect of rapid promotion. Decrees of 15 July and 26 August 1877 announced that promotions to lieutenant-colonel would also be effected by selection and not seniority, and the following January a special examination was instituted for promotion from captain to major.[49]

Uppermost in Mezzacapo's mind was the fear of a possible European war. Mounting tension between Russia and Turkey, which led to war in April 1877, and fears that Austria-Hungary might profit from the unstable situation by seizing Bosnia and Herzegovina from Turkey, led

to increasingly vociferous distrust of Austria and to mounting irredentism. Victor Emmanuel was eager for Italy to get something out of the
Russo–Turkish war because of his wish 'to crown his life with a victory
which will give the army the prestige and the power which it lacks in the
world's eyes'.[50] The king, Depretis and Crispi all pinned their hopes on
inducing Bismarck to participate in a dismemberment of Austria–
Hungary, a chimera which Crispi pursued out of frustration at Italy's
weakness in international affairs. 'If our leaders had not failed us in
1866', he wrote to Depretis,

> and we conquered in Venetia and on the Adriatic, the Austrians would
> not dare to write and speak of us as they do, the Italian army would be
> a power in Europe, which today it is not, and Italy's voice would
> command greater respect than it does in the different cabinets.[51]

Crispi, who suffered from something akin to international paranoia,
feared a reactionary clerical success in the French elections of 1877, after
which France would attack Italy. He was also convinced that Austria–
Hungary merely waited on the first opportunity to recapture the fortress
of Verona, lost in 1866.

Crispi's fears were wild but not entirely baseless. In February 1877 the
Italian ambassador in Vienna, Di Robilant, reported that Austria was
concentrating 50 000 troops at Graz, and the following month the
military attaché reported evidence that the government was preparing
for war in the near future. The probable enemy seemed to be Russia but
Italy might also be involved, since Austrian officers were convinced that
it was their neighbour's intention to enter into an alliance with Russia.[52]
In July and early August the attaché reported that preparations were
continuing for a mobilisation to the south, and the commander at
Verona, Pianell, recorded signs that Austria was readying herself for
action: they included the laying-in by tobacconists of special stamps for
use by the military in Trieste.[53] Danger also loomed in the west. In April
reports came from the Italian consuls at Marseilles and Villafranca of
French military preparations and in September Primerano reported that
parties of French soldiers had been crossing the frontier near Tour-
noux.[54]

As the international scene darkened, military planners for the first
time gave close attention to the defence of peninsular Italy. The French
were presumed to be the attackers, their purpose to excite the 'dormant
aspirations' of the south by attacking Florence, Rome or Naples – most
probably the latter.[55] The picture which emerged was not a comforting

one. On the Alpine frontier the structure of the valleys would keep the enemy split into separate columns until he gained the plains; in the south the enemy would be in a single mass – probably two army corps – with no immediately obvious objective and the defending troops would have to be split up to cover a number of possible targets. Ideally all available troops should be concentrated in the Po Valley for the main battle. However, Italy was too recently united, and her patriotism too weak, to risk such a strategy. So four regular divisions were allocated to cover Pisa, Rome, Naples and Palermo, supported by four divisions of the mobile militia. This would prevent the disruption of mobilisation, protect the training of the militia, and prevent the enemy gaining his objectives cheaply. Fortifications played a notable part in the plan: 'the fortifications of Rome will be able to delay an invader and provide time to unite mobile forces in sufficient strength to attack him in open field'.[56]

Alarmed and anxious lest Italy be attacked or fail to get compensation for an Austrian advance in the Balkans, Crispi went to Berlin on behalf of the king and Depretis to seek an alliance against Vienna and discovered on 6 September 1877 that Bismarck was unwilling to lift a finger against her. Austro-Italian relations now worsened rapidly. In December the *Neue Freie Presse* reported Andrassy as having announced that if the irredentist movement kept up its activities Austria would retake the Quadrilateral; although this was at once denied it greatly annoyed Victor Emmanuel. The death of the king on 9 January 1878 removed what was thought, wrongly, to be a restraining influence on the irrédentists. In the same month Vienna discovered Crispi's abortive mission to Bismarck the previous September. In March Cairoli, a leading irredentist, became premier and the decline in Italian-Austrian relations approached crisis proportions.

With Depretis's departure Mezzacapo vacated the war ministry, to be replaced by the man he had put in charge of the fortifications of Rome, Giovanni Bruzzo. Mezzacapo had not been content merely to continue Ricotti's reforms.[57] He had reverted to the traditional Piedmontese preference for quality over quantity, reinforcing the first line rather than the reserves. He had also paid considerable attention to improving Italy's cumbersome mobilisation process, increasing the number of military commands and simplifying the task of the military districts. And he had, on 30 June 1876, passed a law creating the territorial militia, though it did not finally appear until April 1880.

Ricotti's attempt to reconstruct Italian military policy had been reversed but Italy's fundamental problems remained unsolved. They were outlined in 1878 by Gandolfi, *relatore* of the military budget. Italy, he pointed out, would remain strategically weak as long as national feeling was not sufficiently diffused to allow of a regional system of recruitment, as long as the communications net remained incomplete, and until a naval force existed which could ensure that deployment was not interrupted by coastal attacks.[58] The army, viewing the bulk of Italian society as militarily unreliable and the frontiers as indefensible, took refuge in expensive fortifications – an occupation force which was itself under siege.

3 Entering the Triple Alliance

Italy's military entered the 1880s as servants of an independent kingdom with no treaty commitments. In keeping with their stance in the previous decade, they saw their overriding strategic task as providing Italy with adequate military security in the face of threats from both Austria-Hungary and France. Either power could launch a seaborne invasion of Italy, and both high command and public were acutely alert to this danger. As far as land frontiers went, Italy's choice seemed to be to meet an attack in the Po Valley or to adopt a forward defence and fight for Italian freedom in the mountains themselves. In the debates over a national defence policy which took place in 1880–87, a conservative military group strove to continue established practice and spend Italy's defence monies building expensive fortifications to guard against both dangers. However, the soldiers exercised only partial control over their own affairs, and they were also to be confronted with new and potentially onerous military obligations.

While the military looked to physical security, the politicians looked to diplomacy and sought allies for Italy in the harsh world of Bismarckian Europe. In 1882, in response to French moves in North Africa, Italy joined Austria-Hungary and Germany to form the Triple Alliance. Superficially, the effects of the success of the military conservatives and of alliance membership were beneficial for the army: its political status rose and – more gratifyingly – the military budget increased to 23 per cent of state expenditure in these years. For these reasons the 1880s have been called 'the happiest years for the Italian army'.[1] However, membership of the Triple Alliance carried a requirement to look beyond Italy's frontiers; and it involved a potential loss of autonomy. A conservative and defensive-minded military faced the possibility that it might be drawn into military adventurism, either in Europe or elsewhere, by politicians eager to escape from the legacy of 1866 and make Italy's voice heard among the Great Powers. While the soldiers concentrated on where to build their forts, voices began to mount that Italy faced a choice: 'either to remain under the burden of unmerited defeats, or . . . be swept up in a great war which would provide the occasion to demonstrate her true military capacity'.[2]

Anti-Austrian feeling mounted during 1878 when Corti returned from the Congress of Berlin with 'clean hands'. The substitution of Austrian for Turkish rule in the provinces of Bosnia and Herzegovina marked a set-back for Italy; her only achievement was to prevent outright Austrian annexation of the two provinces.[3] Unease turned into genuine alarm in the autumn of 1879 with the publication in a semi-official Austrian military journal of an article by the former Austrian military attaché at Rome, Alois von Haymerle, entitled *Italicae Res* which concluded that Italy might attempt an attack on Austria at any moment, aimed at annexing Italian-speaking territory.[4] What gave *Italicae Res* its special force in Italian eyes was the fact that the author's brother was Baron von Haymerle, the Austrian foreign minister. It was mistakenly assumed in official circles that the Austrian government could only have sanctioned its publication in order to stimulate national susceptibilities and jealousies. In fact at that time Baron von Haymerle was anxious to improve relations between the two powers. The pamphlet had a profound effect on the war ministry, where Bonelli and his colleagues thought for a while that Austria was about to attack the Veneto.

A searching re-examination of the military position in the aftermath of the Austrian war scare showed how much remained to be done despite the Ricotti reforms: the period under arms had been shortened to save money, reserve troops were untrained, stocks and materials were insufficient, the territorial militia existed only on paper, and the officer corps was in a critical condition.[5] Money was simply too tight to call-up Ricotti's large force: with an annual contingent of 65 000 conscripts, a permanent element of 37 000 men, and a budget for only 190 000, third-year recruits had to be sent on leave in September and new recruits not called up until January. The obvious solution – to reduce service to two years – was ruled out due to the weakness of Italian patriotism.[6] Italy had to look to her defences, but the treasury was alert to the consequences: hence Count Maffei's remark, 'any addition to the war budget or armaments of Italy would be interpreted abroad as a sign that Italy was harbouring some aggressive designs'.[7] Behind this lay the stark fact that Italy lacked the wealth to fulfil ambitious schemes.

Vienna now gave Rome a thinly veiled warning. Austrian troops were moved up to the Tyrolean frontier, and the Austro-Hungarian war minister, Bylandt-Rhydt, called in the Italian military attaché, Colonel Lanza, early in March. Bylandt opened by expressing his belief in the Italian government's condemnation of the irredentists – 'saying this he had the air of someone who thinks exactly the opposite', added Lanza in parenthesis – and went on to reassure the Italians that Vienna was not looking to regain the Veneto and that war was regarded as likely to be a calamity. His actions, he said, were intended only to prevent any disturbance of the tranquillity between the two neighbouring powers by 'a bunch of seditious activists'.[8] In Rome in the same month seven bills were laid before the chamber of deputies for further military expenditure, of which the lion's share was to go on fixed defences: 18 million lire on frontier defence works, 4 million lire on coastal defence works and 3 million lire on defending the capital itself.

The war scare of 1879 passed but the danger of war did not dissolve. From Berlin it appeared that irredentism was stirring up Austrian feeling to the point at which Vienna might adopt 'a more decided and provocative policy towards us'. The Italian ambassador there, Count di Launay, felt that Italy could draw only one conclusion from the state of European politics: 'the necessity for a prudent policy and for armaments'.[9] A further shadow on the diplomatic horizon was the widespread belief in Germany that war with France was inevitable sooner or later.

The need to strengthen Italy's military power seemed pressing. The most obvious solution was to shorten the term of service, thereby permitting the calling-up of a larger annual class at no extra cost. After Bernardino Milon became war minister in July 1880 he was invited by the chamber of deputies to consider reducing the term of service, but refused to do so. The majority of the high command believed that any reduction below three years would gravely damage the solidity of the army; and the conservative press backed this up by claiming that inadequate primary education meant that recruits would not have the requisite sense of duty and that in any case Italy lacked the railways to transport larger armies.[10] Significantly, the minority of soldiers who argued for two-year service saw the army as an offensive instrument not a defensive one.

The strength of the defensive pre-occupation with fortifications was underlined when the chamber of deputies voted in June 1880 on the seven bills put before it three months earlier. Asked to discuss proposals for the expenditure of 80 170 000 lire on fortifications and armaments, the chamber forebore to question the calculations of the military experts and maintained a patriotic silence.[11] Given the money, the decision had to be made how to spend it, and in October 1880 Milon set up a special commission under Pianell to study the Alpine defences of the north-eastern frontier. It worked rapidly and reported at the end of the month that the first priority was to fortify the val d'Adige; the upper Piave was of secondary importance and the Tagliamento was regarded as a third priority, to be defended with permanent works. Pianell told the minister somewhat pointedly that block forts, an expansion of the Alpine militia, the division of the frontier into strategic zones under commanders who could study their problems in peacetime, an increase in mountain artillery and additional supplies and munitions were all needed.[12]

On 24 November 1880 another commission was set up, under the presidency of Luigi Mezzacapo, to organise the north-eastern defences. Its eight members included five former ministers of war and the man destined shortly to become the first chief of the Italian general staff, Enrico Cosenz. Ricotti suggested that the Adige should be the main defensive line against Austria, and urged that none of the fortresses be too big, lest they act as magnets and draw troops from the main armies of manoeuvre.[13] Bertolè-Viale pointed out that due to Austria's railway construction she could mobilise more divisions more quickly on the Friuli frontier than the Tyrol. From that frontier eight separate roads led to the Piave. Cosenz agreed with the implications of this analysis and suggested a main baseline along the Po, resting on Mantua and Peschiera.[14]

Information had come from Vienna earlier in the year that any Austrian offensive would be launched across the Isonzo and that the Tyrol would serve only as flank protection and as a threat against an Italian defence.[15] As the committee began to reach this conclusion for itself, Bruzzo made a strong appeal for a more advanced line of defence than the Po-Adige position. He gained some support from Luigi Mezzacapo, who remarked that he could suppose that unforeseeable circumstances might make an offensive necessary. Cosenz examined the problem and reported that he favoured a defensive line on the Piave. The commission quickly agreed that this should become the first line of defence, with bridgeheads on the left bank and fortifications at Mestre to protect Venice. Despite the echoes of Metz which it aroused in some minds, and the fear that an army might be locked up in such a fort and play no further part in field operations, the committee agreed to fortify Verona to protect the left flank of the army, and the Adige became the agreed second-line of defence. In his summing-up Luigi Mezzacapo congratulated the commission on having devised a scheme of defence capable of paralysing and repulsing any attack. He did not point out that the large sums to be spent on fortification effectively deprived the army of the reserves it would need to launch its counter-attack.

Austria-Hungary was not Italy's only worry, and in July 1881 Emilio Ferrero, Milon's successor, set up another commission – again under the presidency of Luigi Mezzacapo – to study the problem of defence against France. Once again the defensive-mindedness of the military conservatives was demonstrated, but this time it ran into opposition. A major clash developed between Cosenz and Mezzacapo, rooted in the way in which military problems were analysed. Cosenz argued that enemy landings would pose the most dangerous threat along the Italian Riviera because they would directly influence the main land operations. Mezzacapo countered that the dangers of attack from the sea were wider than was usually supposed: for example Sicily could be taken with 200 000 men and from there the war could be carried to the peninsula. Pianell shared his view, but Cosenz was unconvinced, observing that 'to operate in this way, the enemy would need to employ a great deal of time, which would be all to the advantage of the defence'.[16]

The navy could not offer much in the way of support for Cosenz. Admiral Saint-Bon pointed out that the Italian coast was long and wide open, and from it an attacker could much more easily reach the centre of gravity than if he attacked across the mountains. In his opinion the French would begin a war by bombarding one or more of the great maritime cities, when, 'under the pressure of an irresistible current of public opinion, our fleet would be fatally driven to sacrifice itself to impede such a bombardment'.[17] Once the fleet was destroyed, France could easily land 150 000 men. Saint-Bon also pointed out that if the Po armies were defeated they could fall back and conduct a successive defensive at various points, whereas the fall of Rome would be a decisive political blow.

Cosenz struggled to attain a maximum concentration of nine corps in the decisive theatre of the Po Valley, but Mezzacapo would not abandon his obsession with invasion and manipulated the order of business to overcome opposition. Having lost the proposal that the peninsular theatre was more important than the Po Valley by nine votes to one, he immediately asked whether Sicily should therefore be left void of first-line troops. The committee would not take such a risk and agreed unanimously to leave one brigade there, whereupon Mezzacapo asked whether the same applied to Naples. When the committee indicated that it did, he switched to Rome and asked for three brigades there. When he met sharp resistance in asking for yet another division for La Spezia, he at once ended the day's session.[18] The next day, when the committee reconvened, he reverted to the question of the Rome garrison.

Bertolè-Viale now brought about a revolution in Italian strategy. He pointed out that the French needed only eight days to mobilise, whereas Italy needed ten and then faced the task of transporting her troops up the peninsula to the north-west corner of the country. The French would be able to cross the frontier between ten and 14 days after mobilisation, launch a decisive attack from the 16th day, and could emerge on to the plains on the 21st or 22nd day. Faced with hard and unpleasant facts, the committee adopted an idea voiced earlier by Pianell: that resistance in the mountain zone should be as prolonged as possible.[19] It agreed to base seven corps on Turin, Alba and Acqui, with an eighth garrisoning La Spezia and Acqui, a ninth in Tuscany and a tenth divided between Rome, Naples and Sicily.

The commission had abandoned the strategy of the previous decade, of delaying the enemy in the mountain zone and then manoeuvring against separate enemy columns on the Paduan plain, in favour of a forward strategy of *resistenza ad oltranza* in the mountains. As a consequence, fortification policy had to change: mountain forts were no longer temporary barriers designed only to slow down an advancing enemy, but secure bases for counter-offensives. At the same time fortifications on the peninsula remained important as the threat of invasion mounted in the 1880s, not in place of the Alpine danger but in addition to it.[20]

A new strategy meant new fortifications, and another commission was set up, again under the chairmanship of Luigi Mezzacapo, to produce recommendations. There were two sections of the frontier to consider: the western arc running from the valley of the Dora Baltea down to the Maritime Alps, and the southern arc centred on the head of the Tanaro valley and on Genoa. French military building at Albertville and the construction of new railway lines dictated the line of greatest danger, and it was decided to fortify the western arc, while the southern one was protected chiefly with men.

The danger of invasion from the sea combined with a land attack along the Cornice made the Tanora a vulnerable conduit through which enemy troops might interfere with Italian reserves mobilising and deploying to the north. A commission chaired by Ricotti that summer had recommended a mobile defence for this area, but Mezzacapo pronounced firmly in favour of permanent works – and admitted that he was in the minority – 'partly because by this means possession of the area would be more assured, and partly because this could be achieved without immobilising a large number of mobile troops'.[21]

In reporting the committee's deliberations, Mezzacapo did not hesitate to stress his own opinions where they differed from those of his colleagues. Mostly he was among the minority which wanted additional fortifications. He argued in support of his position that the more the needs of defence could be met with permanent works, the more mobile troops would be available to take the field. This was a specious claim:

fortifications swallowed money and troops. But it convinced cautious military conservatives. Following his recommendations the war minister presented a bill in December 1881 calling for 55 million lire to be spent over five years on the most urgent fortifications, including 11 million for Rome and 17 million for block forts, as well as 32 500 000 lire for artillery. In June 1882 these measures were approved.

On 1 April 1881 the war ministry passed into the hands of Emilio Ferrero. Ferrero's political credentials were impeccable: yet another product of the Turin military academy, he had been decorated at Novara in 1849, seen service in the Crimea and commanded a brigade in King Umberto's corps in 1866, doing well at the battle of Villafranca, before commanding a division in Cadorna's assault on Rome in 1870. Ferrero arrived at a moment of high tension, for early in May the French took over the protectorate of Tunis. Italy's fears of a landing on her vulnerable sea-board, now more exposed than ever, increased.[22] Public demands that Italy make more provision for her defence mounted and the politicians were warned that they had better look to the country's defences.

There were two options open; either to spend yet more money on defence or to seek the protection of an alliance. The latter course looked unpromising. Vienna had resolved her difficulties with the Dual Alliance in October 1879, and two years later von Haymerle had been succeeded as foreign minister by Kalnoky, a devout clerical who seemed no friend of Italy. Nor did Berlin look much better. Bismarck was showing distinct signs of approval of France's Tunisian move as it lessened the threat of *révanchisme* in Europe; and the Italian military attaché reported that the emperor treated the French, Russian and Austrian attachés intimately but had time only for a few words with him *en passant*, putting him on a par with the Spanish, Japanese and Chinese.[23]

Despite considerable public feeling against allying with former enemies, Italy's diplomats chose to seek support from Berlin and Vienna. But to gain that support she had to contribute something to the common cause. As one newspaper put it: 'We must at all costs wipe out the ugly memories of 1866 and show evidence that an alliance with us will be of real use'.[24] In terms of numbers, Italy was militarily weak. In 1880 almost all European states possessed one army corps for every 2 million inhabitants; by this formula she should have possessed fifteen or sixteen corps, whereas she had only ten.[25] Calculations such as these did not take account of the lack of resources, a small manufacturing base and an accumulated national debt; but arguments based on what Italy could afford cut little ice when security and status were both at issue.

Ferrero responded to the situation by making two changes in military organisation. First, the standing army was expanded from ten to twelve corps by calling up more men but giving them less training, against the advice of von Moltke.[26] Sticking to a three-year term of service, Ferrero increased the size of the first category from 65 000 to 76 000 but allowed part of it – an average of one-sixth during the 1880s – to serve for between eighteen months to two years. Some 20 000 category II recruits were called for between two and six months training each year, and two more grounds were devised for removal to category III, which now amounted to some 25 per cent of the annual list.[27] Alongside this, the 180 000 men of the mobile militia were formed into ten divisions and became an integral part of the army, and the territorial militia was formed into 350 battalions to cover the coasts against enemy landings and to maintain internal order, thus freeing troops for active duty.

Ferrero's reforms weakened the army, as Ricotti pointed out. Italian battalions were now smaller than French, German or Russian ones since the numerical size of the army had not increased by the necessary 20 per cent. Also the Italian army already had only one gun for every 415 men, compared to the Austrian ratio of one per 382 men, the German of one per 330 men, and the French of one per 312 men; Ferrero's proposals would worsen the artillery ratio to one gun for every 438 men.[28] The conservatives responded angrily, labelling Ricotti and his supporters 'counterfeit Prussians' for their concern with mere numbers.[29] Ferrero justified his changes by arguing that increasing the size of the infantry companies and the artillery and cavalry would only produce an improvement in 'tactical power', whereas his system had augmented Italy's 'strategic power'.[30]

The prospect of partnership with Germany and Austria-Hungary – and therefore of staff conversations and joint planning – also raised the issue of reform of Italy's clumsy and complicated staff system. In January 1880 Carlo Corsi, writing about the so-called 'Prussian revolution', had called for the creation of an independent chief of the general staff. With the rise of the French threat and calls for military reform, the time had come to do away with the committees which for so long had taken such decisions as had been made. What was needed was a proper chief of the general staff, leaving the war minister free to concentrate on administering the budget.[31]

A more powerful planning head of the army could be an important contribution to making Italy alliance-worthy. Moreover, in war the traditional Italian problem of who would take over-all command still remained. In such imprecise circumstances, a chief of general staff could be 'a most useful implement of war, the supreme complement of a good system of strategic preparation, of a well-ordered military state'.[32] Characteristically Ferrero took a half-measure and decided to resuscitate the moribund Committee of the General Staff, selecting as Cialdini's successor Lieutenant-General Enrico Cosenz. The new appointment was greeted with a mixture of pleasure and anticipation. It was no coincidence that it was announced during King Umberto's visit to Vienna in late October 1881.

The new venture started badly. When the committee was first convened under Cosenz's presidency on 5 November, Pianell, one of the most senior and respected of Italian generals, was absent. Annoyed at being passed over in the search for Cialdini's replacement in favour of an officer of less seniority, he had resigned.[33] In fact, although Cosenz's new post could excite envy it was far from powerful: if, for example, a general of a higher grade or greater seniority was called on to the committee the president had to vacate the chair in his favour. Nor was his role in time of war at all clear.

The war minister had traditionally been the overlord of the Italian army and the king's lieutenant. Any move towards a Prussian-style chief of the general staff would threaten ministerial pre-eminence, and Ferrero was not prepared to step that far. Accordingly, article 15 of the law on the organisation of the army and administrative services of 26 November 1881 carefully reinforced the minister's position by placing the chief of staff under his authority. The new scheme included no plans to increase the number of general staff personnel. Furthermore, the fact that the power to summon the committee rested with the minister meant that Cosenz's post was something of a sham.[34]

While the military anguished over modest reforms, Italy's politicians set out to resolve the situation by diplomatic means. On 23 December 1881, in the aftermath of Umberto's successful visit to Vienna and with Bismarck's flattering references to the Pope ringing alarm bells in Rome, Blanc, secretary-general of the foreign ministry, asked Austria-Hungary for an alliance. The timing was good. Austrian nervousness of Russia had been intensified by a revolt in Bosnia over the imposition of conscription, which had lasted from November 1881 to March 1882. Popular feeling against Vienna ran high in Russia, with the interior minister, the court, the royal household and the army all apparently ready to fight. Bismarck, worried about a visit paid to Paris by the bellicose slavophile Russian general Skobelev, and confronted by the spectre of a Franco–Italian–Russian alliance, encouraged the Italian move.

On 20 May 1882 Italy entered the Triple Alliance. Under the terms of the agreement, which ran for five years, Germany and Austria-Hungary were bound to come to her help if she were attacked by France without direct provocation; if France attacked Germany, Italy promised assistance; if two non-signatory powers (France and Russia) attacked one member of the alliance without direct provocation this was deemed a *casus foederis* which brought the obligation to assist into effect; and if Russia attacked Austria-Hungary, Italy promised nothing more than benevolent neutrality unless France joined the war. Relations with Vienna improved at once: a week after the signature of the alliance the emperor went out of his way to praise the new Italian army laws and to express his appreciation for the goodwill shown at a ceremony for the Austrian dead at Montebello.[35]

To argue that the Triple Alliance gave Italy 'something she did not really need, namely the promise of support against a French attack', and that such a guarantee 'was in fact useless since the French at no time dreamt of attacking Italy' is to disregard Italy's strategic and military dilemma, and her perception of her security needs.[36] Her sense of vulnerability was strong enough to overcome a palpable reluctance to unite with Vienna. Her need to take a place alongside the great powers was strongly felt. The Triple Alliance catered to both these facts.

Ferrero's proposals to expand the army to twelve corps and to reorganise the *Milizia mobile* were carried into being in laws of 29 June 1882 and 8 July 1883. Meanwhile more committees recommended more fortifications. In February 1882 a report recommended fortifying Taranto, Venice and Ancona – the latter to guard Rome against a landing on the east coast. In November a committee under Pianell pointed out that the French could land 70 000 troops at Viareggio or Leghorn in the last days of an Italian mobilisation, and an equivalent number some eight to ten days later. It therefore recommended fortifying the landward side of Leghorn and securing all the passes of the Tuscan Appennines west of the line from Bologna to Florence against attack from north and south alike, thus enabling Italy to resist an Austrian invasion which had crossed the Po or a French invasion across the Maritime Alps. The committee also recommended two more fortified lines to the north, one around Casale-Alessandria and the second on the heights above Stradella and the lower Ticino.[37]

This was, to say the least, a generous plan and Ferrero asked for a 'lesser' version, giving Ricotti the chance to voice his now customary reservations about too much fortification and his belief in an army with fewer, larger units. He suggested fortifying only Bologna and Stradella.

After some opposition from Pianell, Bruzzo found a way round the *impasse* and an order of priority was agreed. The fear of invasion did not diminish, and in September 1882 the customs service was organised into companies and battalions and placed under military discipline in preparation for a role in the defence of the coasts and frontiers.[38]

The half-measure of replacing Cialdini with Cosenz had satisfied no one, so Ferrero went a step further – and in so doing instituted potentially the most important of all the nineteenth-century military reforms. A royal decree published on 29 July 1882 set out in full the duties of the newly created chief of the Italian general staff. He was given supreme responsibility, under the war minister, for all preparatory studies for war; full command over the general staff corps, its recruitment, activities and advancement; and direction of the studies of the *Scuola di guerra*, in which future general staff officers would be educated. He was also empowered to propose commissions of general officers of the army and navy, of which he would always be a member, to examine specific military questions; and he was further empowered to make proposals to the minister of war about the formation of the army and to establish, in accord with the minister, general regulations for mobilisation and plans for deployment in accordance with various hypotheses.[39]

The move had enormous politico–military significance for, along with the expansion to twelve corps, it was to be Italy's military 'dowry' to the Triple Alliance.[40] Perhaps its most important aspect was the power given to the new chief of staff not merely to study defence problems but to draw up war plans to meet them. However, the job had limitations – notably the subservience it demanded towards the war minister – and as a result its occupant would need to be able to get on with his minister, but also to hold his own against him in professional matters if need be. Independence, experience and a high military reputation enabled Enrico Cosenz to sustain a position which might have collapsed around the ears of a less well-qualified occupant.

The first chief of the Italian general staff had an unusual background. In the first place, he was not Piedmontese; born in Gaeta on 12 January 1820, he had attended the Nunziatella and served in the Bourbon army before joining Manin in the defence of Venice in 1848. Exiled for ten years, he had returned to fight with Garibaldi's *Cacciatori* in 1859, and with the 'Thousand' in Sicily the following year. Transferring back into the Piedmontese army, Cosenz had avoided the disaster at Custoza and emerged from the campaign as one of the few senior officers of proven capacity. In 1870 he took part in the capture of Rome, commanding a division there for the next seven years and then an army corps in Turin. He had been carefully looked over and approved for high office by Victor Emmanuel II and Prince Umberto during manoeuvres in 1877.

As well as being brave and lucky, Cosenz was also an intellectual soldier. By 1875 he had published one book on the war of 1866 and three on the Franco–Prussian war of 1870. A patriot of irreproachable colours, Cosenz added one further quality to his already lengthy list: he had never 'played politics'. He had been made a senator in 1872 – a sign of royal favour and a qualification for advancement to the highest reaches of the army – but although he had more than once been invited to join the government he had always declined.

Cosenz was named chief of the general staff on 3 August 1882 and began his term of office, which was to last eleven years, on 1 September. He said later that no one before him had given any thought to how the army would be deployed in a war and that on entering office he found only a list drawn up by Ricotti of the places where it was to concentrate.[41] This was not strictly accurate, but a great deal remained to be done and Cosenz at once set about reviewing plans for deployment and advanced defence, as well as the rail movements necessary to transport the army to the theatre of war. Within a year of taking up his new post, he had also published a revised set of combat regulations. They were initially criticised as overly defensive and laying too little emphasis on the counter-attack, but the revised regulations issued in July 1885 remedied this defect, absolutely condemning passive resistance and insisting that defensive action could never be considered as anything other than a preparation for the offence.[42] Cosenz also directed his first manoeuvres, uniting two complete army corps for the first time, and drew praise from both Swiss and Austrian observers for his handling of the army.[43]

In April 1882 Ferrero revealed to the chamber of deputies that the Alps were no longer considered merely as an obstacle to an invading force but as a zone of active defence, with forts serving as bases from which to launch counter-offensives. As the autumn elections approached the politicians played on feelings of vulnerability and campaigned for a tougher military policy. Crispi urged the electorate to choose deputies who would vote the funds to complete the necessary fortifications and armaments as soon as possible, and Niccola Marselli told his electoral college that Europe valued Italy at nought and made or unmade diplomatic arrangements without regard to her. Marselli pointed out that belonging to an alliance brought new military obligations as well as political benefits:

the value of an Italian alliance rests on the firm resolution to send a strong Italian army beyond the Alps which can, in the shortest possible time, join in the battles which will decide the destiny of Europe.[44]

An offensive strategy cut straight across the traditional conservative pre-occupation with defence. It was also wishful thinking in 1882, since Italian railways were incapable of sustaining it.[45]

Defence remained the pre-occupation of the highest military authorities, and in May 1883 an examination of the strategic position of the south and the islands found that Naples would be easy prey for an enemy and recommended a programme of fortifications centred on Capua, Messina and Brindisi. The overall national programme was so enormous that the commission voted for a reduced scheme, despite Luigi Mezzacapo's objection that this was a political act and therefore properly the function of the war minister. The cost still came out at 613 million lire, with a further 260 million lire required for artillery, so the list was cut by providing only for the outer defences: the Alps, the Ligurian coast, Lucca, Leghorn, Rome, Capua, Messina and Taranto. Of the internal defences only Verona was retained. The bill now amounted to 420 million lire spread over six years. Depretis thought the figure wildly unrealistic and eventually got Ferrero to accept 225 million lire over five years. When the project was finally put to parliament in May 1884 the finance minister, Magliani, would only cover a bill of 205 million lire. This final reduction was too much for Ferrero, and he resigned on 20 October 1884.

As Marselli had pointed out, membership of the Triple Alliance propelled Italy into active involvement in the affairs of Berlin and Vienna. Austria began to signal her belief that she might be plunged into war at any moment, and pressure for faster military preparations came from the Italian foreign ministry.[46] Ferrero responded that all the necessary arrangements were in hand for the army to undertake either 'an extremely effective defence' or a 'daring offensive, combined with the action of allies' – which was a considerable exaggeration. He also requested an exchange of views with Italy's allies in order to give a more clearly determined scope to the preparatory operations.[47] The growing self-confidence of the French army and the clear indications that, in the event of war, it would be allied with Russia added to the pressure.

Military policy had now to take account of diplomatic agreements, and towards the end of 1883 Cosenz began to explore a more aggressive strategy, sounding out the German military attaché in Rome about transporting the Italian army direct to the principal front on the Rhine. The German general staff failed to follow up this initiative and he was forced to go back to the Alpine offensive plan; but the following April Major von Engelbricht reported that he was still anxious to help the Germans as quickly as possible and to draw off a part of the French forces.[48] Linking up directly with German forces posed enormous difficulties since it meant either breaking Swiss neutrality or making use of the Austrian railways, and neither option looked at all promising.

Public pressure to expand the army and improve Italy's defences began to mount. Bruzzo argued passionately that Italy would never believe in her own powers, and nor would anyone else, until she was no longer exposed to the perils of invasion.[49] Another general, Araldi, attacked the current proposals as feeble and idiotic and suggested fortifying all the mountain passes – a ruinously expensive venture.[50] Perucchetti, a more sober and respected voice, was strongly in favour of fighting a main action in the Alps, but also supported a policy of fortifications, seeing the defences of Rome as entirely valid and recommending fixed works on the north-east and north-western frontiers and the coasts as well as inland.[51] These ideas, far from diminishing the fear of invasion, actually increased it: the better the contest Italy put up in the Alps – the argument ran – the more likely an invader was to try the sea, particularly now that France possessed Tunis.

Although now allied with Austria-Hungary, the Italian military remained fearful of her. Cosenz conducted a detailed study of war against her and produced some discouraging findings. Austria could muster 48 divisions to Italy's 33 and could make use of six railway lines to carry them to the Isonzo, whereas Italy had only two for a deployment on the Piave and one if she deployed further east. Better railways meant Italy could deploy more effectively on the Tyrol, but this would leave the Veneto open to an enemy advance through Friuli. In a localised war, therefore, Italy had to adopt the defensive on both frontiers.[52]

The speed with which the Austrians could place troops on the Isonzo, and the consequent disruption of any Italian mobilisation forward of the Piave, dictated the Italian line of deployment. By the 21st day of mobilisation, Italy could have 15 divisions on the Piave to Austria's nine; the worst she had to fear was an Austrian attack before the remaining army corps, composed largely of mobile militia had arrived. In that case she would have to weigh the odds of fighting a decisive battle there and then or ceding ground to gain time to fight with larger forces. The general staff believed that a battle on the Piave would probably go Italy's way, since it represented a natural defensive position and was being further improved with fortifications; if, however, things turned out less than favourably then Italian troops would retreat to the Adige and fight there.[53]

In contemplating an offensive strategy – alongside an ally or after a successful defence – Cosenz aimed to strike for Vienna. To do this it would be necessary to occupy the Tyrol, since 'an advance on Vienna could not be carried out unless the army was guaranteed against the consequences of an enemy offensive into the valley of the Po by way of the Tyrol'.[54] Italian troops would move on Toblach and then detach two army corps to cut the wedge of the Tyrol at the top by investing Franzenfeste, interrupting the Brenner railway and taking Bolzano, thereby avoiding the well-fortified southern salient. While this was happening the remainder of the Italian army would fight the enemy on the Isonzo. This scheme, which was probably way beyond Italian capabilities, remained the basis of war plans against Austria until the 1890s. Cosenz began practising the necessary manoeuvres at once, changing the summer exercises of the war academy from a defensive retreat in the Valtelline to an offensive in the Val d'Adige and beyond the Isonzo and an attack on the Austrian Tyrol.[55]

By now Cosenz was working with a new minister, for after Ferrero's resignation Ricotti had reappeared. He at once reverted to his man-power policy and spent what money was available on expanding infantry companies from 86 to 100 men. When General Pelloux attacked him in the chamber of deputies for accepting an extra 30 million a year on the budget and defended Ferrero for demanding at least 45, Ricotti poured scorn on those who wanted to spend vast amounts on fortifications and artillery and pointed out that if the thirteen major sites for fortification currently under consideration were equipped according to stated requirements they would need 150 000 fortress artillerymen – ten times the number available. Confusingly, both sides in the debate claimed to have Cosenz's support.[56]

Ricotti was opinionated and overbearing, and by November 1884 there were strong rumours that he and Cosenz were not getting along. In March 1885 he unilaterally withdrew a bill to expand the size of the cavalry and artillery, prompting the observation that the recently created post of chief of the general staff was having little influence in matters where its competence ought to be recognised and established.[57] Seven months later Cosenz's deputy, General Ricci, resigned, ostensibly on grounds of ill-health but actually because he found Ricotti too difficult to work with. A year later Ricotti set up special commissions to examine the organisation of the cavalry and the artillery, thereby side-stepping the existing committee of artillery and engineers, the inspector-general of cavalry and Cosenz all in one go.[58]

The undercurrents of dissatisfaction at Ricotti's attitude towards the role and the powers of the chief of general staff came to a head in the chamber of deputies on 18 December 1886, when Ricotti faced demands that Cosenz be given more power. Ricotti was prepared to hand over some powers to a commander-in-chief of the army, but would not renounce the smallest part of his responsibility:

> The only person responsible to Parliament and to the country for preparations for war is the minister, just as the only person responsible for the results of such a war is the commander-in-chief, although that responsibility is partly borne by the minister who has selected him.[59]

He believed that harmony between the minister and the chief of general staff should come through custom and usage, not by legal prescription; if such harmony did not exist, then the chief of staff must go. Having restated the traditional view of the war minister's function, Ricotti skillfully deflected the attack by drawing the issue on to the plain of personalities and insisting that Cosenz's high moral character and intellectual ability imposed a deference upon any minister which would make conflict impossible.[60]

Even Ricotti, who was very much a radical in the debate over the value of fixed fortifications, came down on the same side as the conservatives over this issue. As a result, further reform was impossible. While the war minister reigned supreme, planning lacked consistency and coherence because of his powers to consult other sources of advice – or none. And the problem of consistency was worsened by the impermanence of ministers: there were five between 1878 and 1881 alone. Finally, war ministers were always pre-occupied with parliamentary battles against the civilian deputies or against their military rivals and critics in the senate. Altogether, the need for a classic chief of the general staff was strong; but the resistance was even stronger.

While the dispute simmered, Cosenz got on with strategic planning and also found time to look carefully into the education being offered to future staff officers at the war academy, forcing the commandant to suppress the literary studies course and expand military history as well as reintroducing an obligatory course in social studies. He also arranged for conferences to be held for final-year students dealing with hitherto neglected topics such as discipline and military morale.[61] In 1887 he managed to reduce the course from three years to two, bringing it into line with current European practices. He faced considerable problems in recruiting qualified staff officers: in 1888, there were only fifty-eight candidates for the war academy, of whom thirty failed the entry tests.[62] The staff began slowly to grow in importance, but not in popularity: numerous articles in journals and periodicals in the 1880s attacked the *oligarchia militare* which dominated the army, composed of the general staff, the engineers and the artillery.

In March 1887 the Triple Alliance fell due for renewal. Two years earlier, in August 1885, Bismarck and Kalnoky had agreed that renewal was worth while but also that Italy had already obtained the bargain she deserved and should be given no new concessions. In the intervening months, however, international circumstances had altered in two respects and the Italian foreign minister, Di Robilant, skillfully used them to improve Italy's position. The brief but stormy career of General Boulanger as French war minister between January 1886 and July 1887 rang alarm bells in Berlin which echoed in Rome. And Italy also drew advantage from the growing rift between Austria-Hungary and Russia. In the spring of 1886 hints appeared in the Russian press, apparently planted by the general staff, that war between the two powers would soon occur, and by November Russia's policy of contesting the Balkans with Vienna seemed to betoken the end of the Three Emperors' League. Early in 1887 news of a partial mobilisation of the Warsaw military district heightened the tension.[63] At this point, Bismarck intervened.

The German chancellor had been alarmed by the news of a French offer of a joint alliance with Italy in the Mediterranean, made in October 1886, and prepared to woo Italy by extending Germany's obligations and forcing Austria to do the same. Knowing of Rome's concern at the possible partition of the Balkans between Russia and Austria-Hungary, of the tide of popular feeling against Vienna, and of the depth of Italian fears about a possible French attack, Bismarck moved swiftly to avoid the recurring spectre of a French-Italian-Russian agreement which would do much to resolve Italy's alarms. In January 1887 he made it plain that Germany would not back Austria's eastern policy. He also pointed out that Italy might not be able to afford Austria much help but could certainly do her a great deal of harm. Kalnoky gave way, and on 20 February 1887 the Triple Alliance was renewed for a further five years. In separate agreements Germany extended the *casus foederis* to cover a French advance in North Africa and Austria-Hungary accepted that any change in the status quo in the Balkans would automatically trigger reciprocal compensation for the power not initiating such a change.[64] Eight days earlier Di Robilant had secured a British guarantee of the status quo in the Mediterranean, to which Spain also adhered.

Di Robilant's skilful diplomacy had created a 'truly formidable defensive system' to secure Italy against French aggression;[65] but, though successful in its European policy, Depretis's government was tottering towards collapse as a consequence of misadventures in Africa. Adopting his time-honoured formula of *transformismo* in an attempt to out-manoeuvre opposition, the premier sacked both Ricotti and Di Robilant in order to broaden his cabinet, bringing Bertolè-Viale to the war ministry to warm press approval. At the same time he warned parliament that the military forces of the European powers were increasing, as a result of which

we have been forced to recognise the urgent need to make provisions which will require heavy expenditure, in order to complete our military organisation, strengthen its solidity and improve its armament . . .[66]

Depretis was responding to the debate on a new three-year military service law then taking place in France, and to the bellicose posture being adopted by General Boulanger. The international situation gave a further impetus to Italian military spending, which had been on an upward spiral since 1882 and reached its nineteenth-century zenith of 560 million lire, or 38 per cent of the country's revenue, in 1888–89. By then new hands had taken over the reins of government. In July 1887 Depretis was succeeded as premier by the volatile Francesco Crispi, whose policy of military adventurism was ultimately to lead the Italian army to disaster.

In keeping with a pattern of civil–military relations in which the crown was the bridge between army and state, and foreign and military policy were kept in separate compartments, the creation of the Triple Alliance suddenly faced Italy's soldiers with new strategic horizons and uncomfortable obligations to co-operate with Vienna. Superficially this wrought important changes in Italian military organisation. In reality those changes were little more than cosmetic. Ferrero's expansion of the army to 12 corps was the worst possible compromise in the traditional debate over quality versus quantity; and the newly-created chief of the general staff lacked institutional authority and independence. The generals lost none of their strategic timidity; in Europe, at least, they felt at an overwhelming disadvantage. Their preference for fortifications, and their failure even to contemplate spending part of the military budget on building railways to speed up mobilisation, demonstrated a deeply-engrained conservatism. That conservatism was the product of tradition; but it also represented a sense of unease about the temper of the instrument they commanded.

4 Crispi at the Helm

When Francesco Crispi began his first term as premier in August 1887, the British embassy in Rome warned London that the new incumbent 'may be considered as somewhat "wild" in his ideas of foreign policy, at all events as compared with the Foreign Ministers of European states with whom he has to deal'.[1] Italy's foreign policy, which he conducted as minister of foreign affairs until the fall of his second ministry in 1891, was shaped by adventurism and by an overpowering Francophobia; in 1885 the French raised duties on grain and animal imports, and in March 1888 Crispi introduced a high general tariff in retaliation, starting a trade war which lasted a decade. When not trying to start a shooting war in Europe, Crispi was convinced that one was about to break out. Under his hand, the links between Italy and Germany tightened.

As Crispi came to power Italy entered a decade of instability. An agricultural crisis was compounded by the collapse of a speculative building boom in 1888 which in turn affected the banks. Deficits mounted and economy became the order of the day after 1890, with the military being forced to bear their share. At the same time industrial strikes and agrarian agitation began to increase. An alarming political dimension was added to these seismic shocks as, in the early 1890s, the nascent socialist party set out to persuade labour that it must undertake a political as well as an economic struggle if it was to improve its position in Italian society. By the time that Crispi entered his third premiership in 1893 he faced the spectre of mounting numbers of workers' syndicalist associations, both socialist and Catholic. To a man of Crispi's disposition, red and black threats were equally alarming. To the army they represented a new and unwelcome extension of its responsibilities.

Manoeuvres held during the summer of 1887 as Crispi was settling into office emphasised Italy's strategic vulnerability. Military and naval exercises along the Tyrrhenian coast showed how easy it would be for France to land troops in central and southern Italy, and cut rail and telegraphic communications in the peninsula.[2] Rumour was at least as potent as analysis in stimulating Crispi to action, and after less than two months in office, he heard from Berlin of an understanding between France and Switzerland over the occupation of districts to the north of Savoy in the event of a war between France and Italy.[3] He rushed to

55

Bismarck and on 2 October – according to his own version of events – the two men agreed to create an Italo-German military convention.

Two weeks after his return Crispi wrote to the chief of the German general staff, Helmuth von Moltke, inviting him to outline a scheme of accord. Bismarck swiftly intervened and at his direction von Moltke replied that the issue was too delicate for communications to be anything other than oral.[4] The German attitude was one of wary caution: their military attaché in Rome reported at the end of October that it was far from clear how genuinely the Italians wanted military co-operation. Thus the war plan drawn up by von Moltke in November mentioned military involvement by Italy only in the context of an attack on Lyons.[5] However, Berlin clearly scented military advantage in Crispi's approach, for at the end of the month the German ambassador in Rome, Solms, began to try to persuade Italy to deploy troops alongside Germany in the main theatre rather than wasting them in fruitless peripheral operations.[6]

Crispi had already suggested to von Moltke that two Italian officers go to Berlin to discuss closer strategic co-operation and accordingly Lieutenant-Colonels Dabormida and Albertone – Cosenz's past and present military secretaries – went to Germany on 24 December to begin conversations. Russian military manoeuvres along the Austrian frontier provided a backdrop which Bismarck skilfully highlighted. Despite reassuring noises from the Russian military attaché in Vienna, the German chancellor heightened tension by urging that Austrian troops be moved into Galicia. That the crisis was being orchestrated was clear to Rome from the reports of the Italian military attaché in St Petersburg, who continually reassured his superiors that no untoward troop movements were taking place in Russia despite Italian press reports to the contrary.[7]

On 27 December the Italian delegation proposed that, in the event of a war with France under the terms of the Triple Alliance, Italy should furnish six army corps to co-operate directly with German troops on the Rhine. This offer, which came as something of a surprise to Berlin, necessitated making Austrian railway lines available to transport Italian troops direct to the western front. Berlin approached Vienna about transport co-operation and simultaneously suggested that the conversations be widened to include Austrian representatives.[8] Austria was at first unwilling to take part in three-way conversations, but came to realise that Italian troops operating on the Rhine would free German forces for a campaign in the east. On this basis she consented to put three railway lines at Italy's disposal from the tenth day of mobilisation, each capable of carrying ten trains a day. However, she retained the right not to co-operate with her partners if a war remained confined to the west and did not involve Russia and herself.[9] A *mémoire* recording the points of agreement was duly signed on 28 January 1888.

The military convention was diplomatically useful to both Bismarck and Crispi, but almost at once military voices were raised on both sides questioning its practicality. While Colonel Goiran was in Vienna negotiating the details of the railway agreement the Austrian and German military attachés in Rome both cast doubts on Italy's capacity to re-arm to the necessary levels, pointing out particularly that the Italian army lacked artillery and horses.[10] The new war minister, Bertolè-Viale, also had reservations. He believed that Italy could only make such an undertaking as long as France did not take the offensive against her with forces so large as to require all Italy's forces to confront them.[11] When these reservations were reported to Berlin, Bismarck grew testy.

Crispi now became alarmed lest the French stand neutral on the main front at the start of hostilities and apply all their efforts to crushing Italy by land and sea. He hinted darkly that he had reason to believe that such a plan was favoured by certain circles in France.[12] Bismarck disagreed, and von Moltke thought the only danger lay in French disruption of Italy's already slow mobilisation procedures. Even so, an attack on Italy by twelve French corps would be as favourable for the partnership as it would be risky for France. Italian fears on this score could not be stilled by bland musings from the safety of Berlin, however; and they were about to be sharpened as relations between France and Italy took a turn for the worse.

News of Italy's military approach to Germany leaked in Paris in mid-January and the French at once unleashed a stock-market war. At the same time the French fleet concentrated at Toulon and the threat of a French attack on Italy's coastline was only dissolved when a British naval squadron arrived in Genoa in March. Crispi's sense of insecurity mounted, heightened by clear signs of Franco-Russian *rapprochement*. He concluded that Italy's interests could best be served by a preventive war against France, and on 24 March, at the premier's orders, Cosenz instructed Goiran to go to Berlin and explore the possibility of a joint war outside the terms of the Triple Alliance. Such a war offered Crispi a way to escape the twin perils confronting him: to continue arming Italy at the present pace and rush headlong into bankruptcy, or to give up and hand over dominance of the Mediterranean to France. Crispi's schemes collapsed when Bismarck refused to contemplate the idea.[13]

Crispi was far from alone in fearing a French attack. The aggressive ideas of Admiral Aube, current head of the French navy, who had made clear his readiness to bombard undefended coastal cities in the event of war, were well known and were built into the plot of a popular novel entitled *Rome and Berlin*, published at this time in Paris, in which a French fleet bombarded the Italian coast, mounted an expedition on Rome and defeated the combined Italian and German fleets. This book 'fed the fantasms which had tormented Italian military and politicians for decades'.[14] On 30 May 1888, Nicotera put down a motion in the chamber of deputies calling on the government to take all the measures necessary to defend the great maritime cities without delay. Basing his remarks on Rope's novel, he painted an alarming picture in which the Italian fleet was decoyed away from its stations, when nothing would protect the major ports from a French landing except heavy fortifications.[15] In reply, General Luigi Pelloux, whilst accepting that the general European situation 'is such as not to leave much hope of possible harmonisation', pointed out that Italy had to consider whether she could afford to add to her already enormous expenses. Any monies available should go, he felt, to the navy.[16]

During the debate on coastal defence one of the deputies, General Mattei, who was also inspector-general of artillery, seized the opportunity to parade the financial advantages of using mobile batteries for coastal defence and accused the war minister of having ignored an official letter he had sent on the subject. Fixed defences were the official policy and Pelloux speedily demolished Mattei's ideas; but nevertheless Bertolè-Viale was forced to promise a special commission which would examine the problems of defending maritime cities in order to avoid charges of suppressing embarrassing dissent. This episode highlighted a problem which plagued war ministers, who faced in the chamber not only their predecessors but also deputies who were serving officers, able to use parliament to challenge them on matters of technical policy. Differences of opinion which were properly professional matters were exposed to political debate and this made it impossible for the army to present a unified front to politicians and to the public. In this case the dispute between the two men rumbled on until the following January when, after Mattei had voted against military credits, the war minister sacked him.[17]

Tension between Austria and Russia continued to mount during the first half of 1888, and the Italian military attaché at St Petersburg reported demands that fortifications on the Austro–German border be brought to full readiness and news that two new army corps were to be created immediately after the summer manoeuvres and stationed on the German frontier.[18] Alarmed by the threat from France and by the apparent imminence of a major European conflagration, Crispi introduced a massive military budget for the year 1888/9. Total military expenditure amounted to 560 million lire and, at a time when the trade war with France was gravely weakening the country's economy, the inevitable consequence was a deficit of 488 million lire – the largest since 1866. This rate of military spending was insupportable and military budgets shrank rapidly from 38 per cent of total state expenditure in 1889 to 28 per cent in 1890 and 20 per cent by 1894.[19]

The importance of relations between Rome and Berlin was emphasised by Wilhelm II's visit in mid-October. Italy wanted to put on a convincing show of military determination, but unhappily the Kaiser arrived just at the time when the army cut its least impressive figure due to the release of conscripts for the winter. A poor display greeted Wilhelm and the soldiers were not given prominence in the official celebrations. However, the officers who formed part of the Kaiser's entourage were apparently pleasantly surprised to find that the Italian army was better than they had been led to expect.[20]

Official and unofficial signs of a closer military relationship between Italy and Germany now began to appear. Cosenz was awarded the German order of the Red Eagle, first class, and the Prussian grand cordon of the Black Eagle; and in October General von Gottberg was spotted visiting Rome in disguise. He was widely believed to be attempting to persuade the Italian military authorities to switch to territorial mobilisation, which would enable an army corps to be brought up to full strength in a few days rather than three weeks.[21]

Despite the new agreement, strategic planning developed along well-established lines. Autumn manoeuvres dealt with an enemy moving on Florence from Bologna and being met by a southern army coming up the valley of the Arno.[22] Shortly afterwards a new deployment plan for war against France completely disregarded operations on the Rhine. The revised scheme divided Italian forces into four armies; three corps based on Alba and Alessandria; three at Turin; three guarding Verona; and four watching Bologna. The object was to string out a defensive net, with troops allotted to the protection of vulnerable coastal points as well as defensive positions from which counter-attacks could be launched.[23] Consenz was too cautious to place any great reliance on the Rhine option; as he once pointed out, a system took years to finalise, during which time interests and alliances could change many times.[24]

Fear of French attack persisted and some circles regarded it as inevitable. Crispi, deeply concerned lest war break out before Italy was adequately prepared, urged his war minister to adopt territorial mobilisation. He brushed aside the fears of those who thought Italian patriotism still too weak to risk the dangerous fragmentation such a system would entail: 'The national sentiment is profound in all classes of the population', he told Bertolè-Viale, 'and the different elements have been so thoroughly mingled by twenty-nine conscriptions that their fusion is now complete'.[25] Crispi was willing to take a chance and extend a system already operating in the artillery and Alpini – and save money in the process. His soldiers – and many civilians – were not.

The French conscription law of 1889, which shortened the period of military service to three years and increased the proportion of the annual contingent serving it from half to three-quarters, was not calculated to induce tranquillity in a mind as volatile as Crispi's, and an incident with France in June, involving the rights of French fishermen at Tunis, heightened his anxiety. It was immediately followed by hints from the Pope that he was contemplating leaving Rome – precisely the kind of occurrence which Crispi feared would be the pretext for a French attack. On 10 July he wrote to Bertolè-Viale pointing out the high rate of desertion in the Alpini and the inadequacy of some of those holding the highest rank in the army. He felt a sense of immense foreboding:

> Europe, at the present time, is a volcano, which may burst into irruption without a moment's warning, and we must be prepared. The threat of war is ever with us.

France, he believed, had made all the preparations necessary to launch an attack by sea and by land.[26]

A report on 12 July from an agent inside the Vatican that a French attack was imminent – for which Crispi sought no independent confirmation – provided the stimulus to action. The king was informed of the danger next day and advised to form an emergency war council consisting of the premier, the navy and war ministers and the chief of the general staff. During the days which followed, preliminary measures to mobilise the army went into effect and the fleet was placed in a state of readiness. The concentration of Russian troops on the Austro-Hungarian frontier heightened Crispi's nervousness, and he now feared war in both east and west. Crispi was calmed by Giolitti, who pointed out that France could gain nothing from such an attack, by messages from Germany relaying Bismarck's incredulity at the idea, and by reports from Italian embassies abroad that there existed no real evidence of any aggressive intention on France's part. Most important of all, the French made no move.[27]

Crispi's diplomacy suddenly confronted the army with a new aggressive role. If the premier's cheque were ever cashed, it would have to honour commitments it was not large enough or powerful enough to meet. And size apart, the army's internal condition was poor. An officer corps of which at times as many as half were ex-rankers, and in which the middle classes were notably reluctant to serve, was a ready prey to division. Morale and cohesion were further lowered by pay and promotion problems and by restrictive and contradictory internal regulations. A marked absence of intellectuality and of concern for professional improvement also played its part in lowering military professionalism.

Ferrero's expansion and the need to stock two extra army corps produced some four thousand new subalterns by the mid-1880s. For a very short time at the start of the 1890s promotions flowed quickly, and a captain's stars came after only eight or nine years; then the 'bulge' began to choke the army. By the start of the twentieth century the official age for promotion from lieutenant to captain was 35, the actual age was nearer 39, and some officers would be 50 years old before reaching the coveted rank.[28] The promotions-stakes also magnified differences of social origin: infantry lieutenants from the military schools could reach captain four or five years earlier than ex-rankers. In the artillery and engineers, ranker officers could never hope to advance beyond a captaincy.[29]

Military pay-rates had been set in 1861 and raised in 1883; a second-lieutenant earned 1800 lire a year, a captain 3200 lire and a colonel 7000 lire. Among state employees only diplomats and naval officers were better paid; and middle-ranking Italian officers earned more than their French or Austro-Hungarian equivalents. Yet there was considerable dissatisfaction and no little poverty – military memoirs depict a junior officer corps too poor to buy civilian clothes, clad in second-hand overcoats until a military co-operative society was founded in 1890, In practice, Italian officers were poorer than the published scales suggest. The state retained 15 per cent of the salary of all newly nominated second-lieutenants for six months – at a time when they were required to kit themselves out from top-to-toe – and 25 per cent of each subsequent augmentation. The situation was exacerbated by the agonising slowness with which the court of accounts registered promotion decrees, holding back badly needed pay increases for a year and more.[30] Nor was there much hope of enjoying the fruits of high rank: with no legal age limits, old soldiers did not fade away in retirement. By the mid-1890s most colonels were over 50, the majority of major-generals were 60 or more, and 13 lieutenant-generals had passed their 64th birthdays – one was 77.[31] At all levels the Italian officer corps showed its age.

Among the many difficulties under which the Italian officer had to labour, none was more painful than the marriage question. Following Piedmontese practice, officers had to get permission to marry; this was granted only when they could furnish evidence of an annual income in addition to pay, fixed on a sliding scale according to rank. For most officers this meant finding a wife with a dowry. The system was purely one of social control, and it produced bizarre consequences: a lieutenant with 1800 lire a year in pay and the requisite additional 2000 lire could marry, but a major earning 4400 could not do so until he found an extra 1200 lire. To avoid condemnation to bachelorhood, officers frequently contracted illegal civil marriages, or religious marriages which the state did not recognise and were thus doubly illegal. Periodic amnesties simply encouraged them to break the law. By 1894 there were 3833 married and 10 920 unmarried officers in the army, and a further 450 were awaiting pardon for having contracted civil or religious marriages without permission.[32]

A foreign observer noted that even where talent and genius were found in the Italian officer corps, 'they are seldom accompanied with perseverance, method, application and determination'.[33] A lack of intellectuality followed not simply from the class background of the officer corps, but from a lack of official stimulus to study. Junior officers found their days filled with instruction, inspection and training of troops. Senior officers had their hands tied by red tape and excessive bureaucratisation. The only form of intellectual activity which received any encouragement was the conference: a lecture, almost always by a junior officer, given before an invited audience of soldiers and civilians which was commonly regarded as an opportunity to make a social mark. It generally consisted of a reading of some portion of military regulations or a piece of research so esoteric that it went straight over the heads of the audience.[34] Anything outside narrowly conceived professional obligations was thoroughly suspect: one junior officer, caught by his colonel reading a book entitled *Contemporary Socialism*, received an unambiguous warning:

Anyone who concerns himself with things which are irrelevant to his profession is not a good officer; anyone who interests himself in these ideas is in for a nasty future. So watch out![35]

All this produced an officer corps fractured by dissatisfaction and discouraged from committing its intellect to the service of the profession. Liable to the loss of their commissions in the courts if they accepted a duel or at the hands of regimental disciplinary councils if they refused one, conscious of one law for themselves and another for their generals, denied much hope of reward for professional competence, Italian junior officers spent their spare time obsessively studying army lists and scanning notices of decorations, terrified lest they end their days wearing the same order as the inventor of a new shoe polish.

In the ranks, mixing together recruits from different regions did not reduce antagonisms. Regional rivalries offered a potential for disaster which was tragically realised in the affair of Pizzofalcone. The disaster occurred on 13 April 1884 at a barracks near Naples. It began when a group of northerners surrounded two Calabrians and started to crack jokes about the south. One of the two, a non-commissioned officer named Misdea, went to his barracks, returned with a rifle and fired over fifty shots, killing seven other soldiers. At his trial Misdea, whose Calabrian accent was so thick that some members of the tribunal could not understand what he was saying, showed unmistakable signs of epilepsy and what was described as 'moral imbecility'. Despite this, the extreme deprivation of his background and the provocation to which he had been subjected, he was sentenced to death and shot. Even while the trial was going on, a *carabiniere* was killed at Pizzofalcone in similar circumstances.

The trial raised awkward questions about the state of the army. Why had nobody tried to stop Misdea? Why were loaded rifles left lying around in barracks? Why was there no organised attempt on the part of other non-commissioned officers to deal with the disturbance? And why had the officers not intervened before the affair had reached heights of passion which could only lead to tragedy? These questions were left unanswered, and the army's only apparent response was to decree in May 1885 that soldiers should not have live rounds to hand all the time, but should draw them from company lockers when they were needed.[36] To later eyes, Pizzofalcone suggests that the policy of using conscription as a 'national crucible' was deeply flawed.

Poor physical conditions combined with neglect to make the ranker's life an unenviable one. Insanitary barracks and a poor diet contributed to high mortality rates: in the year ending 30 June 1887, 417 Italian soldiers died on active service whilst another 1776 died of illness and a further fifty-seven committed suicide. It was not uncommon for European armies to have higher mortality rates than their parent societies, but the condition persisted in the Italian army well into the 1890s. By 1893 the death rate in the Italian army was 11.1 per thousand, more than double that of Germany and higher than either France or Russia, but lower than either Austria or Spain. The two most common causes of death were tuberculosis and typhus.[37] Whilst this situation was partly the consequence of official neglect, it also reflected the fact that Italian units often had to garrison pestilential areas where sanitation was primitive and disease endemic.

The structure of recruitment altered only slightly during the 1880s. The proportion of those exempted from military service on family and other non-physical grounds increased from one-fifth at the beginning of the decade to one-quarter at the end. The absentee rate hovered around 3 per cent until 1889, when it suddenly leapt to more than 5 per cent. The most striking change was in the number of conscripts who were supposed to serve the full term. In 1883 the ratio of chest measurement in proportion to height was reduced, and as a result the rate of rejection shrank from 26 per cent to 16.8 per cent. Because of this and other factors the size of the annual intake rose from 67 000 after Ferrero's reorganisation to 95 000 by 1891. With more people being funnelled into the first and third categories, the middle category dwindled to a few thousand, and in 1892 it was suppressed altogether.[38]

The use of the army for policing, which increased markedly during the 1890s, had always been a recognised part of military duties and troops were familiar with the experience of helping the *carabinieri* with crowds which got out of hand, as when the drawing of lottery numbers was suspended.[39] Under Crispi's rule, civil-military confrontation changed significantly. Workers' riots at Terni in May 1889 foreshadowed the domestic turmoil which characterised the next decade, and produced a string of arguments which were to become all too familiar as the army was increasingly ordered into action to prop up political authority. The government was strongly criticised for allowing full freedom of expression and then having to use the army to suppress the consequences: it was a tactic which divorced the soldier from the citizen and encouraged the public to regard the extremist parties as more important than they really were, when a little skill could result in avoiding the politics of confrontation. If this recipe for order was somewhat naive, the criticism of the effects of government policy on the army was and remained valid. Having to perform policing duties deprived troops of their small amount of free time, exposed them to injury in situations in which their only means of response was inappropriate and excessive, interrupted their training and lowered their morale. If the government wanted to copy the

English system of freedom of expression, one newspaper suggested, then the police must provide the means of control and the country must pay the extra cost.[40]

The fall of Crispi's second administration on 5 February 1891 gave him a brief respite before he had to confront the consequences of political activism and social distress. Over the next two years, developments in both spheres accelerated the progress towards crisis. Marxist socialism first appeared in Milan in 1890 and within two years a genuine workers' movement was being created. At a congress held in Reggio Emilia in September 1893 the newly formed Italian Socialist Party confirmed its political programme: class war, organised resistance to capital, socialisation and an end to collaboration with all bourgeois parties. At the same time, far away in the south, the harsh effects of the trade war against France were producing a spontaneous reaction no less inclined towards the politics of confrontation. As the sales of wine, fruit and sulpher declined, landlords passed on the cost to the peasants in the form of higher rents and increases in local taxation. The peasants reacted by founding local *fasci* to resist these encroachments, and by October 1893 there were 162 such groups in Sicily spear-heading a twin assault on the agrarian capitalists by strikes and through local elections.

As these developments were beginning their brief but spectacular process of maturation a right-wing administration headed by Rudinì came into office to succeed Crispi, with economy and financial retrenchment as its watchwords. As war minister the new premier chose Major-General Luigi Pelloux, who announced that, as far as his department was concerned, the necessary savings were to come from military reform. Despite his defence of Ferrero a few years earlier, Pelloux now belonged to the minority of generals who were prepared to serve as war minister without demanding more money as a pre-condition for joining the government. The major issue confronting him was whether the 12 army corps were to be retained, as the links with Germany seemed to require, and if so, how money was to be saved without unduly diminishing their effectiveness.

The appearance of a new political regime only a year before the Triple Alliance was due for renewal sent tremors of apprehension through conservative ranks, for it seemed to presage a departure from Crispi's policy of firm adherence to Berlin and Vienna. Domenico Farini, the highly influential president of the senate, lobbied energetically to persuade Rudinì that the alliance of conservative powers was essential for Italy's future internal and external security.[41] Berlin was equally concerned and the Italian military attaché there was harried by senior officials, from which he deduced that two things were pre-occupying the Germans:

(1)   Whether the *total force* and *availability* of the Italian army and fleet will be reduced;

(2)   Whether the sentiments of the men now in power will be as benevolently disposed towards the Triple Alliance as were their predecessors.[42]

Conservative fears were allayed when Rudinì renewed the alliance in May 1891, a year early, under the same terms.

The military links between Italy and her allies now began to tighten. A joint working-party re-examined the railway timetables in October 1891 and updated them, speeding up movement on the three lines by between two and five days. Italy was chronically short of rolling stock, and in the revised agreement Germany undertook to supply 201 engines and 2942 wagons to make up the deficiency. It was probably at this conference that Italy indicated that her contribution on the Rhine was likely to consist of five infantry corps rather than the original six.[43] The railway agreements were further updated in October 1893 and again in January 1896, and conversations also took place with the Austrian general staff in June 1892 about transporting troops across Austrian territory.[44]

During 1891 von Waldersee was replaced as chief of the German general staff by Alfred von Schlieffen. In July Schlieffen requested details of the work done by the Italian general staff on the problems of supplying troops by rail, and in November he sent Cosenz details of the forts of Epinal and Belfort, the likely targets of an Italian force operating on the Rhine.[45] At the same time, the advantages of strategic co-operation with the Germans became more apparent. The Italian staff ride of 1891 suggested that the Rhine option might be the best – indeed the only – way in which to attack France with any hope of success. An Italian offensive across the Maritime Alps would confront geographical obstacles and fortifications which together 'compose an imposing – one might even say formidable – complex of conditions, faced by which the thought of attacks is brought up short in confusion'.[46]

As military involvement with the central powers deepened Italy came under pressure to speed up her mobilisation and deployment times by adopting regional recruitment: in April 1891 Archduke Albrecht of Austria-Hungary, a keen student of Italian military affairs, suggested that Italy consider abandoning her regional system.[47] As time went on, such hints increased. However, any departure from traditional practice greatly alarmed the conservatives, who had the ear of the king. A proposal by Rudinì to do away with the military districts and save money produced a horrified outburst from Farini:

> an organisation without districts would lead to a territorial organisation, which would be extremely dangerous for national unity; and . . . even if this were not the case, it would be very damaging to locate certain units in unhealthy parts of the country forever . . .[48]

Farini's point was a good one: parts of Italy were still liable to regular outbreaks of cholera so bad that on occasion annual manoeuvres had to be cancelled, and the health hazards in the mosquito-ridden regions around Rome and elsewhere were severe. But behind these rational objections to a change in military policy lay the deep-seated fear that the end of national recruitment would spell the end of national unity.[49]

Pelloux fully recognised the drawbacks of the current system and proposed that, on mobilisation for war, regiments should be filled with men from the districts where they were stationed, but he fell from office with Rudinì's successor, Giolitti, in December 1893 before he had time to attempt to change the recruiting system.[50] His successor, Mocenni, set up a commission of general officers in 1894 which pronounced in favour of regional recruitment. The following year Mocenni tried to implement this recommendation but ran headlong into the opposition of parliament, which did not share his optimism about the solidity of Italian nationalism. With rioting in Sicily and industrial unrest in the north, there was no hope of introducing regional recruitment and every incentive to spread Sicilian recruits through the army rather than concentrate them together. Crispi, now in office for the last time, smartly dropped preparations to divide Italy into fourteen different military regions.[51] National recruitment, despite all its drawbacks, remained in force – one issue over which liberals and conservatives were united.[52]

Pelloux had to provide the troops to flesh out twelve army corps in wartime and also save money. He squared the circle by the simple expedient of calling up recruits late and allowing them to leave early. As a consequence the numbers of men in the ranks during the winter months each year shrank substantially. This so-called *forza minima* had considerable military disadvantages: as well as leaving Italy with a weak standing army during the winter it made training difficult and unsatisfactory, since skeleton battalions had to be grouped together for manoeuvres to make up normal combat-sized units.[53] In an attempt to make the best use of the manpower available, Pelloux introduced a new category of subsidiary service from whose almost untrained ranks all non-active wartime jobs would be filled

One way to maintain units at full strength and make some savings in the process would have been to reduce the army to ten corps. Rudinì had been in office scarcely four months before he came up with this idea. He tested it on Farini and Cosenz and ran into outright opposition. Cosenz pointed out that Italy had an agreement to send five corps to the Rhine in the event of war; she could not therefore contemplate such a reduction. Ricotti, brought along to strengthen Rudinì's hand, argued that in war a few large battalions could defeat many weak ones, but his views cut no ice with the military establishment and were not much appreciated by Farini, who pointed out that outsiders would assume Italy had reduced its army by one-sixth. The political effects of such a move outweighed its military advantages.[54]

To Farini, and to the court faction surrounding King Umberto, order and stability in Italy rested on three pillars: the monarchy, the army and the Triple Alliance. Any action which threatened to weaken the army posed a multi-faceted threat to foreign and domestic policy and was simply unacceptable. Umberto became even more convinced of the need to preserve the 12 corps after he visited Berlin in the summer of 1892 and talked to Schlieffen about Germany's plans for a massive attack on France in the event of war. He returned home determined that there must be no reduction in the size of the army and openly sided with Cosenz against Rudinì.

Pelloux, sandwiched between the premier and the king, managed to save 27 million lire on the military budget between 1891 and 1893, mostly by dint of living from hand to mouth. Committed to maintaining the officer corps at full strength in order to be able to expand the army in the event of war, he economised on barrack-construction, fortification, artillery replacement and the provision of mobilisation stores. Cutting corners in this way produced relatively small savings at the cost of considerable internal friction. Nothing demonstrated this more clearly than the case of the captain's horse.

Ricotti had passed a law in April 1886 granting the right of free forage for a horse to the six senior captains in every infantry and grenadier regiment.[55] This was a very necessary measure for, given the average age of infantry captains by the 1890s, it was questionable whether many of them would be able to stand up to the rigours of campaigning for very long without such an essential aid to combat. The news that Pelloux was contemplating doing away with the allowance therefore produced a wave of consternation which reached as far as Berlin: even Wilhelm II expressed doubts about the wisdom of depriving the captain of his horse.[56] Nonetheless Pelloux abolished the allowance in the teeth of bitter criticism, saving some one-and-a-half million lire in the process. The episode showed how difficult was Pelloux's task of making economies, and its result was to lower officer morale yet further.

In 1892, half-way through Pelloux's period of office, Cosenz, who was now 72 years of age and rather deaf, suggested that it was time to select his successor, and recommended his protégé, Domenico Primerano. Primerano was in many ways a replica of his patron. Born in Naples in 1829, he too had been educated at the Nunziatella and had served in the Bourbon artillery before joining Garibaldi's 'Thousand' at Cosenz's personal invitation. Transferring to the Italian army, he had been Cadorna's chief of staff in 1870 and later Mezzacapo's secretary-general at the war ministry. Deeply worried about military finances, he had earlier refused to join one of Crispi's administrations and was reluctant to take the post of chief of the general staff for the same reason. Succumbing to persuasion by Pelloux, he took office on 3 November 1893 and at once began to make much more of a nuisance of himself than his predecessor, demanding more money and an increase in the influence and authority of his new office.[57]

Shortly after Primerano's appointment Giolitti's first administration collapsed and in December 1893 Crispi came back to power for the third and last time. He returned at a moment when tension with France was high. The pitched battle fought at Aigues Mortes near Marseilles in August 1893, in which thirty Italian workers were killed, produced a deep wave of public anger. Franco-Italian military relations were poor and Paris got hot under the collar when an Italian prince attended German manoeuvres at Metz in September. In the same month the Italian military attaché in Paris went with his foreign colleagues on a trip to Beauvais. The Russians, seated in the leading vehicle, were greeted with great popular enthusiasm, the Germans with marked hostility, and Panizzardi with shouts of 'Down with the maccheronis'.[58] The press showed growing alarm at the continual increase of French troops and war material along the common frontier; and French moves to build a major naval base at Bizerte during 1893 caused widespread fears that Italy was about to experience another Tunis. Franco-Italian tensions could be detected with senses much less keen than Crispi's.

Anxiety about French intentions was clearly reflected in military exercises and planning. The annual grand manoeuvres in the summer of 1892 had featured a battle in the valley of the Tiber between Orvieto and Perugia to defend Rome, but the following year Cosenz's last staff ride took as its scenario a landing in south-west Sicily by a French expeditionary force launched from Tunis and Bizerte with the object of capturing Palermo and Castrogiovanni. The exercise proved that this would not be a decisive move in a major war and that the worst Italy had to fear was a *coup-de-main*, no danger as long as a bridgehead was maintained on the island.[59] The staff ride the following year explored the prospects for a French attack launched along the Moncenisio before Italy was fully mobilised and exposed the weakness of Italian defensive works and the pressing need for more artillery.[60] The ride conducted in 1895, which studied the fate of Italian offensives aimed at Nice and Albertville and contemporaneous with successful German action on the Rhine, confirmed French superiority along that stretch of frontier and produced the recommendation that Italy must have more barrier forts, more roads and more mountain troops if the French were not to overwhelm her.[61]

Crispi liked to control military policy, and on taking office again he cast about for a successor to Pelloux. Primerano would undoubtedly ask for more money, which would put Crispi in an extremely awkward position in parliament; and Ettore Pedotti, a Lombard general currently in command of the war academy, refused the post because of the economies he expected to have to make. On 15 December 1893 Crispi settled on Stanislao Mocenni, who was prepared to accept a cut of 16 million in the war budget. A Tuscan – Farini labelled him 'one of the most frivolous (*leggerissimo*) of the frivolous Tuscans' – Mocenni had been born in Siena in 1837 and entered the Italian army in 1860 by way of the army of central Italy. He lacked a power-base from which to resist the Piedmontese bloc and proved wholly incapable of standing up to Crispi, who used him as little more than a messenger-boy.

The military economies Pelloux had made had alarmed Germany, and those of his successor increased that alarm. Mocenni cut numbers and time with the colours, so that companies fell in size to only seventy men. By July 1895 the German military attaché in Rome was openly reproving the king for permitting the Italian army to grow weaker at a time when the French army was getting stronger.[62] After grand manoeuvres that summer the Germans made their views even plainer: Italian officers had insufficient experience of command, a consequence of the brief period during which the army was at *forza massima*; and Italian generals lacked the opportunity to judge the performance of their supply and support services because manoeuvres were always held with makeshift staffs which included officers from other commands.[63] Nevertheless co-operation continued at the planning level, with the dispatch from Berlin of studies of France and of routes which a German invasion might take.

Crispi needed a strong army less to assuage foreign demands than to deal with mounting domestic discontent. On 4 January 1894 he declared a state of siege in Sicily and ten days later did the same at Massa and Carrara when 200 reservists, called up because of the Sicilian situation, refused to entrain for the south. His sense of paranoia was exacerbated by reports that Sicilian rioters were teaming up with French and Russian agents who were trying to break up the Triple Alliance. In May 1894 eleven leaders of the Sicilian riots were tried, found guilty and sentenced to long terms in prison. Anarchist outbursts in Rome during the summer and the assassination of President Carnot by an Italian in June added to the spiralling tension.

Crispi responded by dissolving the Socialist Party in October 1894 and by proroguing parliament two months later after revelations implicating him in the banking scandal which had unseated Giolitti. The prolonged crisis united premier and king and propelled the army willy-nilly into the foreground of politics. By 1895 the court was in the grip of a siege-mentality and saw everything in black and red: the church was trying to expand its influence, while the socialists were attacking the very foundations of post-Risorgimento Italy. In this turmoil crown and army were locked together for, as Farini told the king in July 1895, 'If the army is weakened, all is lost. As long as the army stands firm, there is nothing to fear'.[64]

Desperately in need of a stronger army, Crispi sought to overcome cabinet reservations and increase spending once more, despite the economic consequences of the trade war with France. He urged his treasury minister. Sidney Sonnino, to find some means of remedying Italian impotence in the face of great danger:

> Will there be war? There is no doubt of it. Only the day when it will break out remains unknown. The great powers are ready for the terrible event, and we cannot delude ourselves that they will wait for us to catch them up.[65]

Sonnino refused to cut expenditure elsewhere and would not support any proposal to raise extra money from taxation. He thought it deplorable that Italy had spent 740 million lire on fortifications between 1877 and 1894 and was now being told they were useless.[66] He believed that advanced defence would be better secured by using manpower rather than building fixed fortifications and that the army could advantageously be reduced in size; better eighty or a hundred thousand men in a full state of readiness for war than twelve incomplete corps. Italy should devise a system of advanced mobilisation on the Alps and send two full corps to the Rhine as soon as possible after war broke out. Speed, Sonnino believed, mattered more than mere numbers.[67]

These ideas were not far removed from Ricotti's, but rather than give them the consideration they deserved, Crispi fell back on undiluted alarmism:

> Along the French frontier, from Nice to Besançon, there are 300,000 men of all arms, fully equipped and ready to march. So, if tomorrow we had a general who was intelligent, expert and courageous, he would be defeated, because when the enemy enters Italy nothing will stand in his way for twenty-one days. And in twenty-one days the French will have taken our greatest cities.

He called for more weapons, more railway transport and more men under arms. If the coming war were fought without Italian participation, he concluded darkly, then whoever won it would take compensation from her.[68]

Crispi's demands were sufficiently similar to the conclusions reached by the most recent staff rides to suggest that he was aware of their findings, and he certainly had the new chief of staff's backing in his call for military expansion. Primerano feared that an army reduced to ten corps would produce no real economies but would 'completely upset our entire mobilisation system and would be an absolute disaster, materially and morally, both inside and country and outside it'. Like Crispi, he thought a European conflagration inevitable, and suggested that the civil ministries temporarily give up part of their programme in order to help out.[69]

Crispi's hold on power was growing ever more precarious, for although the elections held in May 1895 were a personal triumph for him the socialists tripled their vote and elected fifteen deputies, among them three of the imprisoned leaders of the Sicilian *fasci*. Co-operation between socialists and radicals signalled political reefs ahead, and Crispi seemed to have no answer to the situation other than to fall back on the army. In the short term, an active military policy seemed to offer a way out of his troubles. In a desperate attempt to recover his personal political standing and to distract the Italian people, Crispi turned to the army and demanded a great victory in Africa.

5 African Adventure

When Italy occupied Assab on the Red Sea coast in 1879, no colonial blueprint existed in Rome. In the years that followed a series of chance events created an opportunity which Italy's diplomats misperceived and were unable to resist. Taking little account of their country's military capacity and none whatsoever of the local enemies they faced, civilian politicians used the army in a status-induced gamble without ever weighing political benefit against military costs. What began as naked opportunism was later used as a distraction from social problems at home, a substitute for war with France and a safety valve for irredentism.

Unlike British or French imperialism, Italy's African gamble was motivated by her desire to rank as a Great Power rather than by economic, strategic or geopolitical calculations. Without a clear and consistent political purpose, a sound strategy was impossible. Without a colonial army, which Italy never created, it was impossible to build up a fund of operational expertise or to establish a psychological commitment to the colony on which to create a successful native policy. Intellectually as well as economically, the African adventure was a hand-to-mouth affair.

The collapse of Egyptian rule under the twin assaults of the British and the Mahdi opened the path to Italian expansion on the Red Sea coast. The Mahdia broke out in the Sudan in 1881, and soon all the Egyptian garrisons there were threatened. As the upper Nile collapsed, Egypt's hold over the Red Sea littoral was exposed and undermined. The spread of dervish power presented Britain, who had occupied Egypt in 1882, with difficulties she had not the military resources to resolve. First charge on her energies was the relief of Gordon in Khartoum, and an expedition was under way to rescue him by September 1884. In the circumstances she could not spare troops to take over the Egyptian garrisons on the Red Sea, and before the year was out Italy was told that there would be no objections to her taking Beilul, Zeila and Massaua.[1] Italian diplomats conjured up the vision of a broader Mediterranean partnership with Britain, and on this shaky foundation Mancini launched the army into Ethiopia. 'Why', he asked his critics, 'do you not wish to recognise that in the Red Sea, the closest to the Mediterranean, we can find the key to the latter?'.[2]

On 31 December 1884, using as a pretext the massacre of an Italian expedition somewhere south of Assab two-and-a-half months earlier, Mancini asked Ricotti's opinion on a punitive expedition. Ricotti passed the problem to Cosenz, who suggested sending out several infantry battalions with artillery support to conduct a preliminary reconnaissance; he also remarked that it would be convenient to have troops permanently stationed at Assab.[3] Cosenz justified a permanent military presence on the grounds that the colony would be exposed to native retaliation whenever fleet units left the port, which they frequently did.[4]

With London's agreement to the occupation of Massaua in his pocket, Mancini pressed Ricotti to carry out preliminary studies for the punitive expedition at once. Such a force could also be used, he added mysteriously, for another job the government might give it.[5] On 12 January 1885, the designated commander of the expedition, Lieutenant-Colonel Tancredi Saletta, was called to the war ministry to receive his orders. He was instructed to find out the details of the massacre and assess the prospects of an expedition into the interior, and to garrison Beilul if the navy required it. He was warned not to let the trip assume the proportions of a proper expedition, and told that his main concern was to be the line from Assab towards Haussa.[6] Although he was allowed to read these instructions, Saletta was not given them. However, he was warned that he might have to change objectives *en route* and occupy Massaua.[7]

At this point, clumsy British diplomacy caused Mancini's hopes of a policy of Anglo-Italian co-operation to soar and also opened up a new goal for the Red Sea expedition. On 15 January Sir Savile Lumley, British ambassador in Rome, dropped hints that Italian co-operation against the Mahdists would be welcome. Mancini at once leaped to the conclusion that Britain was signalling her disinterest in the region.[8] News of the failure of the Gordon relief expedition reached London on 5 February and three days later Italy offered to help reconquer the Sudan.

Saletta reached Suakin on the Red Sea on 1 February. The following day he learned that his orders had been changed and that he was now to occupy Massaua.[9] His force numbered 38 officers and 764 men, his guns were at the bottom of the ship's hold underneath 600 tons of stores, and he was largely ignorant of the place he was going to. In Rome, fresh orders were already being formulated on the basis of Mancini's reading of British policy in the Sudan. Saletta was now to master the island of Massaua and make ready for operations inland along three possible lines of advance: south-west towards Andowa (*sic* Adua) and Gondar; west to Kassala and then to Khartoum; and north to Suakin. His attention was particularly drawn to the western route.[10] On 6 February Cosenz was instructed to begin studies for the occupation of Suakin and for a successive advance on Berber and Khartoum.[11]

Mancini's hopes of co-operating with Britain against the dervishes were torpedoed by Russia. As Italian troops were establishing themselves in Massaua tension mounted along the Afghan border, culminating in the Penjdeh incident on 30 March. Britain could not run risks in India to defend the Sudan. On 15 April the cabinet decided to evacuate and by mid-summer Britain's only foothold was at Suakin. Italian offers of help against the dervishes in February, reiterated in March and April, were unwanted. The Italians were left by the British 'as their watch-dog along the Ethiopian Red Sea coast, thus preventing French entry into the Nile basin from the East'.[12]

On 5 February Saletta's two ships entered the harbour at Massaua. Saletta at once began to push inland to defend his base and by August his troops were at Saati, 30 kilometres from the coast. Mancini was well aware of the dangers of expanding too far from Massaua, warning Ricotti early in April:

> The important point to be held as the basis of our action is to do nothing which may disturb our relations with Abyssinia, since it is obvious that a rupture, or even a disturbance, in our relations with that kingdom could create very grave difficulties for our position at Massaua.[13]

When, on 25 August, Ras Alula of Tigre, the local chieftain, demanded that the Italians withdraw from Saati, Ricotti ordered Saletta to retire to avoid getting into difficulties which could swell to unforeseeable proportions. However, he was not to take this step if he thought it would adversely affect the Italian position.[14] Saletta replied firmly that any sign of Italy's being prepared to enter into negotiations would be interpreted as weakness and that he was decisively against abandoning the spot. The new foreign minister, Di Robilant, accepted his judgement.[15]

On 12 November 1885 Major-General Carlo Genè arrived to take over from Saletta. The new commander, who had previously been director of the Institute of Military Geography, had in his pocket instructions from the foreign ministry to maintain positions already occupied but to take no others.[16] During the first half of 1886 Genè obeyed orders, content to woo the local chieftain, Menelik of Showa, a rival of the emperor Johannis, but then he succumbed to the belief that the man on the spot was the best judge of policy and pushed forward, taking Zula and Ua-a. In an attempt to force an Italian withdrawal from Saati, Alula threatened to kill the explorer Count Salimbeni, who had fallen into his hands, if the forts were not abandoned by 18 January 1887. Genè warned Di Robilant, who ordered him to take all the steps necessary to prevent any harm coming to the three-man party and to make it known that the necessary reinforcements would be forthcoming to teach Alula a severe lesson. Encouraged by this support, Genè garrisoned Saati with regular Italian troops.[17] Alula responded to the challenge. Fighting began around Saati on 25 January and the garrison commander, Major Boretti, at once telegraphed for reinforcements.

At 5.20 a.m. the following morning a relief column of 540 Italian troops under the command of Lieutenant-Colonel De Cristoferis marched out from Monkullo to relieve Boretti. It had been on the road for two-and-a-half hours, and was about an hour's march from Saati, when De Cristoferis learned that 5–12 000 Ethiopians barred his path. Within half-an-hour his force ran into the hordes of Ras Alula. One of his two Gatling guns jammed at once and the other after only half-an-hour. Meanwhile, his troops, some of whom had been in Africa for only 48 hours, fired their best cartridges while the enemy was out of range and were left with 'barrack' cartridges – partly-charged rounds for dealing with rioters which did not produce mortal wounds.

Finally De Cristoferis ordered a withdrawal to the low hill of Dogali. Up to that point the Ethiopians had fought at long range; now they closed in, the native irregulars panicked and fled, and the column was annihilated. At about the hour that De Cristoferis's men were meeting their end, Di Robilant was confidently informing the chamber of deputies that Genè was 'in a position to teach anyone who attacked him a severe lesson'.[18]

Genè, like many of the commanders who followed him, underestimated his opponents. However, the affair at Dogali set the pattern for Italian tactics for the next ten years. From it were drawn three major lessons: that Italian forces should never retreat in the face of the enemy; that they should always make maximum use of artillery, thought to be their great advantage; and that they should always try to take the counter-offensive from the shelter of *Zeribe* – stone-built field fortifications.[19] These tactics served the Italians well until 1896, when they were abandoned with disastrous consequences.

After Dogali, Genè at once pulled his troops back, despite a report from Boretti that the tribesmen had withdrawn, and telegraphed Di Robilant that the colony was now in a true state of war. He urged a strong forward move to take rapid and complete revenge. Two years' experience had shown that it was impossible to live in peace with the natives, and the cost of a punitive move would be worth it in the long run:

> There is no doubt that a secure position on the Ethiopian heights will give considerable influence in Africa, which all nations now want, to the power which has the foresight to secure it in time.[20]

To carry out his advance, Genè asked for a force of eight to ten thousand men and suggested recruiting the dervishes as allies.

Di Robilant felt that an unsuccessful adventure could have very grave consequences for Italy, and knew she could not spare the resources necessary to be sure of success in view of the dark European scene 'on which the future of our country may perhaps depend'. Moreover, to ally with the dervishes would destroy Italy's good relations with Britain. Genè was ordered simply to take all the necessary steps to defend Massaua.[21] Two months later, he was removed and Saletta returned to take up command.

One of the causes of Italy's military disaster in Africa was her inability to provide enough resources to maintain a firm hold on the colony. Evidence of this is apparent in the reaction to Dogali. Although many deputies were ready out of patriotism to vote funds for Africa, doubters pointed out that the European situation looked particularly menacing and that it might be unwise to send an expeditionary force of up to ten thousand men out of the country at that moment.[22] Ricotti's solution to the problem of reinforcing Africa while not interfering with mobilisation arrangements for a European war – to send a company from each of sixteen different regiments – set a very bad precedent which was followed for the next decade, as a result of which African units lacked cohesion.

Saletta, by now a general, took command at Massaua on 23 April 1887. He was now free from foreign office restraint, for a royal decree of 17 April had put the local commander under the sole authority of the war minister. Like many of the African generals, Saletta soon grew restless, and after a month he sent Bertolè-Viale proposals for further military action in the autumn, either to occupy the altopiano at Asmara or to take over control of Bogos or Keren. With Crispi now premier, Rome was in a receptive mood. In July Saletta was told that the government wanted to re-take Saati and Ua-a, abandoned after Dogali, 'without however embroiling us in a major war in the interior which would require great sacrifices and would not offer us enough by way of recompense'. Saletta saw difficulties in such an operation: the two objectives were 26 and 51 kilometres away from Massaua along difficult roads, and 60 kilometres apart. He offered the government three choices: a fully-fledged invasion of Ethiopia, the occupation of Bogos; or remaining in Massaua and making it strong enough to keep the local tribesmen at arm's length with the aid of the *corpo coloniale* of native ascaris he had established in July. Personally, he favoured taking the third course and then waiting on events – 'for example, a revolution in the interior of Abyssinia' – before undertaking decisive action.[23]

Saletta's proposals did not match Crispi's political needs, and on 28 September he was informed that General Di San Marzano was being sent out with a force of 12 500 men. The new commander knew that the government had decided to undertake a military action in Africa which would 'vindicate our military prestige, but will not commit us to a war to the finish with the idea of conquering Abyssinia'. His orders were to re-occupy Saati and connect it by rail to Monkullo and Massaua. Once this had been achieved the government intended to reduce its forces to the level necessary to garrison the forts and maintain the occupation.[24]

By the end of December, Di San Marzano was ready to make his move. He had at his disposal 14 000 Italian infantry, 38 guns and 28 machine guns, as well as balloons, searchlights, land-mines and the new 70/87 model Vetterlì rifle. He was expecting to face up to 75 000 men with rifles and 10 000 with lances. Already the transfer of technology which was equipping the Ethiopians with ever-increasing amounts of modern European weapons was beginning to make the Italian task hazardous.[25]

Di San Marzano pushed out four kilometres beyond Monkullo to the Plain of Monkeys. There he halted on 9 December on hearing that the local bands of Ras Mikael, Ras Hailu Mariam, Mengesha and the Imperial Guard – in all, perhaps 200 000 men – were moving against him. Refusing to bow to the urgings of two of his subordinate commanders, Baratieri and Genè, who wanted to drive rapidly for Saati, he advanced slowly and cautiously, building entrenched camps fortified with metal towers every day to protect his troops. By the beginning of February he had re-occupied Saati, and on 15 March his engineers completed the vital rail connection.[26]

At the end of March Emperor Johannis appeared before Saati with some 80 000 troops. Di San Marzano wisely resisted the temptation to sally out from behind his fortifications and instead treated with the Negus, passing on Italy's claims to Saati, Ua-a and Ailet. Johannis was in a weak position. He knew of Italian negotiations with Menelik and feared an alliance between the two. He also knew of the success of the mahdists in the north-east, where they had defeated Tekla Haimanot of Gojjam at the Battle of Sar Wulla and sacked Gondar. Finally he was all too well aware that his army lacked the capability to capture a fortified position – fortifications had played little part in the open warfare of the Ethiopians. Short of provisions, he began a disastrous retreat on 2 April during which his transport animals died of rinderpest, unknowingly imported by the Italians in cattle bought from India.[27]

Once Johannis retired from Saati Di San Marzano's task was completed, and he and the extra troops were recalled to Italy, leaving General Antonio Baldissera in command. Baldissera began an upward move on to the altopiano by occupying Zula on 1 August 1888 and encouraging a friendly local chieftain to take Keren. Within a week he suffered a set-back when a punitive expedition against a recalcitrant local ruler went wrong. A column of native troops was caught at Saganeiti and all five officers and 250 of the 400 men were massacred. Believing that his movements had been betrayed, Baldissera set a Lieutenant Livraghi to find the culprit, unleashing a reign of terror which lasted three years. Livraghi carried out murders, summary executions and the massacre of entire native bands in Italian pay which were suspected of wanting to desert. The episode revealed the brutal cynicism which coloured Italian military colonialism. It also reflected Baldissera's unbounded ambition: during the course of Livraghi's trial he admitted that his ultimate goal was the conquest of all Ethiopia.[28]

Whenever forward-minded military commanders could appeal to a sympathetic political leadership, the potential for disaster in Ethiopia existed. In January 1889, Crispi lighted with alacrity on the idea of a further forward move to occupy Asmara. Bertolè-Viale blocked his way. The war minister believed that neither funds nor forces were sufficient to protect Italy in Europe whilst adventuring in Africa:

> However you look at it, it appears to me that we ought not to undertake an enterprise so full of dangers and difficulties, which could expose the country to the sad figure of having to abandon to an enemy territory of which it has just taken possession. For Italy this would be the height of weakness.[29]

Crispi replied disingenuously that he was not thinking of a regular campaign leading to fixed occupation, but of a 'reconnaissance march'. Alluding to his own Garibaldino past, and to the results which daring could bring, he suggested the erection of temporary fortifications which would protect the colony from surprise and serve as a base for renewed action when circumstances turned in Italy's favour.[30]

As Baldissera was planning his march on to the altopiano news arrived of an accord between Johannis and Menelik, and Rome at once countermanded the order to advance. Faced with internal dissension and two external enemies, Johannis had decided to deal first with the dervishes. On 9 March 1889 he met the mahdist forces in battle at Metemma and was mortally wounded at the moment of Ethiopian victory. His army at once retreated and the following day his body was discovered and decapitated and his head borne off to Khartoum. Menelik, his successor, profited most from Johannis' last battle, not only because it opened up a path to the throne but also because it was a decisive set-back for the dervish armies which were too exhausted to invade Ethiopia in their turn.

When news of the Negus' death arrived in Italy on 1 April 1889 Crispi tried again to get a forward push but was resisted by the combined efforts of the war minister and the ministers of public works, finance and the treasury, all of whom were worried about the huge budget deficits which had already been amassed. Bertolè-Viale forestalled Crispi's bid to persuade the cabinet to his way of thinking by reading out a report from Baldissera which concluded that Italy would lose nothing by waiting. Unwilling to risk a political crisis by jettisoning his war minister, Crispi looked for backing in parliament, winning a major success in an African debate on 7 May. Caught between the recklessness of the premier and the enthusiasm of parliament, Bertolè-Viale was forced to agree to the occupation of Keren and Asmara, completed by 7 August 1889.

On Christmas Eve Major-General Baldassare Orero took up command at Massaua, and on 1 January 1890 the colony was formally named Eritrea. Hearing that Mengesha and Alula were both retreating, Orero proposed marching on Adua. He wanted to get there by 26 January – the anniversary of Dogali – to demonstrate Italy's military power, and he also wanted to punish Alula, the person responsible for the massacre. Crispi, intent on taking advantage of what could, if necessary, be disclaimed as a local forward initiative, sent Orero a series of equivocal telegrams outlining Bertolè-Viale's opposition to such a move but tacitly urging the local commander forward. Manipulative tactics of this sort, which encouraged field commanders to act rashly, were to be an even more marked feature of the second Adua campaign.[31]

On 27 January 1890 the main body of Orero's troops entered Adua. Crispi telegraphed his congratulations, but to his annoyance Orero retreated two days later. The forward move greatly alarmed Menelik, who discovered in July that the Italians had perpetrated a linguistic trick on him in the Treaty of Wichale (1889) and now claimed to represent Ethiopia to the outside world. He complained to the European powers, gaining the promise of shipments of French arms which included Hotchkiss quick-firing artillery, and more arms from Russia. His position was gradually growing stronger thanks to his swelling arsenal of modern weapons, and Orero's advance had forced Ras Mengesha of Tigre into his camp. On 27 February 1893 he notified the Italian government that he intended to terminate the Treaty of Wichale the following year.[32]

Shortly after Orero's abortive parade on Adua, one plank of Crispi's African policy gave way. In March 1890 Salisbury openly warned the Italians that Britain had not abandoned her title to the Sudan. Crispi fought hard for equal partnership on the upper Nile – while an Italian force overwhelmed the dervishes at the battle of Agordat on 27 June 1890 – but negotiations collapsed when Salisbury refused to accept the Italian contention that British rights to Kassala had 'lapsed' and that Italian occupation of the town was necessary for the defence of Eritrea. Crispi then fell from office and his successor, Rudinì, struck a deal to hand Kassala back to the Egyptian government when it was in a position to re-occupy it.[33] Dreams of taking the Sudan, one of the objectives for which Italy went to Eritrea in the first place, were now shattered.

Orero was succeeded on 4 June 1890 by Major-General Antonio Gandolfi, and when Rudinì took over from Crispi he was run on a much tighter rein. Rudinì was prepared to pull out of Eritrea altogether because of its expense but was opposed by the conservative circles surrounding the king, who would only accept such a move if Italy had previously gained a resounding success elsewhere.[34] While he was trying fruitlessly to divest Italy of Eritrea, Rudinì ordered Gandolfi to stay put inside the Massaua–Keren–Asmara triangle and avoid complications. He also reverted to a policy begun by Baldissera and wooed Ras Mengesha of Tigre. Since Mengesha was the natural son of Johannis, this move challenged Menelik's throne and therefore hardened his hostility towards the Italians.

On 28 February 1892 Oreste Baratieri, Gandolfi's second-in-command, succeeded to the post of commander-in-chief and governor. Sensitive and difficult, Baratieri had the authority as governor to assume direct command of military operations and he used it to reduce the military commander, Arimondi, to little more than a chief of staff, making himself virtually a military dictator.[35] He took a hard line against Menelik, following the Tigrean policy of allying with Ras

Mengesha, and strongly opposed any withdrawal of the colony's boundaries. In this he had the support of Baldissera, who wanted to push out to Lake Tana and create a 'second Italy'.[36]

Baratieri's immediate problem was not the Ethiopians but the dervishes, some 12 000 of whom attacked the fort of Adigrat on 21 December 1893. After a fruitless assault, they settled down to sack a nearby village. Realising that his force would probably be overwhelmed in a night assault, Arimondi sallied out in an all-or-nothing attack. By 2.20 p.m. the battle was over; the bodies of a thousand dervishes lay on the field at a cost of 110 Italian dead. Arimondi's victory was due largely to the fact that the dervishes were used to fighting the squares of the Anglo-Egyptian forces and found it difficult to cope with the elasticity of the Italian extended order, which could avoid the weight of a charge.[37] The victory delighted court circles and Umberto made Arimondi a general. From this time on, Baratieri grew increasingly jealous of his subordinate's reputation.

Smarting at Arimondi's success, Baratieri now suggested that the colony could be more securely defended by moving outwards. The foreign ministry warned him against pushing towards the Sudan:

Any government which exposed the Italian flag to a provocative war against the Dervishes would commit unpardonable mistakes. To reinforce Agordat with defensive works, to make it capable of concentrating the bulk of Italian forces there, to make of it – in a word – another Keren further along the road to Kassala, would not be an act of conservation but of provocation.[38]

However, Crispi secretly encouraged Baratieri's ambitions to attack Kassala, passing him news which suggested that a new dervish attack was at hand.[39] By July, Baratieri was clearly contemplating an attack on Kassala, but admitted that the Ethiopians might use the opportunity to attack him themselves. The war minister, Mocenni, who was totally ignorant of government policy, had no clear idea of how to react: 'It is a seductive idea', he noted, 'but not one to be undertaken lightly, given that it could have grave consequences'.[40]

Hitherto, African military policy had been formulated without reference to the views of the chief of general staff. On 14 July 1894 Cosenz's successor, Primerano, broke with tradition and wrote to the war minister warning him against the Kassala operation: Italy lacked the means to deal a decisive blow against the dervishes, and would find herself facing two threats with only limited force at her disposal.[41]

However, he was already too late. Two days earlier Mocenni had telegraphed Crispi's approval for Baratieri to take what measures he thought fit. Premier and governor – both ex-Garibaldini – were now the senior and junior partners in a conspiracy of expansion.

Baratieri took a force of ascaris and set off at once for Kassala. The battle began at 3 a.m. on 17 July and lasted some six hours, then the dervish garrison fled. A week later Baratieri withdrew, leaving behind him a force of a thousand men and two guns under the command of Major Turitto. Unlike Arimondi, he had won a hollow victory for, after the defeat of Ahmed Ali at Adigrat, the dervishes had pulled back to Omdurman. Reinforcements set out for Kassala eight days before the battle, but failed to arrive in time. Baratieri had beaten a token force.

Baratieri had been able to move against the dervishes in the first half of 1894 chiefly because of the apparent quiescence of the Ethiopians. He failed to appreciate the strides Menelik was making, both materially and politically. By late 1894, thanks to French and Russian activity, the Ethiopian market was so saturated with guns that stocks were going unsold.[42] Menelik was also reaping the fruits of a policy designed to promote reconciliation among the warring factions of the empire. First Tekla Haymanot renewed his vows of loyalty and then, early in June 1894, Mengesha came to Addis Ababa to seek pardon for his dealings with the Italians. He brought with him Alula, Bahta Agos and Wolda Mikael. Menelik had achieved almost complete unity within his empire, and in doing so had laid the foundation of Italian defeat.

Suspecting Mengesha's loyalty, Baratieri launched a reconnaissance in force to Adua, arriving there on 28 December but being forced by logistic difficulties to leave again four days later. Mengesha followed him and, moving his troops at night, Baratieri met the Ethiopians at Koatit on 13 January 1895. The day ended indecisively, but Mengesha's forces were caught at Senafe two days later, and the first Italian artillery salvo blew his tent to pieces. He fled, leaving behind correspondence suggesting that he had been incited to revolt by Menelik.[43] In two days of battle the Italian forces had fired off 153 725 rounds of rifle-ammunition; with Ethiopian losses calculated at 1500 dead and 3000 wounded, only one shot in thirty-four had hit the mark.[44] Crispi, looking for domestic advantage in foreign success, congratulated Baratieri for acting like 'a true Garibaldino' in defeating superior numbers, but pointed out that Tigre now lay open and that it would be an 'indulgence' not to want to occupy it.[45] Mocenni shared this view.[46]

Baratieri responded by recommending expansion to incorporate Adua and the holy city of Axum as boundaries of the colony. For once,

Crispi did not egg him on. Awaiting elections on 26 May, he could not increase the colony's budget beyond 9 million lire, the maximum Sonnino was prepared to accept. Accordingly Adigrat was set as the limit of the Italian sphere; any expansion was to be funded by local tribute. When Baratieri complained, Crispi retorted tartly that Napoleon made war 'on the money of those he defeated', a singularly inappropriate analogy.[47] Frustrated in his attempts to swell Italy's sphere of influence, Baratieri asked on 23 April to be recalled. His request was refused.

Baratieri now sought a defined policy in Africa, but in asking for government guidance he scarcely put the alternatives impartially:

Either a defensive war which, for a hundred reasons, will force us onto the offensive and therefore to territorial conquests, to expansion, to a definitive solution of the problem, to a weakening of our enemies in the south and by repercussion those to the west; or peace, with considerable sacrifices of territory, whenever such a peace might be concluded and when it would not carry within it the seeds of new wars and greater sacrifices.[48]

Victory would secure 'a vast and fertile country for Italian colonisation' but even to defend the colony would require preparations for war.[49] He pushed hard for more resources but met with resolute refusals from Mocenni and Blanc. Finally, on 7 July he made it clear that unless he was given an increase in the garrison to face the coming war he would resign.

Baratieri was recalled to Rome for consultations but after seven weeks news from Arimondi that things were worsening forced him to return to Eritrea. On 14 September, the day before he left, he met Crispi and Mocenni at Naples but got little in the way of positive guidance. Instead he reassured them: 'Have no fears; I am lucky, and under me, even in Africa, everything must go well'.[50] Three days later Menelik ordered a general mobilisation.

In Rome, Mocenni recognised that Baratieri was in a difficult position which was only partly of his own making. He thought Menelik would have to attack by mid-December if he were not to lose his authority.

For my part, because of my own caste of mind and because of the old maxim that he who attacks defends himself better, I would incline to fight a great war to a finish which would leave no doubt about the victory.[51]

Holding such views, Crispi's war minister was temperamentally disinclined to act as a restraint on the premier in the way that Bertolé-Viale had done. Fertile ground was being prepared in which to sow the seeds of disaster.

Baratieri decided to make Adigrat the pivot of the colony's defence against the massing Ethiopians. A series of forward positions was established, the outermost of which, commanded by Major Pietro Toselli, was at Amba Alagi. Baratieri intended that Toselli withdraw to Makalle if hostiles appeared. This instruction was either misunderstood or deliberately ignored by Arimondi, who had recently quarrelled with the governor, and Toselli was left with the impression that he must hold Amba Alagi at all costs. He expected Arimondi to come to his aid in case of trouble, but Arimondi was expressly forbidden to move beyond Makalle by Baratieri, who ordered him to tell Toselli to fall back as the Ethiopian hordes massed around him. Toselli never got this order, possibly because Arimondi never sent it.[52]

By the evening of 6 December 1895, with 30 000 Ethiopians surrounding the garrison of 2350 men and no orders from Makalle, Toselli's officers sensed that they were done for. The battle of Amba Alagi began at dawn the next morning. By 11 a.m. Toselli was out-flanked, many of his officers were dead and his artillery was down to its last rounds. At 12.40 p.m., having fought for six hours and realising that he would get no help, he gave the order to retreat towards Makalle. Most of the deaths occurred during this retreat at the troops – retiring down a valley – were fired on from both sides by the Ethiopians. Toselli perished, along with 1500 ascaris, 20 white soldiers and almost all the officers. Leaving Major Galliano and a garrison of some 2000 at Makalle, Arimondi withdrew to Adigrat.

Defeat in Africa stirred the government to action, not least because of the jubilant press reports in St Petersburg and Paris. Mocenni telegraphed asking exactly what reinforcements Baratieri needed, to which the governor responded somewhat lamely that he could not say since he did not know the enemy's intentions.[53] Baratieri's plan to mass ten thousand men at Makalle and counter-attack the Showans or attack their flank if they marched on Adua had collapsed. If the enemy attacked him, he proposed to fight; if they split their forces, he would attack one of their columns; if they marched towards Mareb, he would launch a flank-attack.[54] Mocenni was ready to send reinforcements, but Baratieri was reluctant to ask for them until the situation became clearer.

Indecision at the front was now compounded by lack of direction from the rear. Mocenni urged Baratieri to be prudent and told him to be guided by military opportunity and by the need not to get fully committed and risk another disaster.[55] Crispi's telegrams in the week before Christmas were extremely confusing, first announcing that the government did not intend to follow an expansionist policy and then urging Baratieri to assess enemy strength in order to decide whether or not to take the offensive: 'Let us think of victory – only that is our duty at this moment'.[56] A memorandum from Primerano recommending the dispatch of three full regiments, together with transport, preparation of a second expedition and the provision of more money was ignored.[57] On Christmas Day the premier warned Baratieri, in yet another confusing *volte-face*, that an offensive needed more troops than were currently available.

Baratieri had built up a force of 4 522 Italian troops, 10 324 ascaris and twenty-two guns at Adigrat by the time that he arrived there himself on 10 January 1896. Meanwhile Galliano, with 1350 soldiers and four guns at his disposal, worked desperately to improve the defences of Makalle, carrying out summary executions to speed up the process. His position was hopeless. The perimeter wall was overlooked by heights surrounding the fort and the two wells which supplied the garrison's drinking-water lay 400 metres outside the defences. On 6 January Ethiopian troops began to arrive and two days later they occupied the wells and began an artillery duel with the Italian guns. From that moment it was only a question of time before thirst forced Galliano to surrender.

On 18 January, his water-supply on the point of exhaustion, Galliano proposed either blowing up the fort or trying to break out. His officers voted to break out and the desperate action was planned for the 20th, but the day before it was due to take place Galliano was told that the siege was over and his men had safe-conducts back to the Italian lines. Menelik, prepared to try to reach a diplomatic settlement, had agreed that the garrison should be spared and escorted back to Adigrat.[58] Galliano's men were given 500 mules and an escort but the Italians believed he was slowing them down by making them await the survivors before moving against the Ethiopians.

The Italians had consistently underestimated the military capacity of the Ethiopians, but Ethiopian artillery-fire on Makalle showed how much native armies had improved since 1888, when large numbers had not dared to attack the fort at Saati. Now, as the Italians learned, the Ethiopians were equipped with 37 mm quick-firing artillery, much more up-to-date than the Italian 75 mm mountain artillery, which was more accurate and could throw charges eight or nine times as far but had a much slower rate of fire.[59]

Baratieri's strategy was to hold a large army on the plateau and to react to Ethiopian moves; but the longer the Italian force kept the field, and the larger it grew, the more important the supply question became. Early in December Baldissera pointed out that supply services from Massaua to the highlands presented uncommon problems and could at any moment produce a crucial situation. The ideal man to take charge, he suggested, was Albertone.[60] On 22 December Albertone was ordered to Africa, but when he arrived he was given a brigade of infantry instead. This was one small example of the series of misjudgements which were about to lead Baratieri and his army to disaster.

The day after Albertone left for Eritrea, Mocenni proposed that Baldissera replace Baratieri, in whom he had no faith and who appeared to have no faith in himself any more. Baldissera advised against replacing Baratieri at once as his unstable character might make him do something foolish. He also believed that the campaign would turn out to be short, since the Ethiopians would be forced to retreat as Johannis had done in 1888 and Menelik in 1890.[61] Baldissera was finally appointed governor of Eritrea by royal decree on 22 February, and sailed from Brindisi the following day. He arrived at Massaua on 4 March, three days after the battle of Adua.

The fact that Baratieri knew of his iminent replacement by Baldissera might explain why he sought battle with Menelik and thereby brought about his own downfall.[62] Contemporaries certainly expected that the news, if it reached him, might force the issue.[63] However, Baratieri himself said that he did not know of his removal until 5 March, and neither Salsa nor Valenzano, both of whom saw him at close quarters during these days, believed that he suspected he was about to be replaced.[64] It is theoretically possible for him to have known: the telegram bearing the news was sent to the vice-governor of Massaua on 25 February, and it was well within the capacity of a native runner to have carried the news to Baratieri's field-headquarters in four days.[65] But there is no firm evidence that the governor did know on the eve of Adua that he was about to be sacked, and his defeat is readily explicable without it.

As the siege of Makalle began, Crispi increased the pressure on his unfortunate field-commander. The country, he told Baratieri, expected another victory which would determine the Ethiopian question 'for ever' and he was reminded that he held Italian honour and dignity in his hands: 'I don't ask you your war plan. I only ask you not to repeat our defeats'.[66] At the same time, responding to pressure from public opinion, from the court circle and from Primerano, Mocenni began to send out troops regardless of Baratieri's apparent unwillingness to accept reinforcements. This must have seemed strange in Rome, but it made more sense on the spot, for Baratieri was beginning to experience increasing supply problems. The reason was partly the shortage of pack-animals, but Arimondi was also very critical of Baratieri's decision at the end of 1895 not to renew Bienenfeld's contract but to give the job to a new and inexperienced supply company.[67] More generals arrived with the troops: Dabormida, Albertone and Ellena – the foremost artilleryman in Italy, annoyed to find himself commanding an infantry brigade – as well as a new chief of staff, Colonel Valenzano. All had one thing in common: they lacked African experience.

At the end of January Crispi instructed Baratieri to put the army into a position where it could attack or respond to an attack. At the same time Blanc telegraphed the government's view that no acceptable terms could be sought until after Italy had won a victory. Accordingly at the beginning of February Baratieri began a push on Sauria, which exacerbated his supply problems. His ideas of what might happen were optimistic but hazy: at first he hoped that want of food would cause the huge Ethiopian armies to dissolve, but by the middle of the month he was hoping to force the enemy to attack him.[68]

Salsa, who was conducting pointless negotiations with Menelik, was able to see for himself what kind of enemy the Italians were facing. He estimated their strength at 80 000 rifles, 'carried by a people who are brave and courageous, led by chiefs who are far from stupid and who are showing that they know how to wage war better than one could have supposed'. However, the newly arrived generals and colonels were pushing Baratieri towards a fight. So was Crispi, who telegraphed the news that two more brigades of reinforcements were on their way and added:

> Remember that Amba Alagi and Makalle were two military setbacks, no matter how glorious; and that the honour of Italy and of the Crown are in your hands.[69]

Supply problems now began to take on ever-greater importance. By the end of the third week in February Baratieri had 20 000 troops at Sauria and strung out along the 186-kilometre supply-line to Massaua. Stocks previously built up at Adigrat had run out, and he was relying on the arrival of caravans from the port to sustain his troops on the altopiano. To get foodstuffs forward and return the transport animals to Massaua took twenty-four days; to do this and give the animals adequate rest, Baratieri needed 9000 camels. By 27 February he had only 1700.

Menelik swung around Baratieri's forward position, and moved north-west towards Adua to re-supply his army there. In an exposed position which was both tactically useless and difficult to maintain, Baratieri warned Mocenni on 21 February that he might have to retreat. This was the point at which the government decided to replace him with Baldissera. It was also the point at which Baratieri finally lost his grip on the campaign. By now he was unable to make clear decisions and enforce them. He was neither eating nor sleeping, and according to one of his officers he was 'physically finished'.[70] On 23 February, under pressure from his four brigade commanders, he cancelled the order to retire, and the next day he agreed to a reconnaissance in force towards Adua which achieved nothing. His indecision goaded Crispi into one last, exasperated prod:

This is a military consumption, not a war: little skirmishes in which we are outnumbered by the enemy; gallantry wasted without results. I have no advice to give you because I am not on the spot, but it appears to me that there is no fundamental conception underlying the campaign and I want that remedied. We are ready for any sacrifice to save the honour of the army and the prestige of the crown.[71]

To a man in Baratieri's frame of mind, Crispi's urgent but vague exhortations were merely another cause for anxiety.

On 26 February Valenzano, the chief of staff, met with the supply officers and concluded that stocks would be exhausted within ten days and that camp would therefore have to be struck by 3 March at the latest. The following day Baratieri was warned by telegraph from Adigrat that he would get a caravan of foodstuffs on 2 March with supplies for five days, after which no more could be guaranteed. This news led him to call together his four brigade commanders and the chief of staff for a decisive counsel of war. Afterwards he was accused of summoning this unusual meeting in order to avoid responsibility for the defeat he feared he was about to suffer. In fact, as two witnesses independently confirmed at his court-martial, such gatherings were a habitual occurrence.[72]

The four generals were called to Baratieri's tent on the evening of 28 February 1896, and Valenzano explained the logistical situation to them. Then he put the vital question: advance or retreat? Dabormida spoke first, decidedly against retreat. Albertone and Arimondi were of the same opinion, and Ellena suggested gathering together the largest available force and going out to seek the enemy. Someone said that the nation was expecting a victory and that retreat would be a betrayal.[73]

According to an eyewitness, Valenzano left the commander's tent at the end of the meeting rubbing his hands and exclaiming, 'At last we've got him to attack'.[74]

The pressures on Baratieri were intense. In addition to the immediate problem confronting him, the dervishes were threatening Kassala and behind him the Agame district had risen in revolt two weeks earlier. To retreat might encourage further insurrections, and would have a bad effect on the troops' morale. It would also expose the army to the danger of attack in circumstances in which the Ethiopian armies were at their most effective. Finally, Baratieri was aware that Crispi had been forced to agree to recall parliament, which had been prorogued for two months, on 4 March and needed some political support. Ironically, Menelik's position was every bit as parlous: by the time of the battle of Adua his army was starving, and he had ordered it to strike camp on 2 March.[75]

At 5 p.m. on the afternoon of 29 February, Baratieri called his brigadiers together to receive their orders. He intended to make an offensive demonstration which might tempt the enemy to attack him, or, if they did not, to retreat to Sauria without loss of face; but he also thought it might be possible to attack Menelik's camp in the valley of Mariam Sciavitù. He was misled by false reports from Ethiopian spies that a good half of Menelik's army was away in distant provinces raiding and levying supplies.[76] His mental confusion was reflected in orders which were extremely unclear. On the left Albertone's native brigade (4076 men) was to advance to a hill named Chidane Meret; in the centre Arimondi (2493 men) and behind him Ellena's reserve brigade (4150 men) were to move on Rebbi Arienni, another prominent hill; and on the right Dabormida (3800 men) was also to move on Rebbi Arienni. Confusingly, Baratieri left Arimondi with the option of taking up position behind Albertone and Dabormida if their brigades were sufficient – for what, he did not say.[77] With his orders, Baratieri gave his brigade commanders a sketch-map. The hill indicated on it as Chidane Meret, Albertone's objective, was in fact Enda Chidane Meret, eight kilometres closer to the Ethiopian camp at Adua than its near-namesake, which – along with a number of other hills – was not marked. Another of the seeds of tragedy had been sown.

Albertone left the meeting believing that he was to occupy the heights of Chidane Meret and attack Mariam Sciavitù beyond them together with Dabormida's brigade on his right.[78] He called his battalion commanders together and, according to one of them, announced:

Gentlemen, the move we wanted has finally come. In two hours we leave to attack the enemy at Chidane Meret or beyond, wherever we find him.[79]

Ellena called one of his colonels to announce that the brigade was leaving at 9.30 p.m. that evening for Adua, where the enemy would be encountered.[80] Only Dabormida seems to have shown any signs of concern: an eyewitness saw him return from the generals' meeting looking extremely pre-occupied, and supposed that he might be suffering from a recurrence of an illness which had affected him a short while before.[81]

The night march of 15 kilometres took the troops eight hours, despite a splendid moon, chiefly due to shortage of water. Albertone, instead of marching west towards Chidane Meret, swung north in the direction of Rebbi Arienni, colliding with Arimondi's column and cutting his line of march at about 2.30 a.m. The centre column halted for an hour-and-a-half to let the left-hand column go through, separating Albertone from the bulk of Baratieri's force. Albertone reached his intended destination at 3.30 a.m., and after pausing for an hour recommenced the advance towards Enda Chidane Meret, which he reached at 5.30 a.m. Shortly afterwards, and by now separated from the other columns, he was in action.

Arimondi's column, after its enforced pause, arrived a kilometre-and-a-half from Rebbi Arienni at 6.00 a.m., while Dabormida's brigade, which by 3.00 a.m., was hopelessly lost and dependent on local guides, managed to reach its allotted position an hour before Arimondi.[82] Menelik and his empress, Taitù, were interrupted at divine service at 4.00 a.m., on Sunday, 1 March 1896, with the news of the enemy advance, and while the Italians were blundering into position the Ethiopians were summoned to arms with trumpets captured from the Egyptians in 1875.

The battle of Adua, which was about to commence, was not a single battle but three separate engagements. Baratieri's confused orders and misleading sketch-map created the possibility that the Italians might be split up, and Albertone's deliberate advance to Enda Chidane Meret determined that this would happen. Another accident now helped throw Baratieri's ill-laid plans even further awry. Albertone's advance-guard was under the command of Major Turitto, who was anxious to remedy an undeserved reputation for hesitancy gained in an earlier battle. On reaching Enda Chidane Meret, Turitto saw the Showan advance-guard a little way ahead of him and attacked at once, drawing the rest of the brigade into action earlier than Albertone may have intended.[83]

Turitto's troops began the action at 6.10 a.m. and forty minutes later, as they were retiring onto the main body of the brigade, Albertone sent a message to Baratieri explaining his position. It was one of many sent that day which never reached their destination.[84] Albertone, who was expecting help from Dabormida, was in a weak position. His right flank was out of contact with the main Italian force, both his flanks could be turned with ease, and his men stood on ground overlooked by heights from which the enemy could fire down on them and fronted by a deep river-bed where the Ethiopians could mass unseen.

By 8 a.m. Albertone was fighting off some 30 000 Ethiopians from a horseshoe-shaped position, and within an hour they had gained the heights overlooking it. From here quick-firing artillery, reportedly directed by the empress Taitù in person, was brought into action with deadly effect.[85] At 9.30 a.m. his position was struck by 25 000 fresh Ethiopian troops and at the same time Showan units drove past his right flank, severing it from Arimondi and Dabormida – who were, in any case, in no position to be able to help him. The artillery protected the retreat of the native troops, firing over open sights until, at 11.15 a.m., their ammunition was exhausted. They were massacred where they stood. Albertone was captured at about this time; his brigade no longer existed as a fighting force.[86]

Afterwards Albertone blamed his native troops for lacking fire-discipline and using up their ammunition too soon, and had no doubts as to the cause of his personal disaster:

> I am deeply convinced that if, at Chidane Meret, I had had under my orders a white brigade and not a native one, then the results of its fire would have been much more effective. Standing on a naturally strong position, where there was no need to manoeuvre, the calm and well-aimed fire of white troops would at least have prolonged our resistance for some hours and enabled us to inflict greater casualties on the enemy.[87]

The ascaris were obvious scapegoats for a general who lacked African experience and who had fought a poor engagement, but other eyewitnesses found nothing to complain of in their performance as marksmen that day, when they shot as if on the firing range.[88]

In the centre, Baratieri responded to the growing noise of battle by ordering Arimondi forward to Monte Bellah at 7.45 a.m. Arimondi advanced slowly – a caution which perhaps reflected the fact that he was the most experienced general on the field – and as a result never completed the move, for the enemy arrived there before he did. His troops halted at 9 a.m., and an hour later the first indistinct figures appeared in front of his force 'like grains of white flour'.[89] Unsure whether they were fleeing ascaris or Showans, his men held their fire. They turned out to be the enemy. Within half-an-hour the Ethiopians were lapping at Arimondi's flanks and at 11 a.m. his left, under the command of Galliano, hero of Makalle, broke and he turned to Ellena for help from the reserve.

Ellena could do nothing, for the reserve no longer existed. He had had to detach most of the units under his command to deal with Showan attacks on his right, which had split the centre off from Dabormida's brigade, and now had only five companies left. At this point Baratieri, who had already entirely lost his grip of the battle, was cut off and lost for about an hour. Arimondi fought a defensive battle in a semi-circular position during which his officers, easily distinguishable by their sashes and by the red and blue rank badges on their white uniforms, were rapidly picked off by the enemy. Shortly before 2 p.m., Baratieri, who had now been found and reunited with the centre, allowed a tactical retreat to develop into a general retirement. A brief stand was made, but to little effect, and the rearward movement gathered pace. More troops were lost in this phase of the battle than in all the earlier ones. Baratieri, who had lost his pince-nez, had to be led from the field on a horse. Arimondi and Galliano were among the dead who remained there.

As Baratieri began the retreat, Dabormida was under the delusion that he had won his battle. As the first sounds of firing were heard on Rebbi Arienni at 6.30 a.m., signalling the start of Albertone's battle, Dabormida moved forward. In the labyrinth of hills around Adua it is impossible to tell where the sound of firing is coming from. Probably under the illusion that he was moving towards Albertone when in fact he was moving away from the rest of the army, Dabormida advanced his troops one kilometre too far, opening up a gap through which Showans poured to cut him off from the centre some three hours later.[90] This forward move broke up Baratieri's front, splitting it into three parts. At 8.15 a.m. Baratieri ordered him to move left to join in Albertone's action, but instead, accepting Colonel Valenzano's suggestion of a route which he thought offered a better way to get to Albertone, he moved not left but right. Valenzano had directed him into the valley of Mariam Sciavitù, a funnel which led west, its only openings in the direction of Adua. Dabormida was now in no position to help anyone.

Dabormida's advance-guard was swinging towards Albertone at 9.15 a.m. when it was struck in front and on the right by Ethiopians.

Within twenty minutes it had been destroyed. At the time when Albertone most needed help, Dabormida was four kilometres to the north of him and five kilometres west of Arimondi with a stiff fight on his hands. By 1 p.m. he had fought off a series of counter-attacks with some success, and believed he had won his part of the battle. He was wrong. The enemy attacks had merely been intended to 'fix' him until the main body of Ethiopians and the artillery were free to deal with him and his counter-attacks with the bayonet achieved little other than exhausting his men as the enemy repeatedly slipped away. There was a pause in the battle, during which the Italian troops thought it was all over, and then at 2.15 p.m. they caught sight of two huge masses of Showans coming up on their left. This was the main body of Menelik's army, which had already disposed of the other three brigades. Dabormida fought on against some 50 000 opponents for an hour-and-three-quarters and then at 4 p.m., with both his flanks being enveloped, he launched one last desperate charge before ordering the retreat. He was killed shortly afterwards.[91]

After the battle the Ethiopians fired the grass, flushing out the wounded and those who had been feigning death. Those unable to march back to the enemy camp were shot and expertly emasculated, the trophies being stuck on the end of rifles. Adua cost Italy 289 officers and 4600 Italian troops dead, 500 wounded and 1900 taken prisoner. Native losses were much lighter: 1000 dead, 1000 wounded and 800 captured.[92] Roughly half the field-force had died or been wounded. Among the survivors were 30 Italian soldiers who had been castrated during the battle and 406 ascaris who had had their right hands and left feet cut off after it, to prevent their taking any further part in acts of warfare. Ethiopian losses amounted to perhaps some 4000–6000 dead and 8000 wounded out of a total force which may have numbered 100 000 men.

Baratieri reached Saganeiti on 4 March and Asmara the next day and the remnants of his troops trickled in to Adi Caie and Adi Ugri over the next three days. The retreat had been disorderly and marked by panic once the officers had fallen with only minimal attempts to resist the pursuers.[93]

In 1896 Italy faced the best-armed native state in Africa, in the hands of a highly-skilled political and military leader. Adua happened because political pressure from Crispi drove Baratieri to seek battle when prudence should have dictated otherwise. Once begun it was poorly controlled, magnifying the enemy's superiority. Other European armies fell to native opponents, and other generals made similar mistakes: 20

years earlier and half a world away, George Armstrong Custer – the Albertone of the United States Army – came to grief in a very similar fashion at the Little Big Horn. British or French forces might have lost a similar battle – although they would probably never have been put under the same pressure to fight it. Britain and France would certainly have revenged such a defeat. The hollow kernel of Italy's military imperialism was that she was too weak to do so.

6 'The Most Liberal of Generals'

The Risorgimento pattern of civil–military relations put the army into the political arena as an outpost of the throne. For more than three decades the military remained institutionally passive: individual soldiers sat as senators and deputies, but neither they nor the war ministers tried to exert collective pressure in areas beyond their professional concern. Although Italy passed into the hands of a general in 1898, this did not signal the flowering of dormant military interventionism: Luigi Pelloux's appointment as premier represented a last-ditch attempt by conservative circles to repress the forces released by political change, economic developments and social distress. Loyal to the crown, the army defended the state against its internal enemies – but not without considerable dissatisfaction at the politicians who had put it into a position it preferred to avoid.

Crispi's successors had to deal with the rise of the Socialist Party, and the re-entry of Catholicism into grass-roots politics. Static agricultural output between 1891 and 1898, coupled with an increase of 3 500 000 in the population, produced harsh conditions in the countryside which were exacerbated by a government policy of high consumption taxes and low expenditure. Italian industry, which took off in these years, was unable to keep up with the availability of labour, producing unemployment, underemployment and emigration. To authoritarian liberals, the only answer to red and black threats was a foreign war to pull the nation together.[1] To his credit, Pelloux never succumbed to that deception.

Italy's external position was no easier than her internal situation. A member of the Triple Alliance, she depended on Germany in Europe and British sympathy and goodwill in the Mediterranean to safeguard her against France. This policy held good only as long as there was no conflict between Britain and Germany, but the Congo dispute in 1894 and the Kruger telegram in 1896 signalled increasing discord between London and Berlin. At the same time, British unwillingness to antagonise France evolved into a readiness to reach diplomatic accommodation which endangered Italy's Mediterranean position. The trade-off in March 1899 which allowed France the central Sudan but excluded her from the Nile basin suggested in Rome that a French advance along the north African coast would not be impeded by London. The strategic implications of this were alarming and Pelloux found himself having to make military provisions against France at a moment when the soldiers also became aware of the vulnerability of the north-eastern frontier.

No sooner had Rudinì replaced Crispi in March 1896 than the French problem presented itself in some urgency. The protectorate over Tunis assumed by France in 1881 had cut across the Italo–Tunisian treaty of 1868, which had given special rights to Italians resident there. The treaty expired in the summer of 1896, and Rome learned that the French government had been sounding out the Russian attitude in the event of what were euphemistically termed 'complications' over Tunisia.[2] No help was to be found in London. In the circumstances Rome had but little choice, and on 30 September 1896 she concluded an accord recognising permanent French predominance in Tunis.

Italian military planners had already lived for fifteen years with the threat of an enemy base below Sicily, but this was greatly heightened as the French began to build a naval base at Bizerte. Port construction and a strategic railway link with Tunis had been begun in 1894 but construction difficulties soon developed and progress was slow. Nevertheless the new base posed a threat, and in October and November 1898 Italy made naval preparations to resist a French attack.[3]

French expansionist designs also threatened to engulf Tripoli, in whose fate Italy was developing a special interest. The alarms sounded in April 1896, when Lord Salisbury informed the Italian ambassador, General Ferrero, that he strongly opposed any French advance on Tripoli,

> but that on this as on other questions connected with the *status quo* in the Mediterranean, the course which Her Majesty's Government would think it right to take in any contingency could not be decided until the contingency arose.[4]

In 1898 Italy ended her economic war with France. In May 1899, bereft of British support, she began a long-drawn-out process of negotiation which was finally concluded in January 1901 with an exchange of back-dated notes in which France declared her disinterest in Tripoli in return for a similar Italian declaration over Morocco. The lack of institutional links between the war ministry, the general staff and the ministry of foreign affairs meant that the soldiers continued to work on the French threat without the benefit of any guidance on the aims and intentions of Italian foreign policy.

Ricotti took over the war ministry against the backdrop of Adua. On entering office, he was less concerned with the repercussions of the battle than with reviving his policy of reducing the number of units in the army to consolidate its strength and improve its efficiency. He had powerful external support. Berlin felt grave doubts about whether Italy could carry out her military obligations. Her infantry companies and cavalry squadrons were too many in number and too weak in strength, and there was criticism of money wasted in useless exercises such as recalling the mobile militia for training. The message from Berlin was that Italy would be well advised to reduce her regiments from twelve weak companies to nine strong ones, and not to interfere with a well-established routine by ending the practice of war mobilisation through the military districts.[5]

Ricotti was prepared to keep Ferrero's twelve army corps – indeed, he could hardly do otherwise since they were widely regarded as essential given the terms of the Triple Alliance – but proposed to reduce the number of tactical units by a quarter and to increase the annual intake from 70 000 to 90 000 men. All of this could be done, he calculated, without going beyond his predecessor's budget of 234 million lire. His scheme provoked strong opposition from the court and the army, not least because if it were adopted some 1500 officers would have to be retired. Within four months, when combined with Pelloux's reformism and the reverberations of Adua, it was to cause his fall from office.

Although he could not reform the army, Ricotti did preside over an important rejuvenation of the officer corps. On 27 March 1896 the senate approved a law on promotions which introduced age-limits for the first time. The credit, however, properly belonged to Pelloux, who had introduced the draft law three years earlier. Under its terms lieutenant-generals had to retire at 65, major-generals at 62 and other officers at proportionate ages, down to 50 for captains and 40 for lieutenants. The law was in some respects confusing, for lieutenant-generals in command of army corps need not retire until 68, and there was no clear distinction between past and present tenure of such command. Over-all, it would result in the retirement of 636 officers of the rank of colonel and above and 1098 promotions in the 15 years up to 1910.[6] One of its first victims was the chief of the general staff.

Primerano's role in the *débâcle* at Adua became the subject of attention during a parliamentary debate on 8 May, when the government was asked why the published documents contained no instructions from the chief of the general staff, why the war minister had not thought to consult him and why, if he had not been consulted, he had not thought it his duty to protest. The chief of staff, it appeared, had sat back and watched widespread interference in the army without acting to curb it. Failing to get any support from his former minister, Mocenni, Primerano at once resigned.[7]

Ricotti recognised the dangers of the situation and moved quickly to prevent any up-grading of the chief of staff's authority. In a speech to the chamber on 22 May, he said that he did not know the reason for Primerano's resignation as he had not been told and had not asked. He then reminded his audience that the king was commander-in-chief of the army and that the chief of staff exercised his powers through the war minister. Ricotti made it transparently plain that he would not countenance any increase in the authority of the post of chief of staff, using the specious argument that to do this would necessitate the appointment of a very senior general who, being close to retirement, would not put much effort into the job. Instead he favoured a young general of 50 or 55, who would study preparations for war only.

The following day Ricotti faced a call to give the chief of the general staff more powers; he responded that this would put him in a position to execute a *coup d'état*. This was a shrewd ground on which to appeal to parliamentarians, but it scarcely masked the meretriciousness of Ricotti's argument. The war minister did disclose the broad outlines of the correspondence between Primerano and Mocenni, and then laid the blame for the central mistakes of the war squarely at the feet of the chief of the general staff; 'no preparatory studies were made and we entered the campaign unprepared'. As soon as the new law on seniority came into force, he said, he would have asked Primerano for his resignation.[8]

Primerano was unwilling to use his position as a senator to provoke a direct confrontation with Ricotti, regarding a fight between the heads of the army as unseemly and fatal to military discipline.[9] He spoke in the senate on 11 June, making a skilful plea for a larger role for the chief of staff in an age of mass warfare and pointing out that the minister, with his own general staff section, was currently able to act quite independently of the general staff, of the inspectors of the various arms and even of the army corps commanders. Ricotti responded by reverting to the African episode and remarking that the chief of staff could not make preparations before the war because no one had asked him to do so. Primerano dryly replied that he had already been blamed by the minister in the chamber of deputies for not doing so. Ricotti then tried to recover his position by stating that after Amba Alagi nothing had been arranged, not even the constitution of the reinforcements to be sent out. Primerano reminded him that he had personally put forward a proposal, as Ricotti had admitted to the deputies on 23 May.[10] Ricotti had been made to look something of a fool. Five days later he decided to retire Primerano.[11]

In the wake of the Primerano affair, Ricotti battled to get his army bill through parliament. It passed the senate on 13 June by 70 votes to 36 but only in the teeth of bitter opposition led by Cosenz, Primerano, Mezzacapo and Morra. The likelihood that it would also pass the chamber of deputies brought a concerted action to halt it. General Ponza di San Martino, who had influence with Giolitti's electoral college at Dronero, told Giolitti that unless he opposed the bill he would personally stand against him. The king put pressure on Rudinì to postpone presentation of the bill, and the loyal premier succumbed. Ricotti thereupon resigned on 11 July and was immediately replaced by Luigi Pelloux.[12]

One of Pelloux's first acts in office was to use the new law on seniority, which had come into effect on 2 July, to retire Primerano and sack Mezzacapo. Although there was a slight element of doubt about the legal foundation for both actions, it was felt that the law had to be applied without exception to the pair, aged respectively 67 and 68.[13] Pelloux doubtless welcomed the opportunity afforded by what was in essence his law to introduce fresh blood into the upper ranks of the officer corps. But since both Primerano and Mezzacapo were southerners, his enemies saw the action as Piedmont's revenge for the 'massacre of the Nunziatella' 20 years earlier.

Two months passed before, on 16 September 1896, Pelloux nominated Lieutenant-General Tancredi Saletta as Primerano's successor. Born in Turin on 27 June 1840, Saletta had entered the artillery at the age of 19 and had commanded the Red Sea expedition in 1885; latterly he had served in staff and educational posts, and for the previous 18 months had been Primerano's deputy. Saletta represented exactly the kind of safe appointment envisaged by Ricotti: a technical professional who was neither a senator nor a deputy. Nevertheless, Pelloux recognised the need for new and more effective forms of military consultation and was to make an important innovation in this respect three years later.

The most pressing task was to wind up the war in Eritrea. Treating with Menelik was regarded as anathema by the conservative circles surrounding the king, who were quite prepared to leave the Italian prisoners to their fate. However, Pelloux was determined to settle the issue quickly and peaceably and was prepared to treat on the basis of the Mareb-Bellesa-Muna line as the natural limit of the Tigrine state.[14] Nerrazini brought off a peace treaty with Menelik on 26 October 1896 which annulled Wichale and recognised Ethiopia as a sovereign state, and the frontiers of the colony were finally fixed eight years later. Recognising reality, Pelloux regarded any forward move in Africa as beyond Italy's financial capacity and determined to limit the colony's budget to no more than 7 million a year.[15]

The reverberations of African defeat rumbled on in military and public life for some time. Baratieri's initial report on the battle, read out by Mocenni at a hastily convened cabinet at lunch time on 4 March, turned opinion against him.

> He apparently throws almost all the blame for the defeat on the white soldiers, who allowed themselves to be overcome by panic. He shows a great lack of moral conscience. He does not say why he attacked.[16]

A subsequent report praising the conduct of the white troops only weakened Baratieri's standing still further. Early in June he faced a tribunal in Eritrea, charged under articles 72 and 88 of the military penal code with abandoning to the enemy an army or part of an army under his command – a charge which carried the death penalty. Most of the evidence given at his trial demonstrated that he had blundered as a result of accident and misfortune rather than through deliberate calculation, and the judges found accordingly. Baratieri was held to be free of any criminal responsibility but the tribunal deplored the fact that, in such an unequal combat and in such difficult conditions, command had been invested in a general 'who showed himself so far below the needs of the situation'.[17] Baratieri thereupon retired from the army and from the chamber of deputies.

Pelloux had agreed to accept the post of war minister on condition that he got back the money his predecessor had renounced, raising the military budget to 246 million a year. Short of money to strengthen the twelve corps army but unwilling to reduce them, he presented a draft law on military organisation in December 1896 which harked back to his previous practices. To keep within budget limits, he proposed that infantry companies have a strength of a hundred men for seven months of the year and 65 for the remaining five. The efficiency of the reserves would be improved by calling up more men for training – 100 000 in 1897–98 – so that company strength would rise to 130 during grand manoeuvres. In peacetime Pelloux was prepared to continue with the system of national recruitment; in wartime he proposed to follow the regional mobilisation procedures introduced in 1892. He said nothing about the powers of the chief of the general staff.[18]

Settling the organic structure of the army was only the most politically significant of the problems facing the new minister, for he was confronted by a number of internal issues, some of long standing, which were causing discontent and inefficiency. The first of these was the problem of officers' dowries. Mocenni had put up a draft law to improve the system in April 1894 but had then withdrawn it, and so had Ricotti. Pelloux now pushed through his predecessors' design. Under the old rules a sliding scale had existed, under which second-lieutenants needed 3800 lire a year in order to marry, captains 4800 and colonels 8200. The law introduced on 24 December 1896 replaced this with a flat sum of 4000 lire a year, along with the need to secure royal assent. It thus became progressively easier for officers of the rank of lieutenant and above to marry and marginally more difficult for second-lieutenants to do so. This was an important modification of past practice, but there was nevertheless some justice in the claim that the whole procedure was an archaeological vestige acceptable when the army had formed a caste apart but no longer responsive to the needs of the age.[19]

Pelloux also had to face serious discontent over pensions. Here his position was made extremely complicated by the retirement law which had seen off Primerano and Mezzacapo. A law on pensions passed on 21 February 1895 had decreed the minimum pensionable age for each rank, ranging from 60 for a lieutenant-general and 52 for a colonel to 45 for captains and lieutenants. To get a full pension of four-fifths of active service pay an officer had to serve for 40 years. The law on promotions ensured that only generals and colonels could complete the maximum term and qualify for a full pension; all other officers were caught by the age-limits. The government's powers to retire officers after a number of years in a given rank or put them into auxiliary service, both of which adversely affected pension rights, worsened matters by opening the door to favouritism or accusations of favouritism.[20]

State parsimony made itself felt in a multitude of other ways. Officers returning from the African campaign in 1896 had to take legal action against the government to obtain the field allowances to which they were entitled.[21] The system of 'extraordinary retentions' also caused considerable distress. Officers were often greatly out of pocket when they had to transfer to a new garrison and had to bear such social expenses as the hire of carriages in which to make duty calls. The problems were exacerbated by the slowness with which the Court of Accounts registered decrees of promotion. Pelloux did find some money from a defunct clothing association and used it to provide loans to officers in need, to defray the expenses of those wishing to go on camps and manoeuvres and to supplement funds for corps reunions, but this was only a cosmetic remedy.

Pelloux also faced a mounting problem with respect to non-commissioned officers, although he was never able to do very much about it. They had a right, under a law of 8 July 1883, to a post in government after twelve years' service and both ministries and companies in which the government had an interest were supposed to reserve places for them. This they did not do: in 1897 the *Società dell'Adriatica* railway company should have had 300 ex-soldiers on its books but actually employed only eleven. With unemployment rife non-commissioned officers stayed on in the army, reducing the opportunities for fresh blood. A move to license some non-commissioned officers at 42 in order to create vacancies ran into the pension problem and left the unfortunate licencees with only 50 lire a month to live on. In 1896 some 60 per cent of NCOs already had at least 12 years' service, and by July 1901 more than 1500 were waiting for a job. Pelloux never solved this problem.[22]

Pelloux resigned on 4 December 1897 when the chamber of deputies insisted on amending a draft law on officers' careers. His action was explained at the time as being due to a failure to keep within his budget and subsequently as reflecting a desire to get out of an administration rent with divisions and looking forward to an uncertain future.[23] However, since he had fought hard to introduce legislation which had defeated his predecessors and since he had spoken out four or five times during the course of the debate against the amendment which was finally carried, it is just as likely that he resigned on a point of principle.[24]

While Pelloux fought his parliamentary battles the new chief of staff wrestled with Italy's strategic problems. Saletta's first staff ride along the Nice frontier in 1896 demonstrated the parlous position: a French attack faced only two or three difficult stages of mountain warfare before emerging on the Paduan plain, whereas an Italian attack would find itself tied up in a long-drawn-out campaign in well-defended mountains. Even if they were successful, Italian troops would only gain a foothold on the French periphery.[25] One way out of the dilemma was the Rhine option, but co-operation on this was intermittent and half-hearted. The railway timetables were discussed at meetings in October 1896 and May 1898, and Italian arrival on the Rhine was speeded up by a day; but the Italians found directives for their operations around Verdun vague and the German general staff got nothing back from Rome in return for answering all the Italian queries. In 1898 Saletta re-opened the idea of moving the Third Army through Switzerland to reach the Rhine – a sign of his distrust of Austria – but abandoned it in the face of overwhelming diplomatic and military problems.[26] Instead, Italy focused more closely than ever upon a defensive national strategy.

Staff rides along the French frontier led Saletta to believe that even a straightforward strategic defensive required more frontier fortifications, and in 1898 a special commission was created 'to secure the defence of the routes which cross the frontier and to make arrangements which would allow offensives in the most convenient directions'. Immediately the problem of the inter-relationship between Italian land-power and sea-power obtruded into the discussions. Italy's railway system, deficient in many respects but vital to military mobilisation, was extremely vulnerable to interdiction from the sea. Her coastlines were too long to defend from the land without eating up money and troops, yet many of her major cities were on or near the sea. Naval co-operation was essential – and unforthcoming. Saletta passed on to the navy minister a list of vulnerable points, and was told that 'the means which the navy had at its disposal were insufficient for the task'.[27]

Saletta was determined to secure the French frontier regardless of cost. As each valley was discussed, he produced calculations of the French forces likely to oppose it in wartime. He won increased defences for the northern valleys, sometimes against the better judgement of the commission: the chairman remarked at one point that he could not see why the Vraita Valley needed defending at all since it could only be reached by mule-track.[28] He even got fortifications he did not ask for, the commission deciding that its other recommendations might make a joint French-Swiss attack along the Sempione Valley more attractive.

A major disagreement over the defence of the upper Dora Riparia and Chisone Valleys revealed the importance of public opinion in Italian defence planning. Saletta proposed withdrawing from present advanced positions and read out a letter written by Cosenz in 1889 which criticised spreading out troops along the frontier as liable to have fatal consequences. Several commissioners grew alarmed at the country's reaction if expensive fortifications were abandoned, among them Luigi Pelloux:

> We cannot, politically speaking, tell parliament and the country that up to now we have been following the wrong path, that the defences built at Cesana and at Bardonecchia are not formidable, that they must be abandoned and with them a tract of national territory must be abandoned to enemy invasion; that the considerable sums spent up to now on the defence of the area are of no value and that further financial sacrifices are necessary.[29]

Saletta believed Italy had neither money nor artillery to defend these valleys but lost the argument to Pelloux, and the commissioners agreed to build more advanced works.

The slowness of Italian mobilisation was the justification for yet more expensive fortifications. Yet even the financial prodigality of the commission could not solve the army's problems. The army insisted that the security of both land- and sea-frontiers must be guaranteed for 15 days if the rigid transportation schedule was to be carried out – a condition which could not be met. By the 14th day of mobilisation Italy would have 150 000 men on the frontier, and her offensive could begin the following day; but this put her at a three-day disadvantage, since the Italian general staff calculated that the French would be able to cross the frontier on the 12th day of mobilisation.[30]

Saletta had other problems besides the French. Beck, the Austrian chief of staff, had been working on contingency plans for war with Italy from the end of 1896 and increased Austrian activity along the frontier began to cause alarm. The general staff supposed that, in the event of war with Italy, Austria-Hungary planned rapidly to advance 20 000 troops to occupy the right bank of the Isonzo.[31] The current deployment plan, based on preparatory studies done in 1889 and 1893, strung four Italian armies out between the Adige and the Tagliamento with the bulk of the troops in the area bounded by Venice, Vicenza, Legnago and Rovigo, but it was now somewhat out of date.[32] As part of a major revision of Italian strategy, Saletta turned his gaze on the north-eastern frontier.

A staff ride in the Trentino in 1898 in which Austria defeated Italy and reached the plains produced horrifying evidence of the weakness of Italy's defences. The three routes from the Tyrol into Lombardy were not blocked at all; there was no protective flotilla on Lake Garda; Verona was insufficiently protected to the north; and the valleys of the Brenta, Cismon and upper Piave were dangerously weak and exposed. With few exceptions, existing fortifications were no protection against Austrian attack.[33] Another ride the following year in Friuli and the Veneto ended with an Italian defeat in both attack and defence, partly because a large force had to be detached to defend the weak Trentino frontier. In consequence, Saletta demanded 14 million lire for the defence of the Trentino and another 13 230 000 lire for Friuli.[34]

Saletta's strategy was determined to a considerable degree by mobilisation times. In turn, they were very much the consequence of an under-capitalised and inefficient rail net. The private railway companies were always short of rolling-stock, and preferred to hire wagons from abroad to cope with the annual grape harvest sooner than buy extra units. In February 1899, in the aftermath of the examination of the

French and Austro-Hungarian borders, a special commission assessed the railways' role in mobilisation on either frontier. Although enough coal and wagons existed, the commission urgently recommended more double-tracking, tunnel-ventilation, and the construction of another thirty locomotives. A civilian proposal for a partial mobilisation to test the system was unhesitatingly rejected by the soldiers.[35]

Uninterrupted mobilisation depended upon the strength of Italian sea-power and fear of seaborne attack mounted as the Italian fleet fell from third to seventh place in world rankings in 1900. The Spanish-American war was taken as proving that land forces could not successfully resist a determined invasion attempt, and public anxiety was not quieted when, in summer manoeuvres in 1899, an enemy landing at Civitavecchia was successfully contained by local defences until reinforcements arrived from the Po Valley.[36] Invasion became a popular obsession in Italy as in most of the rest of Europe, and popular novels depicted the French landing at Viareggio, aided by an internal political upheaval, or attempting a landing in Sicily from their Tunis base.[37] De Lanessan's rebuilding programme for the French fleet, which provided for six battleships, five armoured cruisers and a large number of destroyers, torpedo-boats and submarines, added to Italian alarm.

Although defence problems weighed heavily on the military by the end of the century, it was the domestic situation which catapulted Luigi Pelloux into the premiership. Threats to the established order came from both Left and Right. In the north, the Socialist Party was gaining ground: the newspaper *Avanti!*, founded in December 1896, was soon selling 50 000 copies an issue, and by the following March the party had 15 parliamentary seats. In the south, the rural socialism which had burst into flame in 1893–94 continued to challenge the settled order. At the same time the Catholic *Opera dei congressi* began to show an interest in politics, greatly alarming the anti-clerical Right. Finally, spectacular anarchist acts which included the assassination of the Shah of Persia and an attempt on King Umberto's life on 27 April 1897 fed fears of an international plot to destabilise Italy.

Economic distress mounted rapidly during 1897 with the worst harvest since unification. The situation worsened the following spring as freight rates rose due to the Spanish–American war, making imported grain even more expensive. The root problem was the high tax on grain. Zanardelli, the premier, depended on the agrarian–industrialist bloc for power and was therefore unable to lower protective tariffs or reduce taxes on consumption. The army was well aware of the problem, and in April 1898 General Afan de Rivera proposed that the government buy

300 000 quintals of grain on the foreign market and sell it at reduced prices in central and southern Italy. The scheme was wrecked by Luzzati, the treasury minister.[38]

Prices began to rise dramatically: in Turin, a kilo of bread cost a worker half-a-day's pay, in Sicily a whole day's pay. In January 1898 Zanardelli reduced the grain tax and then, as attacks on bakeries, windmills and grain-stores began to increase, the duty was temporarily suspended for two months on 4 May. The action was too little and too late. A wave of agitation swept Italy, beginning as a straightforward *protesta dello stomaco* but fanned in Milan by the funeral of Cavalotti, a popular radical deputy who had been killed in a duel, and by the celebrations marking the fiftieth anniversary of the *cinque giornate* (when Milan had risen against the Austrians in 1848), which brought huge masses on to the streets. The government saw the hand of anarchist conspiracy at work, drawing along the socialists who in turn pulled the republicans. In great alarm, it turned to the only instrument which could maintain its authority. On 3 May the war and interior ministers were authorised to declare a state of siege wherever necessary and within three days 23 Italian provinces were under military jurisdiction.

The army was far from happy at undertaking defence of the government on the streets. The practice of sending troops armed with rifles to deal with crowds of unarmed demonstrators – 'the ridiculous tactic of employing men armed with lightning as if they had in their hands a sausage' – was strongly criticised, and there were demands that soldiers should be used only in the most exceptional cases. The army had a corporate interest in keeping its public-order function to a minimum, since such activities put an extra burden on the military budget at a time when all parties wanted military expenditure held down, and therefore threatened to make unwelcome inroads in military spending. The military world was also alive to the cause of the current upheavals and had its own ideas about how to deal with them: hunger, it was felt, was best suppressed not by force but with bread, and the civil authorities were held guilty of 'phenomenal ineptitude' in dealing with the problems. Once called upon to act, the army saw its task as restoring order as soon as possible. However, it also recognised – more clearly than the government – that a reform of the tax system was urgently necessary.[39]

Trouble broke out in Milan on 6 May when conscripts of the class of 1873 were recalled to the colours. The arrest of two people distributing socialist propaganda led to an attack on a police headquarters, the deployment of a battalion of infantry and then to shooting, in which two people died. A tense situation was made immeasurably worse by the employers' decision to close the factories the following day, thus putting many more workers on to the streets at a time when tempers were running high. After further bloodless demonstrations the police handed over responsibility for maintaining law and order to the local military commander, General Bava Beccaris, and troops spread through the city on Sunday 8 May. Nerves were jittery: the letters 'F' and 'B', put up by the municipal authorities to indicate sewers and drinking water outlets, were taken to be conspirators' signs for 'fire' and 'bombs'.

When barricades began to go up on 9 May Bava Beccaris took action to suppress the non-existent conspiracy. Troops deployed at the edge of the city fired for four hours at what they thought were rebels coming to the aid of the insurgents and shooting at them, but which turned out to be their own echoes. Meanwhile Bava Beccaris launched a full-scale assault on the convent of Porta Monforte, which he believed was sheltering armed insurgents. After blasting a large hole in its walls he captured a group of twenty friars and some forty beggars who had been waiting for free soup. The insurrection – as the authorities termed it – ended the following day when the factories reopened. The tragi-comic affair produced an official casualty list of 80 dead – including one policeman and one soldier (who may have been shot by his own side) – and 450 wounded, although the real figures were almost certainly considerably higher.[40]

The behaviour of the army reservists during the crisis of 1898 suggested that, if there was some sympathy for the rioters, it was not strong enough to prompt men to absent themselves from the ranks. A total of 130 000 were recalled for service and the absentee-rate was only 2.5 percent. This may have been something to do with the fact that for the first time the government made payments to needy families whose breadwinners were called away. However, the absentee-rate for the class of 1876 did rise to 6.46 per cent, an increase of about one-and-a-half points, and of the class of 1877, 6.29 per cent were absent at call-up. A legacy of bitter anti-militarism was given an authoritative impetus with the publication that year of Guglielmo Ferrero's *Il militarismo*, which was enthusiastically received by some parts of the press and led the army to fear that a wedge was being driven between itself and the nation.[42]

Other generals had copied Bava Beccaris in resorting to a state of siege to restore or maintain civil order – among them Heusch in Massa and Carrara and Malacina in Naples – but there was one conspicuous example of a more dextrous approach to the problem of controlling civilians. Luigi Pelloux arrived in Bari on 4 May and managed to maintain order without such a declaration. His example made a notable impression on the official mind. When the government collapsed in mid-June, after the chamber of deputies rejected legislation which would have made the repressive measures permanent, King Umberto did little more than go through the motions of seeking another civilian premier before offering the post to Pelloux, who accepted it on 29 June.

Bringing a soldier in to head the government was as much a sign of the temporary bankruptcy of civilian politics as it was a signal of the king's wish for authoritarian rule. Significantly, Umberto decorated Bava Beccaris but selected Pelloux, a general with a liberal reputation and seventeen years' experience as a deputy, as premier. In accepting the post Pelloux was doing his duty as a Piedmontese officer. He was also taking an opportunity to put the country back on its feet. Bava Beccaris had written to him from Milan:

> I am reading seized correspondence which demonstrates the foolishness and incapacity of the various authorities – but it is not their fault, it is the fault of the parliamentary system as we work it, and of universal cowardice.[43]

At the same time Afan de Rivera had bombarded him with letters expressing the hope that there would be a government with the conscience to restrict some of the freedoms which had been allowed to go too far, particularly freedom of the press.[44] Familiarity with the rough-and-tumble of the lower chamber may have encouraged him to try his hand at ruling, but he lacked one essential skill: the parliamentarian's ability to find a majority to support his policies by manipulating interest-groups.

Pelloux's first ministry – its advent accompanied by an earthquake in Umbria – bore out Sonnino's prediction: 'he wants to pivot on the Centre, leaning to the Left as far as he can and to the Right as far as he must'.[45] Six active generals and admirals, including the premier, shared the cabinet with eight moderate Left civilians. Early measures of restrictive legislation gained an overwhelming vote of confidence and in February 1899 Pelloux tabled bills allowing the government, at its own discretion and without limit of time, to militarise all railway, post and telegraph personnel, thereby making it impossible for them to strike. Backed by the liberal Left as well as by the government parties, the measures passed by 310 votes to 93. As permanent solutions to the problems of social and political inequality, they were recipes for confrontation. Pelloux's formula for political order reflected a soldier's propensity for reinforcing the institutional organs of control rather than rethinking the policies.

In May 1899, following an embarrassing foreign policy gaffe in which Italian claims for a concession in China had been withdrawn by Rome but delivered by the man on the spot, Pelloux resigned and remade his cabinet, confirming the beliefs of those who regarded him as either an out-and-out conservative or a puppet in Sonnino's hands by ditching the Left. The new government ran into spectacular trouble within a month, introducing measures which further eroded freedom of organisation and association and trying to push them through the chamber by summary-voting. The Left developed new tactics of obstructionism to resist, and after wild scenes in the chamber on 30 June, during which Sonnino was felled by a blow to the temple, parliament was prorogued until November. Pelloux's political capital was almost exhausted.

As well as confronting a difficult domestic situation, Pelloux had to grapple with serious and expensive short-comings in Italy's military inventory which threatened to put massive burdens on the budget. Italian field-guns were all out of date compared with the new recoilless quick-firing French '75', Saletta's staff ride in the Trentino in 1898 had revealed the parlous state of the north-eastern defences, and the position on the French frontier was apparently no better. Privately, senior generals considered that it might be necessary to spend 500 000 000 lire on defence.[46] Pelloux was well aware of the competing military demands and in December 1898 he alarmed conservatives with the opinion that the Triple Alliance was only a damaging burden to Italy.

The extent of the strategic problem led Pelloux to take a revolutionary step which greatly improved the machinery for decision-making. A royal decree of 19 July 1899 established a new consultative body, the Supreme Commission for the Defence of the State, to co-ordinate military and naval policies on national defence at the highest level. The new commission had two categories of members: effective members, including the chief of the general staff and the generals designated to command the four armies in wartime; and consultative members, including the inspectors-general of the various specialist arms and the twelve corps commanders. Its creation was an important step in modernising a ramshackle and old-fashioned system of policy-making.[47]

The new commission met for the first time on 30 October 1899 under the presidency of the Prince of Savoy – the future Victor Emmanuel III. Along with four admirals, its members comprised the Pelloux brothers, Saletta and Mirri, the war minister. From the outset fear of the French fleet became the key to Italian strategy-making. Asked whether the Italian fleet could protect exposed railway lines during mobilisation, the admirals were unanimously of the opinion that, in current circumstances, it could not, chiefly because they were entirely unwilling to detach any ships for the task and thus further weaken a fleet which was already inferior to the French Mediterranean squadron. Admiral Morin made the counter-proposal that mobilisation might be completed before the actual outbreak of hostilities and had to be reminded by Luigi Pelloux that general mobilisation was the first act of war, not the last act of peace.

Saletta tried to prise some assistance from the admirals by pointing out that in the event of mobilisation against France the Adriatic would not need to be protected, but could gain only a general agreement that the fleet might in some cases protect limited tracts of railway, with no discussion as to where or how this might be done.[48] The fleet was prepared to resist major landings on the peninsula or in the islands, and the commission quickly reached the happy conclusion that, while it continued to exist in a fighting condition, it would be able to contest major enemy operations as long as it was not called upon to fulfill other, more pressing, strategic tasks.[49]

The protection of the great *piazze marittime* was a major concern, and there was general anxiety lest the French bombard a city such as Genoa to exert political pressure on the government to surrender. The navy was prepared to contemplate contributing to the defence of such cities if they were attacked but adamantly refused to accept any obligation to protect them. Its position was anchored in the contemporary orthodoxy of naval strategy which required that the fleet be held together for the main action, and its stance was concisely justified by Admiral Morin: the enemy would try to gain command of the sea, and it was the navy's job to stop him from doing so.[50] All parties agreed on the urgent need to expand the fleet without delay and on the desirability of aid from allied squadrons.

Saletta revealed his philosophy of national defence during debate on the defence of the south. The commission should decide what was necessary regardless of the financial implications, and the government should proportion means to ends in the light of the political situation. Admiral Morin remarked dryly that Saletta appeared to want the coast littered with small fortifications, and the chief of the general staff lost a vote to fortify Palermo by a large margin.[51] A direct clash took place over what to do about Naples, with the sailors broadly against any further fortifications as being of relatively little utility. The army's preoccupation with the problem of national psychology in defence planning was reflected in General Mirri's response:

the fall of Naples would make such an impression on the country that the question of whether or not to defend it is one of a high political order, even if the proposed fortifications, or those which our financial position will permit us to build, will only partially achieve this end.[52]

The commission concluded by agreeing on the need to establish exactly what function each of the *piazze marittime* performed in the general defence of the state, its importance and whether or not it should be abolished.

The Supreme Commission provided an opportunity for representatives of both services to discuss issues which bore heavily on the army's strategic plans and financial demands, and for the soldiers to acquaint themselves at first hand with the strategic concepts which were the foundations of naval thought. It also provided the opportunity to review a number of assumptions made in the early 1880s and never really questioned thereafter. Its conclusions underlined the importance attached to fortification in Italian prescriptions for national defence, but it had managed to reduce the range and order the priorities in this regard. However, fortifications needed artillery, and so another item was added to an already heavy bill.[53]

The most pressing need was to renew the artillery: Saletta believed that an extra 95 000 000 lire would be required to replace mountain- and field-artillery and howitzers and to refurbish existing siege-guns. First priority was the provision of 530 new 7 cm field-guns; Krupps, whose guns had performed best in trials, could build them in a year, whereas made nationally they would take much longer.[54] Raising the annual intake of conscripts was also desirable, but without more money an increase from 100 000 to 150 000 a year would necessitate reducing the term of service to only 15 or 16 months.[55] Finally, conservative military circles were coming to realise that a citizen-army needed to be run on different lines as Italy entered the new century. The advent of a generation which had never known a divided Italy, together with the mounting impact of socialism, required leadership based on something more positive than mere repressive discipline.[56] Every part of the Italian army seemed in need of reform – and in need of money.

On 31 January 1900 Pelloux demanded an extraordinary budget of 393 000 000 lire, spread over twenty years, for new field-artillery and fortifications for the land and sea frontiers. The prospect of vast new government expenditure united extreme Left, liberal Left and Lombard Right against him. Pelloux's ordering of defence priorities was vulnerable to the prior claim of the fleet for, as one of the most respected military commentators pointed out, the problem of defending Italy 'is not resolved, and is not capable of resolution in a satisfactory manner, until the fleet is in a position to defend the sea frontier as the army defends the land frontier'. A fleet might seem something of a luxury in a war against Germany or Austria-Hungary, but with France as Italy's most likely opponent, it was regarded as a necessity.[57] The German–Austro-Hungarian–Italian naval convention concluded on 5 December 1900, which divided up the Mediterranean, did nothing to ease the dilemma and in any case soon became a dead letter.[58]

Defence problems were pushed to the sidelines by the political crisis which developed during the early months of 1900 as Pelloux sought to pass decree laws and interfere with parliamentary practice by limiting the time allowed to any speaker and giving the president of the chamber powers to stifle opposition. Disorder lasted from February until May, when the government called a general election. It was held early in June, to the accompaniment of a great deal of government interference and manipulation, but when it came to electing a president for the new chamber Pelloux's candidacy could command a majority of only 28. Faced with a revival of all his earlier difficulties, Luigi Pelloux resigned the premiership on 18 June. The assassination of King Umberto on 29 July confirmed the feeling that an era of repression had closed.

The political interests of Italy's generals focused on two objectives: sustaining the monarchy and the Risorgimento settlement, and securing the funds necessary to maintain the army in the best possible order. They looked for a strong and effective government to hold the country together and, by ensuring that the war ministry was always in the hands of a soldier, maintained their freedom from civilian intervention. Pelloux's acceptance of the premiership reflected the failure of civilian politicians to guide socio-economic pressures along the path of controlled evolution. It was not an expression of the army's eagerness to run the country: the role of premier was thrust upon Pelloux by the king, not the other way round. In accepting it he blemished a career in which, so far as the internal needs of the army and the requirement to co-ordinate defence policies were concerned, he showed himself to be both liberal and farsighted.

7 Partners and Rivals

For Italy, the years from 1900 to 1908 saw mounting tension in the army. Structural deficiences in the officer corps remained uncorrected, and professional morale slumped. The continued use of the military to prop up civil power, although less dramatic because of Giolitti's willingness to tolerate strikes, caused mounting unhappiness. Professional frustrations began to turn the soldiers against parliament, which denied them money, blocked small but prized internal reforms, and insisted on using them as school-teachers and policemen. The links which bound the army to the state began to show unmistakable signs of strain.

Italian foreign policy, about which the army was kept largely in the dark, had two aims. One was concisely expressed by Luzzatti in the chamber of deputies in 1907:

> Unbreakable faithfulness to the Triple Alliance, sincere friendship for England and France, and cordial relations with the other powers always remain the bases of our foreign policy.[1]

However, also underlying Italian foreign policy was a desire to play an active part among the Great Powers – the *Consulta* complained with some bitterness in 1902 that 'pour le gouvernement anglais l'Italie est une quantité négligeable'.[2] Its target was Tripoli. In 1902 Prinetti secured a British declaration of uninterest in the area and a free hand from France. The cost was considerable: in the so-called Prinetti-Barrère accords Italy not only gave France a free hand in Morocco, she also bound herself to neutrality if France were attacked or went to war as a result of direct provocation. This left much to interpretation, and Italy was giving a dangerous hostage to fortune.

In the opening years of the twentieth century, the Italian army became obsessed with the problem of defending the north-eastern frontier, a problem compounded by Italian naval inferiority. The defence of Italy demanded a co-ordinated defence policy, but none was devised. Instead, an entirely inconclusive debate developed in which technical dis-agreements over whether modern artillery was or was not capable of fighting off modern warships, and over the role of submarines in coastal defence, rubbed shoulders with political and psychological arguments over the likely effect of the bombardment of a city like Genoa on the national will.[3]

114

As it happened, Italy's first military task of the twentieth century came out of the blue. Among some four hundred Europeans besieged in the Peking Legations in the early summer of 1900 during the Boxer Rebellion were twenty-eight Italians. Prestige alone required Italian participation in a co-ordinated action by the great powers, and on 5 July the war ministry issued instructions for an Italian contingent to be gathered at Naples within two weeks. Haste wrought minor havoc. Units were patched together using large numbers of new conscripts. Ships were badly packed, and sacks of flour in the bottoms of holds were crushed by the weight of other stores on top of them. Typhoid broke out on one ship due to overcrowding. And since the Italians had no concession at Tientsin, they lacked both the means to disembark and supplies when they arrived, and were forced to throw themselves on the goodwill of the other powers.[4] As the force, which numbered 83 officers and 1882 men, only arrived on 29 August, it took no part in the expedition which set out on 4 August and successfully relieved Peking. Italian units did however participate in a number of punitive expeditions. The bulk of the contingent left China on 4 August 1901.

The China expedition demonstrated the deficiencies in army planning: despite the African experience, it had not made adequate preparations to send a small expedition overseas at short notice and proved poor at improvisation. Lacking marines, it had to rely on unseasoned and untrained troops.[5] Administrative and support services were grossly deficient, with shortages of doctors, hospital beds, engineers and communications systems. Italian equipment also demonstrated defects: linen uniforms wore badly, helmets lost their shape and alpine-style boots were too heavy.[6]

The China expedition was an embarrassing side show for the army, whose concerns were increasingly focused on Austria-Hungary. Summing up the lessons of the staff ride of 1900, which envisaged an Italian violation of Swiss neutrality, Saletta highlighted the defensive needs of the north-eastern frontier and claimed that considerable diplomatic advantage would accrue from a massive fortification programme:

> not only can the political future be contemplated calmly and with a sense of security, but our policy, which will be freed from military preoccupations about the capacity of one or other of our frontiers to resist attack, will be free to move in whatever direction best meets the country's interests.[7]

The Supreme Defence Commission examined the problem in December

1900, and heard Saletta develop a strong case for the construction of a series of forts to block an enemy's path.

Six Italian railway lines led up to the Piave, but only two went beyond it. Although Italian forces could be on the river in 26 days, four days earlier than Austria-Hungary, the Austrian armies were larger and could advance into Italy along nine independent routes whereas Italy could use only four beyond the Isonzo and across the Carso. Backed by this somewhat discouraging picture, Saletta carried his requests for fortification of the Natisone and lower Friuli valleys. The commission also agreed to increase the garrison on the eastern frontier.[8]

Saletta wanted to be able to move two army corps up to the Piave quickly without interfering with the rest of the deployment. He also raised the question whether the whole deployment ought not to be shifted forward to the Tagliamento. The double-tracking necessary to move two corps without slowing down the main deployment, together with the purchase of additional locomotives and rolling stock, would cost 44 250 000 lire; to move the whole deployment forward would cost 113 500 000 lire. In the circumstances of the day, military arguments for more railways did not carry much weight, and in this case commercial benefits looked marginal. The commission opted for accelerated deployment of two army corps and expressed the hope that arrangements might be made which would allow deployment on the Tagliamento 'in a not too distant future'.[9]

Saletta wanted fortifications as well as railways so as to be prepared 'in the event of a change in the orientation of our policy'. His bill, excluding railways, amounted to 24 million lire for the north-western frontier, and 33 640 000 for the north and north-east. When he suggested that railway building was even more urgent than fortification he clashed headlong with Luigi Pelloux. The ex-premier felt that, given the huge sums involved, the problem needed further study and the committee backed him, requesting that 'the improvements necessary to increase the capacity of the rail-net be gradually effected, within the limits determined by financial resources'.[10]

The naval representatives came to life when the commission moved on to consider an order of priority for the five *piazze marittimi* of la Maddelena, Genoa, la Spezia, Taranto and Messina, which would cost 39 million to put in order. Admiral Accini stressed the importance of Naples but made it quite clear that the navy did not want to be burdened with the responsibility of having to defend it. Admiral Frigerio wanted all the great coastal cities fortified to give the fleet complete freedom of action. Faced with this uncompromising naval opinion the commission agreed not to decide between the five *piazze* but to carry out 'urgent' work on them all simultaneously.

The quinquennial request for 33 million lire for extraordinary expenditure had already been made, and Saletta pointed out that since urgent works on the north-western frontier and at the *piazze marittime* would require 24 million a start could be made in the north-east with what remained. At that rate, the programme would take fifteen years to complete. However, as Leone Pelloux revealed, shortage of money was not the only cause of delay:

> the slowness in carrying out works for which the necessary funds already exist is often the consequence of the slowness with which studies and plans are drawn up.[11]

As well as planning to defend Italy against Austria-Hungary, Saletta was obliged to consider attacking France. Having already established the difficulties inherent in each of the three direct routes, he examined the possibility of violating Swiss neutrality to turn the Albertville-Grenoble position in the staff ride of 1900, and concluded that 'an Italian offensive against Switzerland would encounter grave difficulties' and that it would be best to respect Swiss neutrality.[12] The staff ride the following year confirmed the dangers of a French attack across the Alps, together with the seizure of Genoa and la Spezia.[13]

At this point, the new king took a hand in military planning, much to everyone's confusion. Victor Emmanuel III did not share his father's attachment to the Triple Alliance and was anxious to revive the rapport with France which had been a feature of Risorgimento. On 24 February 1901 he told the German military attaché that he opposed sending III Army to the Rhine because it would weaken Italy's land frontiers and coastal defences to a dangerous degree. Not three weeks before, Saletta had told von Chelius that the king strongly favoured the Rhine option.[14]

Saletta first suggested that the Italian army could aid Germany better by a vigorous offensive into Savoy and Nice – which he knew to be well-nigh impossible – before finally telling von Chelius on 15 April that 'the military preparations will be continued just as they have been up to now'. During his visit to Germany in the summer of 1902 he told Schlieffen that III Army would be sent to the Rhine by way of Switzerland if it could not make use of the Austrian railways.[15] The whole confused episode, which justifiably raised German doubts, demonstrates how badly co-ordinated Italian military policy was.

During the winter of 1901–02 the general staff drew up a deployment plan for war against Austria-Hungary in the light of the findings of the Supreme Defence Commission. The parlous state of Italian railways left no option but to stand back. Under the new scheme I Army would hold the Trentino while II and III Armies deployed on the Piave and IV Army stood in reserve. The three forward divisions which had been pushed beyond the Piave in the 1889 plan were pulled back. Twelve corps would have to be moved by rail to the north-east, requiring 1556 trains and taking 25 days. The railway transport plan, without which the deployment could not take place, took another two years to come into operation.[16]

While the chief of the general staff was embroiled in the tangles of military planning, the war minister had to deal with the consequences of the army's public order role. Although there were continual confrontations between troops and demonstrators, Giolitti was far less heavy-handed than his predecessors in using the army to maintain civil order. Usually he preferred to use civil authorities, and when he did resort to the army it was generally in an attempt to prevent outbreaks of disorder by nipping them in the bud.[17]

His most extensive use of military powers occurred on 24 February 1902 when he took steps to avoid a damaging general strike on the railways by recalling to arms all employees belonging to the regular army, reserve or militia. The principal railway stations and depots throughout the country were occupied by detachments of infantry, and anyone failing to report for work or quitting without leave was treated as a deserter. Any worker suspended for five or more days by his employer was drafted for service in the nearest infantry corps. When the reservists were recalled for public security duties there were demonstrations in a number of northern cities, caused by rumours that the army was about to be sent to Tripoli. Giolitti solved the problem with pay awards, but the episode strengthened the military view that the government resorted too readily to the army to solve its domestic problems.

The bulk of the officer corps accepted that the army existed both to defend independence and to safeguard the rule of law and took the view that if troops were to be used in civil disputes then they should shoot sooner than yield to intimidation.[18] Moreover, the army could use its role as guarantor of internal peace to demand more money. However, it was displeased at having to defend the property of the very classes which labelled it 'unproductive' and likened it to a vampire sucking at the nation's breast.[19]

There were professional grounds for feeling uneasy about the amount of riot-control the army was having to undertake, which interfered with training and threatened to diminish military effectiveness in the field.[20] There was also a palpable loathing of public security work – 'that odious task' – and resentment towards civilian authorities for being prepared to allow the army to incur the unpopularity which they were unwilling to shoulder themselves. The army wanted clear guidelines which would allow it to steer between the Scylla of frustration at not being allowed to fire at rioters when provoked and the Charybdis of loathing provoked when it did shoot:

> To be portrayed as inept and lacking energy, or else to be tried for murder and cursed as executioners of the poor pleases no one, least of all officers. They would a thousand times prefer to be on a battlefield than in a *piazza* facing rioters.[21]

The problem was never satisfactorily resolved, and was one of many grounds for growing dissatisfaction with civilian politicians.

Just as the army was never happy with the task of quelling disorder, it was also convinced that military service was not an effective tool for combating socialism. The army disliked socialism because of its opposition to military expenditure and because of its belief that Italy should foreswear the offensive and cut the army back to eight regular and eight militia corps. Nonetheless, there was a widespread belief that citizens should be educated in their duties and responsibilities in the family and the school, not in the barracks. The army did not see its task as ensuring that conscripts and reservists were freed of the germs of subversion and did not regard itself as capable of carrying it out: for one thing, only about a quarter of the adult male population did active service, which put a large part of society permanently beyond its reach.[22]

In addition to the public order issue, San Martino and his successors in the war ministry faced a technical problem that seemed at times to have paralysed the army: the need to modernise the artillery. In 1898 Pelloux had announced a competition for a field-gun of approximately 80mm calibre without specifying either a hydraulic brake or an armoured shield for the gun-crew, both features of the new French '75'. By eliminating the need to relay a gun each time it had been fired the hydraulic brake greatly increased the number of rounds which could be fired in a minute; however, Italian artillerists took the view that it acted against the 'simplicity of means' which they revered as the central characteristic of the arm. A representative of the German armaments firm of Krupps, General von Rohne, advised against a recoil-limiting gun-carriage without admitting that his firm was currently unable to make one. Invited to design a field-gun which the Italians could produce themselves, Krupps came up with the fixed-carriage '75A' and in May 1901 60 million lire were set aside to manufacture it. One ground for supporting the programme was that it would improve Italy's standing in the Triple Alliance at a time when renewal and a possible renegotiation of the terms was close at hand.[23]

The 75A, which fired only some six rounds a minute, was obsolete from the outset. The French were on the point of achieving rates of 30 rounds a minute; and higher rates of fire enabled them to reduce their batteries from six guns to four, an enticing economy. All the Great Powers already had or were about to adopt recoilless quick-firing artillery. Its Italian supporters argued that in future pinpoint accuracy would be of less value than rapid fire since artillery would probably not be able to see its target but would be required to hit enemy concentration-areas at the request of forward commanders.[24] Saletta and the general staff wanted power to be the dominant characteristic of the artillery, while the artillerymen preferred to emphasise mobility. The new recoilless 75 seemed to meet both requirements but the artillerists suggested 73, 70 and even 60mm guns, each of which could carry more ammunition than its heavier rivals. After long discussion, one of the new Krupps 75s was tested against the Italian 75A, and found to be superior in all respects.[25]

The old-school artillerists did not give way easily and fiercely criticised the new Krupps gun for lacking the mobility and manageability of its Italian rival. The war minister, Pedotti, chose the worst possible means to resolve the dispute, accepting a recommendation to build a 73mm gun – a calibre no other nation used. At the end of October 1905 the gun was ready and a battery of 73s was tested against a battery of 75s, both furnished by Krupps. The tests clearly showed the ballistic superiority of the German 75, and the following year a commission decided to buy 39 batteries of the '75/906' gun with 320 rounds per gun, together with the rough parts of another 68 batteries which were to be finished in Italian factories.[26] It was characteristic of the whole sorry affair that the cabinet's decision to begin by spending 8 million lire on nine batteries of the new gun was leaked in the press before the new war minister, Viganò, was informed.

Endless delays and the tortuous progression of official committees and commissions began to evoke charges of incompetence and inefficiency on the part of the war ministry and of successive inspectors-general of the artillery. Soon it was being alleged that the 75/906 was a poor purchase since it had a short active life, complicated sights, bad wheels and no protection for the ammunition limbers, and that Krupps had bribed officials to secure its adoption. In an atmosphere laden with suspicion and distrust, the 75/906 was tested against the 75A again. The new gun proved ballistically superior in every test except one, and fired six times faster than its rival.[27] The case for modernisation was at last proven beyond doubt.

The sad saga of the Italian artillery was far from over, however, and in 1909–10 experiments took place to find a gun which used the same ammunition as the 75/906 but could be built in Italy. Models by Krupps and Déport were tested and the French gun – rechristened the 75/911 – proved superior, but neither the rights to build it nor the 50 million lire necessary to do so were available until 1912. When they were, 27 Italian firms formed a consortium to make it but soon ran into technical difficulties which they found it hard to overcome, so that the gun was only just becoming available when Italy entered the war in 1915.[28]

Slow progress and slipshod administration were a feature of Italian arms-procurement. The army finally adopted a 65mm mountain gun in 1911 after seven years' study, and although the need for a modern howitzer had been apparent from 1902 it took nine years to produce a paper programme. The delay in providing the army with machine-guns, though less spectacular, was if anything an even more culpable example of maladministration. The want of them had been cruelly felt at Adua, and by 1907 General dal Verme was lamenting the fact that the Italians still did not have them, although the Swiss had been using them since 1899.[29] Finally, machine-guns were brought in from Vickers in the autumn and winter of 1913.

The delays, hesitations and changes of direction which marked the progress of the artillery question were the result of a complex of factors which included the diffuse system of military administration, a taste for numerous technical committees to deliberate every issue and the imperviousness of the war ministry to technical criticism from outside. The Italian military may also have been too acquiescent in the face of high-pressure salesmanship from Germany. They chose the right field-gun in the end, but paradoxically they were accused by the parliamentary commission of inquiry of exactly the opposite fault from that revealed by the contemporary inquiry into the navy: instead of favouring Italian heavy industry too much, they favoured it too little. In Italy, striking an acceptable balance between these two poles was not easy.

Although the news in 1903 that the French were practising combined manoeuvres at Villafranca which featured an opposed landing caused some concern, Italy's fear of France was fast diminishing. One reason was the improvement in Franco–Italian diplomatic relations. A second was the general staff's calculation that even in the event of war between the alliance systems Italy had little to fear: France would leave two corps to defend the Italian frontier – the Germans thought only one – and would concentrate on the war in the north-east. Thirdly, the general staff was comforted by reports of disarray in the French army in the aftermath of the era of republicanisation under General André: infantry numbers had shrunk, and the officer corps showed clear signs of demoralisation and indiscipline.[30]

Austria looked far more worrying. The Italian general staff ride of 1902 envisaged the army driven from the Piave and defending the northern Appennines, while the Austrians controlled the whole of the Paduan plain.[31] The following year Saletta tested the lower Piave as a defensive position against an Austrian attack from the eastern Tyrol after reinforcements had been sent up to the main Italian armies beyond the Isonzo. The exercise showed that defence would be precarious until the left flank, resting on the mountains, was secure. Saletta suggested strengthening the Friuli frontier to remedy this weakness and allow deployment beyond the Piave.[32]

In June 1903 the war minister asked for a classification of the works needed on the north-eastern frontier in order of urgency. Saletta replied in October that the Supreme Defence Commission had established a programme three years earlier, and asked for detailed information about the direction of foreign policy, the financial means which would be made available and the length of time within which the programme would have to be carried out.[33] The stepping-up of Austrian military activity the following year provided a spur to action. Reports reached Rome of a military build-up in the Tyrol and of rumours that Vienna intended to occupy the sanjak of Novi Bazaar in the spring. Italian alarm was increased with the news that the Austro-Hungarian general staff ride that year would take place along the frontier of the Isonzo and the coasts of Istria and Dalmatia.[34] Large military credits voted by the Austrian parliament produced a strong reaction in Rome.[35]

The Italian general staff ride of 1904 bore out the sense of uneasiness. The Austrians were assumed to have begun secret mobilisation some days before Italy and easily took all the Friuli up to the Tagliamento. Italian forces were pushed back to Livenza, where they won a defensive battle only to find themselves threatened on the flank from Brenta and the Cadore. Italian weakness was revealed everywhere: on Lake Garda, in the Trentino and the upper Piave, on the Tagliamento, at Verona, at

Mantua and along the coasts. The exercise also highlighted deficiencies in the rail network. It was impossible to deploy on the Tagliamento in time, and to deploy on the Piave would take 26 days, but only after 44 million lire had been spent on improvements; to cut six days off the timetable would cost another 50 million. The Austrians were thought capable of massing their troops on the Friuli frontier in 35 days but would be on the starting-line faster once their current programme of railway building was complete.[36]

If Italy were to stand any chance of success in a war against Austria-Hungary, Saletta believed that she must not only spend a great deal more money but also change her recruitment system. He wanted a larger annual intake and a system of regional recruitment-zones, or at least of regional zones for reservists rejoining the army in wartime, and an increased programme of fortification. If these improvements were not made then 'every political aspiration we might have which was contrary to the interests of the neighbouring empire would be unattainable'.[37]

War ministers had to pay more regard to financial realities than chiefs of staff, and on 7 July 1904 General Pedotti asked again for Saletta's suggestions on the most urgent fortifications, noting that temporary works might be an economical solution to the problem. Saletta flatly rejected anything but permanent forts and offered no real guidance on priorities. Pedotti then went behind his back and got the views of the inspectors-general of artillery and engineers. Saletta found out and insisted on the full Supreme Defence Commission programme. However, Parliament was currently debating the state takeover of the railways and Giolitti was unwilling to ask for more funds for defence; so he got the king to ensure that Pedotti neither resigned nor made embarrassing requests for money.[38]

A bitter struggle now developed between the war minister and the chief of the general staff. Pedotti wrote to Saletta on 3 May telling him which defence-works he thought should be erected in the Tyrolese salient and the Cadore. Saletta replied that key works were missing and that the war minister's list was 'unacceptable'. On 12 August he sent his own list, of which the most urgent works were those fronting the Tyrolese salient, which would prevent the Austrians getting to the Po and menacing the line of retreat of an Italian army on the Piave. Pedotti finally gave way and accepted Saletta's programme on 5 December, adding that other works would be built later following the opinions of the chief of staff as to their importance.[39] Nineteen days later he resigned. Caught between Saletta's intransigence and Giolitti's political priorities, his position had become an impossible one.

As a direct consequence of the lessons of the 1904 staff ride the general staff accelerated the deployment of advanced units on the Friuli frontier, strengthened the frontier garrison, allotted another army corps to the eastern frontier in peacetime and pulled back much of the organisation and supply system behind the Tagliamento. These measures still left the mobilisation system unchanged, however, and the military were keen to abandon 'the dangerous system of hurriedly massing there at the moment of war bodies of troops, many of them from far-away places, which are neither homogeneous nor fully complete'.[40] Although militarily desirable, this was politically impossible; by the time of the following year's staff ride, which examined an Austrian attack in the area bounded by Lake Como and the western frontier of the Tyrol and produced another long list of necessary fortifications, the general staff were forced to accept that they could not have territorial mobilisation, despite all its strategic advantages.[41]

Political and military intelligence from Vienna heightened Italian anxieties during the first half of 1906. Austria's ambitions in the Balkans were growing and might bring war with Italy in their train: Lieutenant-Colonel Del Mastro reported from Vienna that

> Austria does not conceal the necessity one day to impose tranquility on Italy, at the moment when, by a forward move in the Balkans she sees Italian public opinion rising against her.[42]

Day-to-day military activities were equally discouraging. In the annual Austrian garrison changeover at the start of the year more troops moved from north to south than vice versa; then in the spring the Austrians tested new mountain guns in the Tyrol. In May, as part of his campaign to win the full programme of fortifications in the north-east, Saletta informed Pedotti that siege artillery was piling up in Franzenfeste and Trento.[43]

As the Austrian threat mounted, the internal health of the officer corps grew worse. Mocenni's marriage legislation had marginally improved the lot of junior officers, and in 1901 the captain's horse had been restored to officers who had been four years in grade, after the chamber of deputies blocked a move to give the allowance to all captains. More important was the promotion-block caused by the expansion of the army in the 1880s. Ponza di San Martino tried to improve promotion prospects by adding 400 captaincies to the lists and cutting the same number of lieutenancies, and by proposing a maximum term of twelve years as a subaltern, but was defeated in parliament and resigned. His successors, Ottolenghi and Pedotti, tinkered with promotions and leave but did nothing to assuage mounting dissatisfaction in the officer corps.

Signs of open dissatisfaction now began to appear. Officers attended the services of a particular priest en masse, or appeared in raw winter weather without their capes; and senior commanders found it increasingly difficult to ensure that their juniors attended garrison balls and found voluntary guards of honour.[44] In 1903 Captain Fabio Ranzi founded the newspaper *Il pensiero militare* as a vehicle for discontent. Within four years over 2000 subalterns were subscribing to it. Ranzi was hounded for his views, and after refusing a challenge from a senior officer which it would have been against military regulations to accept, he was found guilty by a military tribunal of 'lack of honour' and dismissed from the service. He took his case to appeal and after four years won reinstatement.[45] Pedotti forbade serving officers to contribute to Ranzi's newspaper but his successor had to revoke the ruling since disciplinary regulations allowed soldiers to publish what they wished. Nothing was done to improve the lot of junior officers and Viganò, who came to the war ministry in May 1906, claimed that they had no cause for complaint, provoking an open letter of dissent in *Il pensiero militare*.

Among other things, junior officers were deeply frustrated at the use of the army to remedy high rates of Italian illiteracy. They castigated the high command's failure to move with the times and recognise that appeals to loyalty would not move a generation of recruits which had never known a divided Italy. And they felt the need for a more deeply rooted professionalism in the face of a rising level of general culture.[46] Even the king recognised that the old type of officer – 'ignorant, uneducated, stupid, who thought all learning nonsense' – still exercised an unfortunate influence and wished that they would all die out 'as they are such a hindrance'.[47] Discontent bubbled in the army as the international scene darkened.

During the first months of 1906, as Italy conspicuously failed to back her German ally over Morocco, the Italian general staff grew worried about German reactions. On 25 January Saletta sent a message through the German ambassador to the new chief of the German general staff, Helmut von Moltke the younger, asking if the military accords still stood; and next day he took special care to reassure the departing Austrian military attaché that Italy would stick by her undertaking. Von Moltke replied formally that he would stick by the letter of the agreements and attached much importance to good relations between the two staffs, but privately expressed suspicion of Italian intentions.[48]

For his part, Saletta was still taking seriously the option of breaking Swiss neutrality in the event of war to get three army corps to the Rhine if Austria stayed neutral.[49]

Saletta's battle with Pedotti over frontier fortifications revealed the awkward position of the chief of staff when he disagreed with the war minister. Saletta must have won considerable sympathy from the king, for on 4 March 1906 a royal decree gave the chief of the general staff specific responsibility to present to the minister any projects he regarded as necessary or convenient in preparing for war. He was also obliged to formulate his directives on the basis of the recommendations of the Supreme Defence Commission. This decree blocked the minister's right to evade the chief of staff by soliciting alternative professional opinions, and also ensured that the Defence Commission's findings could not simply be ignored. It gave Saletta some leverage, but left the war minister's plea of budgetary constraint intact.[50]

Pedotti's successor, Majnoni d'Intagnano, lasted only five months and was succeeded on 27 May 1906 by Lieutenant-General Ettore Viganò. In July the new minister asked for a complete programme of works necessary for the defence of the state. Saletta replied with what was virtually a reprise of the list of September 1905, calling for the expenditure of 332 million lire on the land frontiers and the *piazze marittime*. Viganò was prepared to ask parliament for 200 million lire – which he believed enough for new artillery, essential fortifications for the north-east, and an improvement in mobilisation-stores – because he would not have to find arguments to justify it; to ask for more would necessitate his plunging into foreign and financial policy to back himself up, which he thought would be *'childishly pretentious'*.[51] He was prepared to spend 12 million on fortification during the coming year and ordered Saletta to preside over a commission to divide it up.

The general staff took the view that it was necessary to know the general plan in order to make best use of the money available. In any case 12 million a year was far too little, and at that rate it would take 12 years to fortify the north-east and more than 20 years to carry out the full programme. There were also weaknesses in the north-west which could not be overlooked. In the 1906 staff ride the French, who had command of the sea, had driven along the Cornice and through the Ligurian Appennines and turned the flank of the main Italian army defending the Alps. More fortifications were therefore needed to bar the route and strengthen Genoa.[52] Viganò was not to be stampeded. He told Saletta that only 80 million could be spent on fortifications between 1906 and 1917, of which 29 million were to go to Venice.[53]

Saletta's demands were gargantuan, and he was undoubtedly overemphasising the value of fortifications in solving Italy's strategic dilemma. But he faced severe problems in hammering together a reasonable deployment plan for war with Austria-Hungary. The location of corps headquarters meant that 13 corps would have to be moved by rail in the event of war in the north-east, but only six in a war with France. Lack of naval protection for coastal railways meant routing as many trains as possible through Rome, Florence and Bologna, which slowed deployment. The best Italy could do was deploy on the Piave by the 25th day of mobilisation, with one corps forward on the Tagliamento.[54] To do this, the army required at least eight days' warning of mobilisation.[55]

Austria-Hungary was both an ally and a potential enemy, which made the question of reliance on Austrian railways to carry III Army to the Rhine a delicate one. It was exacerbated by the violent hostility of the new chief of the Austrian general staff, Conrad von Hötzendorff, towards Italy: after only six months in office, he told Franz Josef and von Moltke that Austria should settle accounts with Italy as soon as possible. Conrad took little pains to conceal his opinions, and the Italian general staff supposed that he was only waiting until he could collect the forces presently strung out along the Russian frontier before launching an attack into Friuli. The vast railway works which accompanied Austrian manoeuvres in Carynthia, quite out of proportion to the numbers of troops involved, prompted Rome to send a secret agent to Galicia in the autumn of 1907 to find out how long it would take Conrad to switch troops from the north to the south. This foray led Saletta to believe he now had only fifteen days in which to deploy the Italian army.[56]

Discussion of Viganò's request for an extraordinary budget of 200 million took place amidst public alarm at the defensive state of Italy's frontiers, and during the parliamentary debate there were open references to the possibility of war with Austria. The deputies were less anxious than the general staff, or at least less willing to devote huge amounts of money to assuaging their anxiety, and on 14 July they voted 10 300 000 lire for *piazze marittime* and 13 620 000 for land forts spread over the years 1907–10. They also established the 'Commission of Seventeen' to examine the whole question of military expenditure – evidence of how badly public confidence had been shattered by the artillery scandal and huge, unceasing fortification bills.

A special conference in July to discuss protecting Venice displayed the deep differences of professional opinion which made it so hard to hammer out even a medium-term policy on defence spending. When the war minister announced that 16 million lire was currently available for coastal defence works and heavy artillery, Saletta said that at least 44 million lire were necessary to put the city in a full state of defence. There were arguments between the naval and military representatives over the calibre of the guns which should be installed and the number of rounds for each gun, and an inconclusive discussion over whether to buy Vickers Armstrong or Krupps. Eventually Saletta was forced much against his will to accept a ceiling of 16 835 000 lire for Venetian defences.[57]

When Saletta put in proposals for spending the money allocated for land-works and for Venice, he was told that rising prices meant the sum available would only pay for 70 per cent of what could have been done the previous year. He reduced his programme; and the general staff concluded gloomily at the end of 1907 that there was not a single line of enemy operations on the western frontier which was securely barred, that the north-east was in a similar position, and that at current rates of progress it would take thirty years to put matters right. Their secret wish was for 350 million lire spread over twenty years, which would secure both frontiers.[58]

As well as having to deal with Saletta's seemingly unquenchable appetite for fortifications, Viganò had to find more men for the public order duties with which the army now seemed permanently burdened. By 1906 only a quarter of the annual class was being called to the colours and absenteeism – a consequence of emigration – was climbing towards 10 per cent.[59] From 1904 the authorities reverted to the old practice of calling up the annual class in the autumn rather than delaying its induction until the following spring in order to cope.

An obvious solution was to call up more men for a shorter period – France reduced her term of service from three years to two at this time – and leading soldiers suggested that two years' or even eighteen months' service would suffice. Significantly, the debate was not cast in terms of the military capacity of short-service troops, as happened in France and Germany. Instead, opponents of shorter service argued that the level of national education was too low to reduce the length of time spent in uniform and that the Italian conscript needed not only technical instruction but also moral education and character-training. Nor was mass conscription without drawbacks: simple, uneducated peasants might be infected with the indiscipline of the factory worker or the scepticism and *nervosismo* of the upper classes.[60] Even progressive liberals, who regarded conscription as a means of educating Italians to civic responsibility, could talk themselves into a position in which they supported a small professional army in order to make money available to improve the lot of the poor and halt the 'shameful' flood of emigrants.[61]

When Viganò entered the war ministry in the summer of 1906, he was put under strong pressure from the general staff to cut the number of exemptions, increase the annual class by 30 000 and extend the age-limit for reserve service from 39 to 42. The planners were acutely aware of Italy's absolute and proportional military weakness: with a population of 33 million she could mobilise 38 divisions; France, with 38 500 000 inhabitants, could raise 75 divisions; Austria-Hungary, with 45 million inhabitants, could put 62 divisions into the field and Germany could field 83 divisions.[62] The following February Viganò tabled a law raising the category I intake to 108 000 a year by drastically cutting back exemptions and reintroduced category II reservists. He failed to carry a two-year service period against strong conservative opposition. A sizeable list of exemptions remained a feature of Italian conscription, but doing away with them would have meant accepting twelve months' service, which most people felt inadequate.[63]

On 3 May 1907, during the debates over military expenditure, Giolitti proposed a parliamentary commission of inquiry into all aspects of military organisation. The 'Commission of Seventeen', established the following month, comprised four generals, one admiral and twelve civilians. It was from those civilians that Giolitti chose Viganò's replacement in December 1907. Senator Severino Casana, then aged 65, a member of an old Piedmontese noble family, was an experienced parliamentarian, modest, unassuming and rich. In breaking a long tradition of military appointments to the war ministry, Giolitti was acknowledging the strength of feeling against the soldiers, who were held guilty of incompetence and possibly corruption. His choice was popular: Casana was regarded as a 'true civilian' who belonged to no military clique or camarilla.[64] Casana moved quickly and in February 1908 royal decrees announced a revolution in defence administration. The rules of the Supreme Defence Commission were rewritten so that the prime minister became a member, presiding as non-voting chairman, an army council was established to give the minister the benefit of collective military advice and the powers of the chief of the general staff were further increased.[65]

A matter of days before Casana assumed office, reports came through that a further five battalions were to be added to the Austrian army corps at Graz. Saletta was sufficiently concerned to ask the attaché in Vienna, San Marzano, for his impressions of Conrad's personality and attitude towards Italy. Spectacularly misled, San Marzano replied that Conrad lacked the natural aversion to Italians shown by so many of his countrymen and believed that the Italian government adhered loyally to the Triple Alliance, although he also feared that a few irredentist demagogues could arouse public opinion 'and . . . in such an eventuality the Italian government would have neither the power nor the authority to resist the wishes of the country'. Less than a month later Conrad urged his war minister to settle accounts with Italy before thinking of any Balkan venture.[66]

During the early weeks of 1908 the international picture continued to darken. On 29 January the military attaché reported that the Rumanian war minister was in Vienna to negotiate a military convention covering joint action against Russia and also, he believed, against Italy. The following month Rome learned from unsubstantiated reports that heavy artillery and fortress materials were being moved from Galicia to the recently constructed forts in the Tyrol. Casana at once sent copies of a general staff report detailing the Austrian military build-up on the frontier to the premier, the foreign minister and the king, gaining a promise from Tittoni to give full support to any measures to increase the country's military potential and strengthen its borders. Tittoni asked only that publicity be avoided in order not to interfere with the conduct of foreign policy.[67]

The case for a substantial increase in military spending, already well known to the government, was also becoming clear to the public and to parliament. At the end of December 1907 the *Corriere della sera* complained that there had never been a comprehensive discussion of the plan for national defence and blamed successive war ministers for failing to present parliament with blunt alternatives; and in January 1908 it revealed that while the Italian naval budget was twice that of Austria-Hungary, Rome spent less than half as much as Vienna on her army. Sonnino pointed out to parliament that the budget had grown by 42 per cent in 13 years but the army's share had increased by only 3.5 per cent.[68] The 'Commission of Seventeen' added its voice to the chorus, recommending that 190 million lire be spent on the north-eastern defences, on improving officers' pay and indemnities and on providing soldiers with better food, clothing and barracks.[69]

Giolitti was left in no doubt about the army's needs when he presided over a reconstructed Supreme Defence Commission in May. Saletta opened the proceedings by putting in a massive bill. For 1236 of the new recoilless field-guns, together with a thousand rounds of ammunition per gun and the necessary limbers, horses and equipment, and for mountain-artillery, howitzers and siege park – all necessary for an offensive in the Trentino – he requested 223 500 000 lire. Fortifications, and the guns to arm them, urgently required 200 million lire and a further 175 million lire in due course. Other urgent needs required an allocation of 225 million lire, of which 74 million had already been provided for up to 1910 in existing budgets, plus 99 million for less urgent requirements. Finally, an additional 41 500 000 lire would be necessary to increase the size of category I and reintroduce category II. Confronted with a demand for one billion lire, the premier coolly remarked that it was impossible to do everything at once and that a programme of priorities must be drawn up which matched financial resources available.[70]

Although the meeting was designed to produce an agreed programme of defence needs, its most striking result was to reveal to the premier the divisions both between and within the services. During the opening discussion on financial requirements the chief of the naval general staff, Admiral Bettolo, proposed that the army take responsibility for defending the continental frontiers while the navy safeguarded the coasts. This went far beyond anything the general staff had managed to get from the navy before and Saletta accepted with alacrity, only to hear General Pedotti point out that in the past the navy had said it could not defend the coasts because of their length. The sailors hurriedly reversed their position, saying that the army must protect the *piazze marittime* by not allowing the enemy fleets to close up to them. Bettolo then revealed that the navy's objective was to be double the size of the Austro-Hungarian fleet and put in a claim of his own for 200 150 000 lire. Later, in the course of discussion on how best to defend Rome, Bettolo stated flatly that without Italian command of the sea an invasion could not be prevented, implying that money spent on coastal fortifications and artillery to defend them was money wasted.[71]

The generals were unable to agree whether the mobile militia should be armed with the new field-gun, or whether the north-eastern frontier should be defended with fully-fledged forts armed with medium artillery or 'local works' equipped with field-artillery. Most damaging of all in civilian eyes must have been their questioning of Saletta's deployment plan. After Saletta had spoken at length about the vulnerability of the Friuli and the Tyrol, General Majnoni suggested that Italian deployment might be safer if it took place further back. Saletta grew very annoyed. To be completely safe, he remarked sarcastically, Italy would have to deploy on the Po, which was inconceivable. Pedotti also expressed doubts about the deployment plan, and Giolitti tried anxiously to stop the discussion:

From the political view we all know that some secrets are not kept, and if a proposition like the one just made [by Majnoni] were accepted and became known it could give rise to dangerous consequences.

However, the argument continued, and after an icy exchange on the responsibilities of the chief of staff to draw up deployment plans and the army commanders to decide battle plans, Saletta's proposal to fortify the lower Friuli was voted down.[72]

Not much was agreed by the Defence Commission, although it did accept without discussion the need to spend 66 million on the defence of Venice. Giolitti brought it to a close by expressing the hope that it would meet more frequently in the future so that the government could be kept informed of the needs of the two services in relation to the defence of the state and the general policy of the country. How the army was supposed to divine what general policy was remained mysterious, for the premier had contributed nothing constructive to the occasion. At no point had he given any indications whatever of government intentions and objectives, even in the most general terms. For his part, Giolitti can only have come away with the impression that the high command was divided on a whole range of questions and that it was no bad thing that a new chief of the general staff was about to succeed Saletta.

Saletta was due to reach retirement age on 27 June 1908, and it had been widely rumoured that Luigi Cadorna would be chosen to succeed him. It was equally widely rumoured that Cadorna was none too keen to have the job as presently defined and in March Ugo Brusati, the king's principal aide-de-camp, wrote asking him to deny 'certain absurd remarks' to the effect that he would only accept the post if the chief of staff's powers under the 1906 decree were expanded and if the king gave up his statutory right to assume the role of commander-in-chief in wartime.[73] Cadorna replied that to suppose that he wanted to exclude the king from command was absurd but that he did want to avoid the 'fatal dualism' of the past. He was willing to take the post only if the chief of the general staff were given complete freedom of action to conduct operations in wartime as well as preparing them in peacetime, and if he could sack any high commander he wanted.[74] All this went far beyond accepted practice, and so the job went to Alberto Pollio, another product of the Nunziatella, on 14 June 1908.

The war budget had been consolidated at 250 000 lire a year between 1906 and 1910, but Viganò had secured an increase of 40 million lire in 1907. Casana now asked parliament for an additional extraordinary budget of 223 million lire to cover frontier fortifications, new artillery and other improvements. His case rested so heavily on the threat posed by Italy's ally that the government forbade customary publication of the parliamentary budget report because it detailed Austria-Hungary's activities along the frontier, demonstrated a railway superiority of seven-to-three in her favour and revealed that she had turned the Trentino into a fortified camp. On 5 July Casana got his money, voted in a single sitting by a sympathetic chamber.[75]

The 1908 staff ride re-affirmed how vulnerable Italy was to Austrian military and naval power. While the bulk of her forces stood on the defensive along the Po after losing a major battle, she had to face a three-division enemy landing on the Adriatic coast between Ancona and Rimini. The manoeuvres ended on the seventh day with the Italians treating for an armistice after having lost a battle at Iesi.[76] While the general staff worked on the mobilisation tables to try to reduce the preparatory period of covert mobilisation from eight days to four, Pollio, showing signs that he intended to be a more active *Triplicista* than his predecessor, personally instituted a reworking of the transport plan to carry III Army to the Rhine. Scarcely had this begun when, on 6 October 1908, Austria-Hungary took advantage of the 'Young Turk' revolution in Constantinople to annex Bosnia-Herzegovina. The forward move into the Balkans which the general staff had been anticipating had now taken place. With it, the Adriatic became a focus of both military and diplomatic concerns. Italy began a search for security and compensation which was to lead the army to Libya.

8 Redressing the Balance

In the years before 1914 the tempo of Italian military planning increased as tension mounted in Europe. It shifted twice in geographical emphasis, but the same sense of strategic vulnerability which had underlain defence plans since unification continued to impose severe constraints on military choice. Internally, last-minute reforms corrected some of the problems which collectively undermined the professionalism of the officer corps. Externally, the army found itself once again in action in a major war overseas after fifteen years of domestic pre-occupation. Paradoxically, that war ended in success but revealed all Italy's military deficiencies.

The annexation of Bosnia and Herzegovina provoked widespread agitation in Italy; article VII of the 1891 version of the Triple Alliance, which provided for Italian 'compensation' for any Austrian forward move in the Balkans, had been public knowledge ever since February 1903.[1] The immediate danger of war subsided when Turkey accepted payment from Austria; but an augury of Italy's troubled future came on 28 December 1908 when an earthquake struck Messina and Calabria, causing heavy casualties and sharpening fears of Austria-Hungary. Articles in the Austrian press suggested that Vienna might profit from this moment of Italian weakness to settle accounts with her neighbour once and for all, and official disclaimers were not believed.[2] Italian official circles supposed that Vienna's military advisers were counselling what would be an easy military expedition against Italy, and the king openly expressed alarm at Austro-Hungarian arms spending.[3] By mid-February it seemed that the Balkan crisis was rapidly coming to a head as the military party pushed for war on the grounds that the current situation was too burdensome to state finances.[4] However, threatened by Conrad's mobilisation of the Austro-Hungarian army and deprived of Russian support, Serbia was forced to accept the annexation of Bosnia-Herzegovina on 31 March 1909.

The Bosnian crisis had an important impact on Italian war-planning. Italian naval planners had been examining the Dalmation coast since 1902 and had devised a plan to occupy Civitavecchia, on the island of Lesina, in 1907.[5] Now the army began to take an active interest in the area. Baldissera suggested that since Italy lacked an effective naval base on the Adriatic, she should prepare an expedition to seize a *punto strategico* on the Dalmation coast. Saletta disagreed: to divert an army corps for such an action would gravely inconvenience a general mobilisation, and in any case he wanted the fleet to protect Italian transport-movements along the Adriatic coast and disrupt those of the enemy around Trieste.[6] The legacy of the Bosnian crisis was a mobilisation plan to ship a special army corps of 40 000 men, 12 000 horses and 1600 carts from Naples to the Dalmation coast. By the autumn of 1909 printed instructions for such an operation were in regular circulation between the services.[7]

In the middle of the crisis, on 4 April, Casana resigned as war minister when Giolitti rejected his request for more funds. His successor, Paolo Spingardi, a 64-year-old Piedmontese general currently commanding the *carabinieri*, proved an effective minister, pushing ahead with army reform with the assistance of reports from the 'Commission of Seventeen'. The category I force was fixed at 225 000 and in May 1909 the war minister approved a new and more restrictive list of illnesses and infirmities allowing exoneration. The stiffer rules had an unequal social effect: one-third of the bourgeoisie went into category I, and 40 per cent of the peasantry.[8] Spingardi also adopted a flat-rate of two years' service, favoured by a minority of the commission and a majority of the officer corps, in June 1910. He did not accept the commission's recommendation that Italy introduce territorial recruitment.

Spingardi inherited a fractured officer corps whose cohesion was further broken down by the opportunities for dissent embodied in the Italian legal system. As part of his programme of 'administrative justice', Crispi had established Section IV of the Council of State in 1890. Its function was to investigate accusations of lack of legal competence, excessive use of legal powers or violations of the law by branches of the executive. Officers went to it in increasing numbers, usually to contest decisions of the promotions boards which put them into retirement or to challenge ministerial rulings which pensioned them off. Between 1906 and 1910, Section IV heard 365 such cases, 295 officers complained to the 'Commission of Seventeen' about incorrect application of the regulations and 258 officers went to special commissions set up by Casana. This system, and the need to have recourse to it, destroyed cohesion in the officer corps and undermined respect for authority.[9]

None of Spingardi's predecessors had done much to remedy the grievances which demoralised the officer corps, but the new war minister began vigorously cleansing the Augean stables. Pay scales were improved, lieutenants with fifteen years' service were automatically promoted captain, a law of July 1912 defined the reasons for loss of rank, elimination from the rolls or revocation of employment and the constitution and procedure of disciplinary courts were tightened up, to the benefit of the accused. In 1913 criteria for promotion were stiffened by making greater use of examinations and limiting promotion for 'exceptional merit', and 'incapability' was at last officially defined. Finally, Spingardi introduced regulations by which suitable qualified sergeant-majors could be nominated to second-lieutenancies.[10]

Spingardi had to accept that the army would frequently be called upon to preserve public order. The extra charge on the military budget that this generated quadrupled between 1903–04 and 1907–08, and during the latter year the army spend nearly 3 million man-days and some 10 per cent of the budget at the service of the political authorities.[11] Demands on the army's time and energies continued to mount and, early in 1910, Spingardi wrote to the premier, Sonnino, to complain that the prefects were making impossible demands for permanent increases in garrisons or detachments of troops to meet what were only momentary needs. He intended to oppose all such requests, he declared.

in order not to change the nature of the office of the army by subordinating the location of troops within national territory to the temporary needs of public security.[12]

There was more to Spingardi's outburst than sheer irritability at the pressures of an unwelcome duty: as he admitted to the senate on 27 June 1910, one of the major obstructions to the introduction of two years' service was that not all available time could be spent in training.[13] His protests had little effect, and the civil authorities continued to use troops not only to contain mounting civil disorder but also to assist in more diverting occasions, such as the Venice air show of 1911.

Italo–French relations remained warm during 1909, and French military missions took part in the celebrations marking the 50th anniversary of the war of 1859. As far as Austria-Hungary was concerned, Italy feared for her Adriatic seaboard and for the next five years Balkan alarm-bells rang in the ears of diplomats, soldiers and sailors. Reports indicated that Austria was improving and renewing her frontier fortifications and creating new mountain regiments. To this was added the threat of Russian expansion in the region as Russian influence in the Balkans began to increase.[14]

War-planning against Austria-Hungary always had to accommodate Italian inferiority, but the Pollio–Spingardi regime began to shift the arena of a land battle nearer to the enemy. In July 1909, war plans envisaged a 24-day mobilisation and deployment at the end of which the bulk of the Italian army would be spread along the Piave.[15] Shortly afterwards, following recommendations of the 'Commission of Seventeen', Pollio and Spingardi constructed defensive fortifications on the Tagliamento. Italian planning was shifting inexorably forward. Pollio also put a high priority on military co-operation with Germany, and the 1910 staff ride featured an Italo–German war against France in which an Italian army of four corps violated Swiss neutrality and advanced on St Gotthard to link up with a German army coming towards Zurich from Schaffhausen.[16]

Diplomatic relations between Italy and Austria-Hungary gradually began to improve, and the war ministry did what it could to defuse tension: when General Di Bernezzo, presenting a regimental standard at Brescia in November 1909, referred to Italians beyond the frontier who were impatiently awaiting their hour of liberation, he was promptly sacked. However, military anxieties remained strong. As Spingardi remarked in October 1910:

A spark – the death of the old emperor and the accession of the new, who is openly hostile to us – could produce a conflagration, even though that would be against the interests of both countries.[17]

Aware of the weakness of Italy's standing army, the soldiers were alarmed by reports from Vienna of a rejuvenation of the imperial officer corps, staff studies of disembarkation operations, the excellence of Austrian mountain-troops and provision in the 1911 military budget for increases in mountain- and fortress-artillery.[18]

Influenced by the Austrian presence at the Swiss manoeuvres in 1910, Pollio set as the scenario for the 1911 staff ride a joint Swiss-Austrian attack between Lake Como and Lake Garda, cutting in behind the mass of the Italian army in the Veneto and striking at Brescia, Bergamo and Milan. This type of operation, he believed, offered the best guide to the future employment of the army in war:

Given the state of development of every country's fixed defences it is to be expected that any war will begin with repeated attacks upon and defence of reinforced positions around a central point which will have been prepared, or perhaps only studied, in peace-time.[19]

In the game, the Italians checked the attack from Switzerland but were beaten on the Tagliamento.

In the early summer of 1911 Pollio's attention was held by the northern border. Within a month, he was preparing for war in North Africa. A long-term diplomatic objective had turned into a military target as a consequence of a combination of domestic pressure and the turns of international politics. In the Italian tradition, civilian politicians rushed the army into what looked like an easy operation to pick up assets which diplomacy alone could not obtain.

In 1910 Italian economic penetration of Tripolitania was interrupted by German attempts to take concessions away from Italy, and by Turkish harassment of Italian citizens and interference with Italian ships.[20] A press campaign, begun by the *Tribuna* in November 1910, urged further economic penetration of the Turkish territories, and it was supported by Enrico Corradini's newly formed Italian National Association. Domestic pressure for war mounted as catholics and moderate socialists swung behind the wave of colonialism generated by the press and economic interests. A war certainly offered the possibility of quieting right-wing dissatisfaction at universal male suffrage, which had recently been proposed, enabling Giolitti to balance between contending forces and win over the Nationalists.[21] However, getting into a position to fight necessitated 'squaring' the Great Powers, for whom mere domestic turmoil would not be a good enough excuse. In the event, diplomatic preparations proved unexpectedly easy.

In moving towards war with Turkey over Libya, Giolitti and Di San Giuliano were greatly influenced by the prospect of loss, not gain. As the second Moroccan crisis developed, French occupation of Fez in May was followed by the arrival of the German gunboat *Panther* off Agadir on 1 July. Any solution to the Franco-German confrontation which gave Morocco to France would leave her with no need for Italian support and therefore no reason to stick to her undertakings to support Italy's claim to Libya. Italian ambitions in North Africa could then be assuaged only at the cost of conceding Austrian claims in the Balkans. In other words, Italy had to seize Libya to avoid being given it by Austria as the bad end of a European deal.[22]

Domestic considerations and foreign policy concerns both pointed in the same direction. At bottom, however, the Libyan war was not a cool act of calculation but a gamble. By mid-September, over-optimistic military advice had convinced Giolitti that a war in Libya would be a walkover. In the spring of 1911 Colonel Marro, the Italian military attaché in Constantinople, reported the internal crisis which was splitting the Turkish Committee of Union and Progress and suggested that the discord was beginning to undermine the Turkish army.[23] In July he advised Rome that Turkey was pre-occupied with Albania and with a rebellion in the Yemen, and wanted to avoid war.[24] And by early September Marro was urging the government to act. Italy's military preparations were known to the Turks; if they were not translated into action, 'they would leave the impression that Italy had given way before the Ottoman threat'.[25] Also, the moment was favourable. To defend Tripolitania the Turks needed money and time – particularly time.[26] Marro's wild over-optimism persuaded Giolitti and Di San Giuliano that a move which they thought desirable would also be easy.

When, in August 1911, Giolitti ordered Pollio to examine the problem of war in Libya from a military point of view, the Italian general staff was well prepared to undertake such an operation. Contingency planning had begun as early as November 1884, when Mancini had ordered preparations to be made to land 30 000 troops at Tripoli, Benghazi and along the coast of Libya.[27] The Red Sea expedition then intervened; but further studies were carried out between 1897 and 1899, based on the assumption that rapid action would be necessary when a propitious moment occurred. In 1909, a variant of the Adriatic plan which entailed landing an expeditionary force of 34 000 men on the Libyan beaches was drawn up and printed. It was revised in 1910 and 1911.[28] Charges that Giolitti and Pollio adopted a casual attitude to the preparation of the Libyan expeditionary force are without foundation.[29]

On 2 September the issue of whether or not Italy should go to war became affected by the question of timing. Di San Giuliano accidentally bumped into the deputy chief of naval staff, Admiral Corsi, in the lobby of the Grand Hotel, Fiuggi, and learned that a landing would have to take place in October or November, or else be put off until the following April. By that time the political situation would have changed totally.[30] On 14 September Giolitti and Di San Giuliano decided to launch an expedition in November. Next day, Marro sent the foreign minister a telegram which was both extremely bellicose and highly optimistic. A sensible minority of Turks recognised that if Italy were sure of Austrian neutrality she could put Constantinople in an extremely awkward political, military and trading situation. The majority, however, were hostile. Turkey would therefore accept a fight,

> even though this is one of the least favourable moments for her to do so (she lacks money, trained reserves, she is badly stricken with cholera and her fleet is unprepared); she will accept with lots of noise, lots of talk, few deeds and above all with intentions which will soon dissolve.

Marro concluded – in capital letters – that if Italy acted now she would be taking no risk but would be ushering a good cause to victory.[31] The same day, Di San Giuliano suggested bringing forward an attack to the first half of October.

By the end of the first week in September the army knew that an expedition to Libya was likely in the very near future, and a week later a flurry of correspondence about orders and equipment began to issue from Pollio's office. At first the general staff thought the Arabs might make common cause with the Turks, but on 19 September Pollio prepared a study of the army's tasks which completely ignored the local Arab population. The Italian army only had to defeat five or six thousand Turkish troops. Pollio believed that they would fight on the spot and then retire towards Constantinople. He discounted the possibility that the enemy might retreat into the interior, threatening the occupying forces and obliging the Italians to carry out expeditions inland and simply did not consider that the Arabs might join in the war alongside the Turks. 'Let us dare', urged the chief of general staff, palpably over-influenced by Marro, 'but let us dare quickly'.[32] In adopting this strategy, Pollio was conforming to Di San Giuliano's political instructions to avoid as far as possible any advance into the interior of Libya. In this way it was hoped that the Arabs might be won over by convincing them that Italy's only enemy was Turkey.[33]

On 23 September the Class of 1888 was recalled to the colours, using postcards prepared two years before after the annexation of Bosnia-Herzegovina. That same day France and Germany signed accords ending their dispute over Morocco. The following day Giolitti sought the king's consent to an ultimatum which gave Turkey 24 hours to accede to Italian claims to political dominance over Tripolitania and Cyrenaica. The Italian fleet was mobilised on the 25th, and the ultimatum was dispatched on the night of 26/27 September. The Turkish Grand Vizier at first tried to avoid reading it, and when forced to do so exclaimed, 'C'est donc la guerre'. In Paris the painter Matilde Serao embraced ambassador Tittoni and cried, 'How wonderful to be Italian!'

Command of the expeditionary Italian force, which numbered 44 408 officers and men, was entrusted to General Carlo Caneva. His orders were to take and hold Tripoli and its immediate surroundings. He was also to occupy Benghazi as soon as possible. Thereafter he could go inland, but must first co-ordinate his movements with the government. Finally he was told that it was highly desirable to separate the Turks from the Arabs and that subsequent operations must look to achieve this.

Watching the departure of a battalion of infantry from Rome on the night of 6 October, the French military attaché was struck by the disorder of the troops:

> the flag without an escort, the men almost *débandés*, marching in ranks of eight, ten or fifteen, smoking, singing, with lots of small flags in the muzzles of their rifles.[34]

He wondered whether they would regain the necessary authority and organisation, and how enthusiastically the crowds would react if the Turks showed more resistance than expected. With some experience of guerrilla war in North Africa, the French expected the campaign to be a lengthy one. Belatedly, this possibility dawned on the Italians: in mid-November, in the course of a series of harsh criticisms about the effects of lack of foresight, Brusati remarked: 'We got ourselves involved in a struggle which could last indefinitely'.[35]

The occupation of Tripoli proved deceptively easy. An Italian destroyer, the *Garibaldino*, sailed into the harbour under a white flag on 29 September and took out all those Italians who wished to leave. After discussions with Captain Pietro Verri of the general staff, who had arrived eight days earlier under a false name to reconnoitre the city, the fleet commander decided not to wait for the arrival of the first half of the main force and began bombarding the town at 3.30 p.m. on the afternoon of 1 October. The contest was one-sided as Turkish artillery was totally outranged. Two days later a force of 1732 sailors under Captain Umberto Cagni landed to receive the city from the German consul. The Turks had gone. Vice-Admiral Ricci, the provisional governor, took over on 7 October, an action painted by the press in terms which made it seem that a happy partnership was developing with the local Arabs, and the first units of the main force arrived four days later. One ill-omen passed unnoticed: when the Italians called in all guns in the city only 700 rifles were recovered.[36]

The Italians enjoyed a sixteen-day honeymoon, during which they occupied the oasis surrounding the city and set up a five kilometre defensive perimeter. To the west and south, where the oasis ended abruptly in desert, they put up lines of trenches and barbed wire; to the east, where there was no clear boundary-line, their positions faced a labyrinth of houses, gardens and orchards. Then, at 8.00 a.m. on 23 October, the Turks and Arabs launched a major assault on the whole Italian line. Diversionary attacks in the west and south distracted the defenders while the main attack went in against the most vulnerable sector – the east. After a day of confused and bloody fighting, in which sailors were rushed from the city to plug gaps in the defence, the attackers were beaten off. The worst of the fighting was at Sciara Sciat, where some 250 Italians were captured, taken to a muslim cemetery and massacred. When the ground was retaken, it was discovered that many of them had been blinded, decapitated, crucified, castrated, eviscerated, burned alive or torn to pieces. In all, the Italians lost some 500 dead and 200 wounded, their enemy several thousand dead.[37]

The Italian high command was taken completely by surprise by Sciara Sciat; before the war began Verri had telegraphed from Tripoli that the Arabs wanted to change masters. The conscripts forming the bulk of the Italian forces were also entirely unprepared for a kind of war with which the French were already too familiar. Officers and men were ignorant of the Arabs and Berbers, and saw in their resistance to conquest and fearlessness of death evidence of their *bestialità*.[38] Panic, and a desire to inflict reprisals on a native populace which had aparently betrayed them, led to a brief orgy of summary executions in which hundreds – perhaps thousands – of Arabs were shot.

News of the Italian massacres created an extremely hostile international environment and confronted Giolitti with the prospect of outside intervention and a compromise settlement. The king, who had been unenthusiastic about the war from the start, pointed out that Turkey might drag things out. Italy needed a *fait accompli* to avoid international complications, so Giolitti responded by unveiling a plan which bore signs of hurried improvisation: Tripolitania would be overwhelmed as quickly as possible, Italian sovereignty declared, and preparations made to occupy Turkish islands or blockade the mainland.[39] A royal decree was rushed out on 5 November 1911 putting Tripolitania and Cyrenaica under the 'full and entire sovereignty of the kingdom of Italy' and the chamber of deputies, which Giolitti had sent on vacation in July, was reassembled on 23 February 1912 to approve the measure retrospectively. However, only military success could convert quasi-legal possession into complete control, and this Caneva was unable to provide.

The Italians spread along the coast in a series of operations which appeared planned but were in fact haphazard, and were characterised by a lack of knowledge of local conditions. Tobruk was taken on 1 October, and over the next eighteen days Derna, Benghazi and Homs also fell into Italian hands. Behind these moves lay the vague expectation that the capture of a few major cities would be enough to end Arab resistance; in taking Homs, Caneva had been hoping that 'once we gained possession of that spot, all the Arab tribes in the vicinity would at once declare for us'.[40]

Unwilling to risk another Adua, and aware that any expedition into the interior would require a colossal effort, Caneva opted for a strategy of letting the enemy wear himself out against Italian defences. 'Our military reputation', he wrote to Pollio early in November, 'which is now so greatly elevated, could be gravely compromised by an important defeat'.[41] The chiefs of the army and navy general staffs had no practical alternative to offer. Both accepted that occupying the Aegean islands, blockading Salonika or Smyrna, or attacking Constantinople were all equally fraught with political difficulties.[42] Italy was staring strategic bankruptcy in the face.

As time passed the possibility of international invervention grew. Tension with Britain and France mounted over the passage – real or imagined – of Turkish men and munitions across Egypt and Tunisia.[43] Giolitti became enraged at Caneva's immobility, which threatened to force Italy into accepting international arbitration.[44] Sidney Sonnino complained to his diary that, with modest expenditure and the aid of a few hundred Arabs, Turkey was pinning down two-and-a-half Italian divisions but even he had no idea how to tackle the difficult task of pacification.[45] Everybody wanted something to be done; nobody knew what.

Belatedly, Pollio realised the importance of an Arab policy and called in one of the most experienced colonial soldiers, Tommaso Salsa, to devise one. Salsa was given a three-fold task: to study the causes of Arab resistance; to devise ways to make them change their minds; and to ensure that the Arab population did not threaten the troops. From Rome, Salsa saw the main military problem as flowing from a sense of weakness which prevented the undertaking of any offensive operations. When he arrived in Tripoli, he decided that poor logistics arrangements explained the immobility of the army.[46] Independent analysis supports him: German calculations suggested that Italy would need 30 000 camels to occupy the interior, whereas she had fewer than 2000.

Under pressure from Giolitti, Caneva now began to push eastward from Tripoli. On 26 November 20 000 troops took Henni and Fort Mesri and a week later, on 4 December, three brigades under the command of General Pecori-Giraldi took the oasis of Ain Zara after nine hours of stiff fighting, begun in pouring rain, at a loss of 23 dead and 107 wounded. By chasing the enemy out of range of Tripoli, Caneva put an end to the perpetual sniping and ambushes from which his troops had suffered for almost three months; however, although the Italians controlled the ground they had not defeated the enemy, who had merely withdrawn.

Ain Zara was only a limited success, and the Italian press began to hint that it was time for naval action against Turkey. The men on the spot saw things differently. Caneva wrote enthusiastically to Ugo Brusati:

> The situation here has radically changed in our favour; the Turks have retreated to the altopiano, the oasis has become peaceful and quiet, and the inhabitants are asking for our protection.[47]

He was optimistic that the Arabs could be separated from the Turks, since the chiefs of some of the desert tribes were already offering to yield, and his optimism was shared by his subordinates.

Buoyed-up with unjustified confidence, Pecori-Giraldi now over-reached himself. On 19 December he sent out a column of 3000 men under Colonel Gustavo Fara to attack Bir Tobras. It got lost, took seven hours to cover less than 15 kilometres, and when it arrived at the oasis it assaulted the wrong positions. Attacked from the rear, Fara dug in, fought until nightfall and then retreated, meeting on his way back a brigade which had been sent to help him and had also got lost. The episode illustrated all the difficulties of desert warfare, into which Pecori-Giraldi had plunged rather too casually. After complaints from Pollio and Caneva, he was sacked and sent back to Italy, apparently the victim of a masonic conspiracy.[48]

As the year ended with no sign of the decisive victory he both wanted and needed, Giolitti grew increasingly anxious. He put about the impression that Italy had plenty of men, plenty of money and plenty of patience, but the British ambassador reported in mid-January that 'a certain nervousness is beginning to be perceptible as to how long the war is likely to continue'.[49] The possibility of international complications loomed when, on 16 January 1912, the French ship *Carthage* was stopped on suspicion of sending aid to the Turks, and two days later her consort the *Manouba* was also detained. On board the ships were a party of the Turkish Red Crescent which contained, to Italian eyes, an unusually large proportion of officers. Relations with France rapidly worsened, and there were rumours that the army on the Alps was preparing to resist a French attack.

Giolitti recalled Caneva at the beginning of February. By the time that he reached Rome, 26 generals and 100 000 Italian troops were hemmed in on the five coastal footholds and were facing an estimated 35 000 Turkish and Arab troops. Although exasperated at Caneva's lack of initiative, Giolitti was unable either to order him into action or to sack him. In the first place, Caneva had the backing of the Italian general staff: although himself impatient at the restraints imposed on Italian strategy by diplomatic considerations and irritated at Caneva's negativism, Pollio accepted his reasons for being reluctant to launch forays into the interior.[50] Secondly, the unusually close relationship between Pollio and Spingardi formed a united front to protect the army, so that Giolitti was unable to split it into rival factions. Not until 3 July 1912 did he feel in a strong enough position to order Spingardi to sack his commander in Libya.

Caneva went back to his waiting game, and the navy took up the initiative. After attacking Hodeida, Kunfidah and Beirut, Admiral Thaon di Revel suggested on 29 February sailing to the Dardanelles and challenging the Turkish fleet to come out by destroying telegraphic communications between the continent and the islands. Admiral Viale, the naval commander-in-chief in the theatre, extended the concept by adding operations against the exterior forts of the Dardanelles and surprise action by torpedo boats against Turkish ships anchored in the Straits. The fleet took the island of Stampalia as a base on 17 April, and the next day a number of Italian ships appeared before the Straits in an attempt to draw out the Turkish fleet, whilst the rest hid behind Imbros. As the Turks wisely refused to be drawn into open waters, the Italian ships fought a two-hour gun-duel with the forts, doing what the French military attaché described as 'conspicuous' damage.

Having failed to entice out the Turkish fleet, the Italian navy reverted to an idea proposed at the end of March by Admiral Faravelli, Viale's predecessor, to occupy the Turkish Aegean islands. Rhodes was taken on 4 May, and Cos, Leros and eight other islands eight days later. Austria-Hungary protested because she had agreed to the occupation of only three Aegean islands, and then on condition that the Dardanelles were left along, but Giolitti had accurately assessed how far he could go and now restrained the navy. Pollio, however, wanted to go further and occupy Chios, which he thought would have a great effect on Turkish determination to continue the war.[51]

Time failed to work for Constantinople as the Turks supposed it would. None of the major powers showed any signs of intervening on her behalf, her troops in the Libyan desert were short of water and pay, and in poor health and she was beginning to experience difficulties in the Balkans. By June 1912 she had another Albanian revolt and a frontier-dispute with Montenegro on her hands, and an even greater menace loomed. Secret treaties between Serbia and Bulgaria on 12 March and

Greece and Bulgaria on 29 May presaged the formation of the Balkan League and the first Balkan war. Both combatants were ready to talk An Italian go-between arrived in Constantinople on 10 June and a little over a month later, on 12 July, the two sides met at Lausanne. The process of hammering out peace terms was to take three months.

The land campaign continued cautiously. Caneva, the shade of Baratieri at his shoulder, made sure he ran no great risks. The capture of Lebda on 2 May was followed by a day-long battle at Gargaresc on 7 June, both successful actions which were not carried through. Thereafter Caneva began a series of operations which continued until mid-August, designed to extend his control along the coast and cut off the caravan routes to the interior, culminating in the seizure of Negdalin which controlled supply routes from Tripoli to the hinterland.

Pollio recommended taking advantage of the Balkan situation to strike directly at Turkey. Since 'there have not been and cannot be decisive battles in Africa', he urged at the end of June that Italy seize Smyrna.[52] Giolitti took no notice, preferring to trust to time – now on Italy's side – and negotiations. On 18 July the navy launched a daring but futile attack on the Turkish fleet at the Dardanelles with a squadron of torpedo boats, and after Caneva was recalled on 31 August the army accelerated its pace. General Briccola began energetically in Cyrenaica, lifting the bombardment of Derna on 17 September with the aid of a brilliant action by Salsa which won him promotion to lieutenant-general; and in Tripolitania General Ragni took the oasis of Zanzur, though with heavy casualties.

Neither the army nor the navy could win Libya for Italy, and Giolitti now pinned his hopes on negotiation. However, he was anxious lest the military ease up, warning the war minister early in August that it might take two or three months before peace was secured and demanding an intensification of action in Cyrenaica.[53] Then Italy had a stroke of luck: on 30 September the Balkan League began mobilisation, and eight days later Montenegro declared war on Turkey. Even so, Constantinople was reluctant to come to terms, and it took diplomatic pressure from Britain, Germany and Austria-Hungary and a threat from Giolitti to attack Smyrna before she would consent to abandon Tripolitania and Cyrenaica to Italy. The Treaty of Lausanne, signed on 18 October 1912, made Libya an Italian possession and also bound Italy to quit the Aegean islands immediately after all Turkish troops had withdrawn from the two North African provinces, which she conspicuously failed to do. Pollio retained an exaggerated faith in Italian arms, and hoped to the last that all the talk of peace in the newspapers was untrue.[54]

Italy emerged from the Libyan war a lucky victor. Her army did not defeat its opponents and failed to impose its will on the enemy. This failure must be explained at three levels. In the field, a force of European conscripts had been expected to adjust to the peculiar conditions of desert warfare in a relatively short time; lacking an operational doctrine to cope with this situation, the Italian high command extemporised with a daring which sometimes crossed the bounds of the foolhardy, or stood rooted in caution in an effort to avoid mistakes. Planning failed at every level: intelligence was inadequate and ill-digested, no comprehensive scheme of campaign was ever drawn up, and logistics were accorded – as so often – the most minor of roles. Behind all this lay the political failure to relate means to aims and think through the question of what kind of defeat would be necessary to force Turkey to relinquish control of Tripolitania and Cyrenaica. Instead, soldiers and politicians partnered one another in a gamble.

Although the Italians had wrested the two provinces from the Turks, they had still not defeated the Arabs. The Senussi and the Bedouin were far from willing to truckle to a decision about their future made in Switzerland, and a long-drawn-out process of pacification began. By October 1913 General Vinari had only managed to clear the Benghazi-Tobruk area of rebels; they in return had shown what they could do by killing General Torelli and his staff on 16 September. The brutal truth was that Italy was unable to subdue her new possession. When the bellicose new minister for the colonies, Ferdinando Martini, put forward a plan in April 1913 for the simultaneous penetration of Cyrenaica from Benghazi, Tolmetta, Derna and Tobruk, Spingardi pointed out that Italy had neither the manpower nor the transport for such a strategy.[55]

Italy's problems in Libya were exacerbated by the appointment of Enver Bey as Turkish war minister in January 1913. Pollio feared that Enver might turn back to Cyrenaica once the Balkan wars ended and Turkey had lost her European Empire.[56] His fears were borne out when, at the end of 1913, reports began to reach Rome of the presence of Turkish officers and men among the Senussi, and by the spring of 1914 it was clear that Enver was sustaining the rebels with money and that arms and ammunition were being transported to the Arabs on Greek ships, which were landing them on the coast between Tobruk and Sollum.[57] The combined activities of Turks and Arabs meant that when war broke out in Europe in August 1914 there were still 50 000 Italian troops in Libya, and little hope of stripping the garrison to swell the field-army.

The Libyan war proved expensive. Some 1500 men died in battle and

2000 from sickness, and a further 4250 were wounded.[58] Its total cost of
1 015 000 000 lire represented half Italy's total annual revenue. The
effects of the African adventure on Italy's strategic deployment in
Europe were no less severe. Initial studies of the Libyan operation had
been based on sending a force of 35 000 but by the spring of 1912 that
number had swollen to over 95 000, and in January the decision not to
interfere with the European frontier corps had to be abandoned. All but
three divisions sent one regiment apiece, along with almost all the
infantry machine-gun sections and support troops, rations, munitions,
clothing in large quantities and the horses which were to be used in a
general mobilisation. Most of the recently trained reservists left Italy,
along with large numbers of *Alpini* and considerable amounts of field-,
mountain- and fortress-artillery. Huge quantities of infantry ammunition also had to go: at one stage, the home army was reduced to only 250
rounds per weapon.[59] Before 1911 Italy had been militarily weak on one
continent; after 1912 she was weak in two.

In the aftermath of the Libyan war, Pollio reassessed Italy's military
commitments to Germany. The rail-plan had been updated in Berlin on
8 June 1911, but during the course of the war against Turkey nothing
had been done to revise or reconsider the plan to send III Army to the
Rhine, even though the drain on the army's resources was soon
apparent. In the autumn of 1912, Pollio began to consider attacking
France across the western Alps or landing troops on the coast of
Provence, and by the end of October he had decided to recommend
ending the Rhine commitment despite opposition from Spingardi, who
feared that a decision not even to send two cavalry divisions might
provoke 'sensitivity'.[60] On 21 November he sent a personal emissary,
Colonel Zupelli, to Berlin to talk to von Moltke.

Pollio did not contemplate a complete strategic reversal: he still
intended to fight, but in a different place. Nor, in view of what was to
happen a month later, is his excuse that Victor Emmanuel wanted Italian
troops kept under Italian command convincing. His real fear was that
the French might land in Italy. The Tyrrhenian coast in particular
offered 'numerous and important objectives for a French attack', and in
September he had special instructions drawn up to use the *Guardia di
Finanza* to aid in coastal defence.[61] Cancelling the Rhine option kept
troops in Italy to counter this threat.

Some of Pollio's strategic anxieties were revealed when Zupelli
suggested that the French might enter Switzerland and threaten the
southern flank of III Army on the Rhine. Von Moltke thought not but
failed to convince the Italians. Zupelli told him that Italy would stick to

the accords in the event of war, but would take the offensive against France across the Alpine frontier or – if she had a command of the sea – by landing in Provence and moving up the Rhone. Pollio put this in writing in a letter to von Moltke on 21 December 1912.[62] In the meantime the Triple Alliance was renewed on 5 December 1912. In accordance with Italian practice, the chief of the general staff was kept entirely in the dark about it and had no idea whether it contained any undertaking to support Austria-Hungary.[63]

In January 1913 General von Waldersee was sent to Rome with orders to 'define more clearly' Italy's future line of military operations.[64] He found Pollio a warm supporter of the Triple Alliance, backed by the king. Although Pollio confirmed his intention to deploy five Italian corps in the western Alps and five more in a landing in Provence, he also told von Waldersee that he could send cavalry, but not infantry, to the Rhine – thus opening a crack in a door he had seemed to close firmly only a month earlier. However, he was still concerned at the vulnerability of the west coast to French landings, and was simultaneously preparing new instructions for coastal defence.[65] The Germans set out to revive the Rhine option, but von Moltke was at pains to leave no doubts as to what a future war might entail: in an interview with the Italian military attaché in March 1913 he outlined Germany's intention to break Belgian neutrality in the event of war, and added that the next war between France and Germany 'will be a question of life or death for us. We shall stop at nothing to gain our end. In the struggle for existence, one does not bother about the means one employs'.[66]

While von Waldersee was wooing the Italians back into the fold a Balkan crisis threatened to catapult the army into another war for which it was not prepared. On 23 April 1913 Montenegro seized Scutari and refused to surrender it to Albania as the Powers had agreed. Di San Giuliano scented an opportunity to put an Italian force into Albania, and three days later the Italian army and navy were ordered to mobilise for immediate action. Pollio complained, with justification, that Italian politicians simply did not realise how long mobilisation took.[67]

Events in Europe and North Africa underlined Italy's military weakness, and on 16 February 1913 Pollio wrote to Spingardi demanding the strengthening of the army, in which it was not uncommon to find companies of 15 men and battalions of 50 or less.[68] In April Spingardi presented a programme designed to increase recruitment to 300 000, as well as improving coastal and frontier fortifications, increasing munitions reserves and organising an air service. Giolitti was not prepared to adopt another massive defence programme without prior professional consideration and debate. Accordingly, he revived the disused Supreme Defence Commission which, after some delay, met on 19 May 1913 with the premier in the chair.

Pollio opened the proceedings by announcing that more fortifications were urgently needed on the western frontier. It was here that Italy would have to attack France and fend off tactical offensives which the French could mount due to their speedier mobilisation. Pollio easily won approval for more forts in some of the north-western valleys, but lost a proposal to improve the coastal defences to Cadorna's suggestion that they be abandoned in favour of upgrading inland fortifications. Spingardi backed his chief of staff in discussion but abstained in the vote. A major difference of opinion then developed over whether or not to improve the defences of Genoa.

Pollio argued strongly for more gun batteries. He was supported by the chief of naval staff, Admiral Thaon di Revel, who believed that fortification was the best defence until such time as the Italian navy equalled that of France, and by the inspectors-general of engineers and artillery. Cadorna wanted no increase in Genoese defences, and even favoured stripping them of artillery. If Genoa were armed she would still be bombarded; and the uprising which might then occur would have a worse effect on national morale than allowing the French to occupy an open city. Also Genoa's strategic function could quite adequately be fulfilled by Appennine fortifications. Pollio lost this argument by six votes to three, and then somewhat undermined his own case by admitting that 'existing fortifications would probably be enough to prevent the very grave occurrence of an enemy landing'.[69]

Pollio got his way with further proposals to fortify La Maddelena, Gaeta, Messina and Taranto, backed by Thaon di Revel; and when the navy minister, Cattolica, declared that in present circumstances there was no need to worry about the defences of Ancona, Giolitti revealed that he too was not immune from the temptation to fortify everything:

> the defence of the state ought to be determined objectively and not in relation to the current political situation, since fortifications could not be improvised and it is therefore necessary to prepare them for all possibilities.[70]

The debates in the supreme Defence Commission displayed the grave deficiencies which handicapped military policy-making in Italy. No commonly agreed doctrine existed on such basic issues as the value of coastal defences, decisions were reached not by searching for consensus but by domination and submission, the views of the chief of staff enjoyed no special status and personality clashes were well-nigh unavoidable. The extent of the disagreements within the high command had been revealed all too plainly to the premier – something Spingardi greatly regretted.[71]

Cadorna was horrified to learn in the course of the discussions that Pollio had abandoned the Rhine option and intended to attack Nice instead. If the attack went ahead, he argued, 'It will only be after a very long time, reckonable as several months, and great deterioration of our troops and equipment, that we shall be able to debouch from the Alpine zone'.[72] By that time major operations on the Rhine could well be over; if France had won them, Italy's success in paralysing four French reserve divisions would be worthless. His conclusion – that Italy should send all the men she could spare to the Rhine and ensure that her flag stood alongside Germany's in the main theatre of war – seems to have changed Pollio's mind somewhat: the transport plan drawn up in July 1913 provided that in the event of war against France 'a large army will deploy in a zone far distant from the others'.[73]

In August 1913 Pollio went to Silesia to attend the German manoeuvres, an occasion which was seized upon by his partners to try to revive the full Italian commitment to the Rhine option. At a meeting on 8 September, Conrad sought to persuade Pollio to reverse his earlier decision. Serbia was growing ever stronger; to handle her, more German troops would be needed from the Rhine, where Italians could replace them. Also the Austrians had co-operated in negotiating the 1913 naval accords and now expected Italy to reciprocate. Pollio was already veering back to the Rhine option for tactical and strategic reasons, and agreed the following day that up to five Italian infantry divisions might operate on the southern German wing.

Later, at a meeting in Salzbrunn, Pollio explained to Wilhelm II why he had decided not to send III Army to the Rhine: with the equivalent of three corps in Libya and a fourth probably necessary, sending another five corps to Germany would have stripped the country of most of its defences. Only three permanent corps would have been left to guard the Alpine frontier and the coasts. 'We could not have supported this burden, while the *first obligation* as a member of the alliance, I said, is *to be honest*.'[74] Pollio offered the Kaiser two divisions of Italian cavalry and said that he was prepared to re-examine the whole question of sending III Army to the Rhine, but in reduced numbers. He further pleased his hosts by adding that, in his opinion, the Triple Alliance must act in war as a single state, since it would be 'a question of existence'.

Despite his protestations, Pollio was being less than straightforward. For one thing, the strategic considerations which had decided him in 1912 were essentially unchanged. Also, despite his apparent enthusiasm for returning to the Rhine, he was still preoccupied with the problem of the western Alps. In the 1913 Italian staff ride, Italian armies attacked Savoy and Nice and the French counter-attacked along the Dora Riparia and Chisone valleys, aiming at Turin. This scenario was based on the Italian general staff's belief that the French military service law of 1913, extending conscription from two years to three, increased the likelihood that France would take the offensive against Italy. The underlying purpose of the ride was therefore to concentrate on the special problems of mountain warfare, for 'whatever the hypothesis of war in Europe, our army will always have to operate first in the mountains'.[75] Things worked out well enough for Pollio to be confident of checking a French offensive and counter-attacking.

In December 1913 General von Waldersee was again sent to Rome to press the case for an Italian army on the Rhine. Pollio personally favoured the plan but would make no promises, since in Italy the military point of view did not prevail over the political. No one had ever asked the politicians' consent to technical plans before, and Pollio was using this pretext to conceal his own indecision. However, the pendulum was swinging back to the Rhine: on 18 December the designated wartime commanders of the four Italian armies met the chief of staff and voted unanimously in favour of the Rhine plan, and during the course of the month Pollio's private secretary, Colonel Montanari, was sent to Vienna to discuss transporting troops across Austria into Germany.[76]

Pollio was still not irrevocably committed to returning to the Rhine, and during the winter of 1913/14 a naval liaison officer was detailed to examine the possibility of landing in France. Time alone ruled out the idea. It would take the navy a month to win command of the sea and a further three months to prepare transports for the necessary 217 000 men. This force would have to land at St Tropez and capture Nice and Marseilles before advancing up the Rhone Valley, by which time the war would probably be over. Italy would have contributed little to the victory, and would receive little at the peace.[77]

Practical considerations were forcing Pollio to accept that if Italy were to co-operate with the central powers in war, the most effective theatre in which to fight was north-east France. At the end of January 1914 a conference at Vienna discussed transporting two cavalry divisions, but the Italians refused as yet to consider the wider issue of transportation for III Army. Then, on 11 February, the German military attaché informed von Moltke that Victor Emmanuel III had consented to send three army corps to the Rhine. Conrad was told five days later.[78] Pollio gave every appearance of satisfaction at this decision, writing to von Moltke that

> if God wills war, Your Excellency and I will have the consolation of having prepared for it in the best way possible, for the good and the glory of our Sovereigns and our peoples.[79]

A major meeting took place in Berlin 10–11 March 1914 between Zuccari, designated commander of III Army, and von Waldersee. Thanks to preliminary discussions with the Austrians, Italian troops could be moved to Alsace within four weeks of the start of mobilisation. The Germans offered heavy artillery and indicated that they wanted the Italians to attack French fortifications blocking the upper Moselle or to counter-attack in Lorraine. Later the Italians claimed to have been careful to stress that Italy would carry out her military obligations only after the *casus foederis* as determined in the terms of the Triple Alliance had occurred.[80]

Although Pollio had moved back into the German orbit, he remained deeply worried about Italian vulnerability to French attack. 'What we have most to fear in the event of war with France', he told Ugo Brusati in mid-May, 'is naval action against our undefended maritime *piazze*'.[81] Corps commanders were ordered to improve railway protection, territorial militia units were told-off as railway guards, and Thaon di Revel was requested to protect the great coastal cities with more submarines.

Although the discussions of the Supreme Defence Commission in May 1913 had secured more fortifications, Pollio was still deeply concerned about general deficiencies in the army and in March 1914, after Spingardi and Giolitti had both resigned, he seized what looked like an opportune moment to present four separate projects: a *programma massimo* which required 551 million of extraordinary expenditure, a 'reduced' programme of 475 million, a 'minimum' programme of 402 million and a *programma ultraminimo* of 198 million lire. There was no likelihood that his ambitious projects would gain assent. Military expenditure had averaged 511 million lire a year between 1907 and 1912, and had risen to 837 million in 1912–13, plus a further 498 million for Libya, which represented 47 per cent of public expenditure.[82] It had to come down. Moreover, in presenting a statement of the Libyan expenses to the chamber on 20 December 1913 the treasury minister, Tedesco, had assured the house that it only remained to complete 'in a small part' the replacement of military stores.[83] Finally, in supporting the new premier, Antonio Salandra, the Right was backing a programme of balanced budgets. The political environment was not one in which to try to reverse a downward trend in state spending.

On 30 March 1914 Pollio sent Salandra a list of provisions he regarded as indispensable. To equal Austria, Italy needed ten more first-line divisions, 30 000 more conscripts a year and a standing army of 345 000 men – an increase of 70 000. Pollio also spelt out Italy's shortage of heavy-, field-, horse-, mountain- and fortress-artillery and pressed for the recall of larger numbers of reservists for annual training. He told Salandra that it was by no means universally believed that the stores had been fully replenished after Libya, and that in any case the war had demonstrated that they needed to be better stocked, since industry had been incapable of keeping up with consumption.[84] Three days later Salandra reassured parliament:

> On 1st January this year the military magazines had been resupplied with their normal stocks, and by means of timely substitutions a large part had been improved in quality and increased in value.[85]

Pollio's repeated appeals to strengthen the army were ignored.

Military links with Germany continued to tighten. Transport officials met in Vienna on 1 April, and nine days later signed an accord to transport three Italian corps across Austria. Now, however, a variant of the Rhine option began to emerge: the use of Italian troops on the eastern front against the Russians. This scheme may have been mentioned during the transport talks, and Pollio himself suggested to the German military attaché early in April that Italy might send troops to aid in a war against Serbia. Wind of this quickly came to Victor Emmanuel's ears and Pollio had to reassure him that it was no more than an idea for internal study. In contemplating such a strategy, Pollio was acting as a loyal partner of Germany and Austria-Hungary. By mid-April he was aware that Conrad believed that the time was not far off when Russia would make a move into Armenia, possibly with Rumanian support.[86] Von Moltke professed to share Conrad's fear, and by the end of May he was openly pressing that the military convention not include fixed locations in Germany for the deployment of Italian troops since the military situation might require their use elsewhere. Calderari reported from Berlin:

this is an idea which Moltke and Waldersee have both been playing with for some time because it would give them the means, if necessary, to deploy the Italian contingent on the Russian front, where Germany is now able to give less help to Austria-Hungary because of the new grouping in Europe.[87]

Pollio was prepared to consider a request to use Italian troops on the eastern front once war had begun; he was not prepared to insert such an undertaking into the military convention. The most he would agree to was an exchange of ideas, into which Conrad read too much.[88]

Pollio may have been prepared to contemplate co-operation with Germany, and even to discuss hypothetical operations on the eastern front, but this did not mean that he had grown any less suspicious of Vienna. In April he forwarded a paper to Brusati listing the roads being built in the Trentino and highlighting the deployment of new guns in the region, doubtless intending it to be seen by the king.[89] Then, on 24 June 1914, he sent war minister Grandi a lengthy memorandum pointing out that there were almost as many Austrian troops on the Italian frontier as there were facing Russia and that in 1914 Vienna had spent nearly one million lire on her land forces. She still threatened Italy, who would be safe – said Pollio – only when she was strong.[90] Shortly afterwards, the events at Sarajevo precipitated a European war for which Italy was almost entirely unprepared, and she was confronted with the question of whether to join the Triple Alliance in war or throw in her lot with the Entente. The pattern of Italian civil–military relations, which held soldiers at arm's length from diplomats, now worked to produce the worst of all possible decisions.

9 From Neutrality to Intervention

Until 1914 Italian military planning was conducted in an atmosphere of functional specialisation. When soldiers and politicians met formally to discuss strategy, which rarely happened, the debates were narrowly technical in scope and the broader underlying considerations were conceived in social terms. The political dimension of strategy was left aside. Thus when the July crisis overwhelmed Europe, Italy was doubly unprepared. Her planning had been largely defensive and she lacked a strategy for aggressive war against Austria-Hungary, which her politicians might require; and she also lacked the habit and experience of debating strategy in political terms. Her civilian leaders were not ready to listen to political arguments from the military; her military did not speak with a single voice; and her soldiers were materially unready to fight. After some ten months, circumstance and tradition combined to put the army once more at the service of the state in a gamble for limited aims.

The news of Franz Ferdinand's assassination at Sarajevo reached the Italian general staff in a telegram from Vienna which was deciphered at 8 p.m. on 28 June. Its impact was minimal, for the army was preoccupied with the problem of public order. Left-wing anti-militarist demonstrations on 7 June and the army's reaction to them had unleashed popular resentments throughout much of central Italy. One Italian general had ignominiously surrendered to the rioters during 'Red Week', and the war minister was seething at the enforced passivity imposed upon the troops. As the Austro-Serbian crisis began, the threat which overhung army and government in Italy was that of a rail strike.

During the first month of the crisis the customary gulf in Italian civil-military relations was widened by the lack of a chief of the general staff. On an inspection visit to Turin, General Pollio suffered a massive heart attack which was wrongly diagnosed as a gastric obstruction, and was given a purgative. By 1 July he was dead. A week later the three designated army commanders and General Grandi met to elect a successor. The result was a tie, with two votes for Luigi Cadorna and two for a much more junior general. The final selection was left to the king, who chose Cadorna.[1] On 27 July he was formally installed as Italy's fifth chief of the general staff and immediately faced the possibility of leading the army into war.

The new chief of staff was in every way different from his predecessor. Born into an aristocratic Piedmontese military family, Cadorna was 63 when he took up the reins of power. Pollio had impressed everyone with his fine physique and soldierly bearing; Cadorna was ugly and inelegant. He nursed a sizeable persecution-complex and was convinced that on various occasions a combination of freemasons and Jews had blocked his promotion. Already a harsh disciplinarian, he trusted no one but maintained absolute faith in his own strategic ideas. He had served neither in Eritrea nor in Libya; and although familiar with much of the military planning, he knew little about the army's physical readiness for war and nothing about the diplomacy of the day.

Cadorna tried to persuade the government to enter the war quickly rather than wait, but his policy broke against the firmness of Di San Giuliano's diplomatic line. In mid-July, before he realised that Austria intended to carry the Serbian crisis to the brink of war and beyond, the foreign minister had decided that in the event of an Austro-Serbian conflict there must be adequate territorial compensation for Italy.[2] This remained his policy after he learned of the harsh terms of the Austrian ultimatum to Serbia on 23 July: in a letter to Victor Emmanuel the following day he emphasised that Italy must get compensation for any Austrian advantage in the Balkans and for Italian involvement in the war, which he regarded as 'possible, but not likely'.[3] Determined to try to bargain Italy's neutrality in return for territorial gains, Salandra and Di San Giuliano were committed to non-intervention by the time that the new chief of staff took office.

Cadorna told the German military attaché, on the day that he assumed office, that he fully accepted all the agreements made by his predecessor. He repeated this undertaking in a letter to von Moltke that same day, assuring Berlin of the bond uniting the alliance partners. In his reply two days later von Moltke speculated that the two armies would soon be united in battle and working towards a common victory.[4] Expectations were being built up in the minds of the military leadership of the Central Powers which Cadorna was to prove unable to gratify.

On the day that Cadorna wrote to von Moltke, Salandra called in his two service ministers and asked them whether they were ready to mobilise. The navy was, but the army was not: General Dino Grandi, Spingardi's successor, hesitated, citing a shortage of uniforms which he claimed not to have known about earlier in the year when he had allowed Salandra to reassure parliament that the Libyan losses had been made good.[5] On 31 July, as Russia went into full mobilisation, the Italian cabinet met and opted for neutrality. This decision had a military rationale. Di San Giuliano was well aware that the Italian navy felt vulnerable to the British and French in the Mediterranean.[6] It was no less vulnerable to the Austrian fleet, a line of argument which had been instrumental in bringing about the Triple Alliance Naval Convention the previous year. However, it was not a decision explicable solely, or even chiefly, on military grounds.

The question of whether or not to throw Italy's military weight into the scales never really arose because the foreign minister could see no clear advantage for Italy in any of the three possible outcomes to the war. 'It would be superfluous to recount the sad consequences that a defeat of the Triple Alliance would produce', he wrote on 2 August.

> Even if it gained a partial victory, it would not be able to give us adequate compensations; and if the alliance won a decisive victory and reduced France and Russia to impotence for many years, there would be neither the interest nor the desire to give us compensations in proportion to our sacrifices.[7]

Given this frame of mind, the extent to which the Italian army was ready to fight was beside the point. Di San Giuliano set the policy-line without considering either the strategic or the psychological significance of early Italian participation in the war. Cadorna had strong views on both.

It is a measure of the poverty of Italian civil–military relations that Cadorna set about his new task in the mistaken belief that Italy would shortly meet her obligations under the Triple Alliance. No politicians consulted him, and no one disabused him. On 29 July he drew up a list of 'urgent military provisions'; they included stripping the Austrian front of fortress artillery and transporting it to the French frontier, and making good from other units the equipment deficiencies of troops destined for Germany.[8] The same day he asked the king's permission to send all forces not necessary for the defence of Italy and Libya to the Franco-German front in the event of war.[9] On 2 August the king approved these decisions, just as the cabinet publicly announced Italy's neutrality.

Cadorna was not alone in expecting to meet the military obligation to Berlin and Vienna. On 31 July the Austrian foreign minister reminded his ambassador in Rome that no instructions had yet been received confirming Pollio's undertaking to Conrad to send Italian units to Galicia as well as the Rhine in the event of war.[10] The following day

Conrad wrote to ask that this commitment be met in view of the 'unforeseen deterioration of the situation' and inquired when the troops would be ready.[11] The news that Italy would remain neutral evoked a mixture of shock and anger in Berlin and Vienna. On 2 August von Moltke thought that, even if Italian troops were not sent to the Rhine, Italy might mobilise on the French frontier. Three days later, shaken that his erstwhile partner had not even gone that far despite Pollio's and Cadorna's undertakings, he wrote angrily to Conrad:

> Italy's felony will be revenged in history. May God grant you victory now, so that you will be able to settle accounts later with these knaves.[12]

Di San Giuliano's policy of temporisation made it likely that Italy would alienate her allies while not fully supporting her erstwhile opponents, Britain and France. Cadorna believed that, win or lose, the Central Powers would never forgive Italy for deserting them.[13] After the war, having supported neither side from the outset, Italy would be distrusted by all and would be unable to count on any fixed alliance. Instead she would have to arm herself even more heavily than in the past. However, there was a way to make the best of the situation: while the strategic position hung in the balance, as it still did in August, Italy's forces might be enough to determine the outcome.[14] The longer mobilisation was delayed, the less likely was it that this situation would persist. Accordingly, Cadorna pressed for war alongside the Entente.

Cadorna's political justifications for abandoning neutrality failed to make any headway against the prevailing currents. He lost a struggle in early August in which he opposed partial mobilisation and argued for full mobilisation after Di San Giuliano convinced Grandi and Thaon di Revel that political logic ruled it out.[15] The principle of Italian compensation for Austria's forward move in the Balkans offered the attractive possibility of being bribed not to fight, and many who later criticised the foreign minister for following a policy which brought the country to the brink of a humiliating catastrophe, among them Luigi Albertini, supported it at the time.[16] Di San Giuliano was in tune with a widespread mood of non-interventionism.

Although rooted in political calculation, Di San Giuliano's policy also had a foundation in assumptions about the war and about the army. The war, he believed, was likely to last a long time. Italy lacked England's or Russia's power to sustain herself in such a war; therefore Di San Giuliano would not break with the Central Powers until he could be sure of victory alongside the Entente.[17] This policy would inevitably make Italy appear grossly opportunistic – a fact Cadorna acknowledged, but Di San Giuliano did not. The foreign secretary also disbelieved his chief of staff's assertion that throwing Italy's military forces into the balance at an early stage in the war might determine the outcome: alongside this suggestion he minuted drily, 'I don't think so'.[18] In view of the army's poor performance in the Libyan war, this attitude had some justification.

If he was to win his struggle to enforce a military policy on the government, Cadorna had to overcome opposition from within the army as well as from outside it. Rapid mobilisation would expose deficiencies which he now knew to be considerable. The army was short of 13 500 officers and 200 000 sets of uniforms; due to the long-running artillery problem, ten of the 36 regiments of field-artillery did not exist; and the reserves and militia were poorly trained and ill-armed.[19] Grandi would not admit the extent of the shortages. He told the cabinet that Italy had more arms and ammunition than she needed, but did acknowledge a lack of 250 000 uniforms – which came as something of a shock, since his predecessor had told the king that the army was only 40 000 short.[20] The shortage of officers was a particularly severe problem: Italy had only one officer for every 25 men, whereas the German ratio was one-to-ten. Grandi's prudent peacetime mentality rebelled at Cadorna's proposal to add another 7500 officers to the army, and in mid-August he rejected it on the grounds that it would cost 32 million lire a year – an 'intolerable burden' – and would have adverse effects on the long-term career structure of the officer corps.[21]

Cadorna's politico–strategic logic demanded a full and rapid Italian mobilisation. Grandi regarded the militia, which amalgamated with conscripts and reserves to make up each wartime corps, as useless. Without them, however, Italy could field only 380 000 men.[22] During the second half of August he proposed three novel alternatives to full mobilisation: mobilising only a limited number of corps, inducting only the younger class of reservists, and mobilising the whole army but halting it in the Po Valley. No plans existed to carry out the first option; the second was impracticable, because the older reservists manned vital service-units; and the Transport Office pointed out on 24 August that the third would take 35 days, twelve days longer than it would take to mobilise on the north-eastern frontier, as well as requiring a further 20 days to shift forward to the Veneto.[23]

Had Grandi not been in a position as war minister to undercut the chief of staff by presenting rival proposals, or had he chosen to back Cadorna, the politicians would have had to confront the military argument for early intervention more directly. Their decision would probably have remained unchanged, but a united military front would have altered the nature of the debate. The structure of Italian military authority prevented this from happening. Cadorna, who feared that the Central Powers were going to win the war and then fall on Italy, believed she should attack Austria while she still could, and pressed for immediate mobilisation on 23, 27 and 28 August. Grandi's opposition made it easier for Salandra to cleave to his political line, and relations between the war minister and the chief of staff began to deteriorate rapidly. Even more annoyed at Grandi's caution, Cadorna swung to the other extreme, like other Italian generals before him. 'In politics and in war (which have many points in common)', he noted after one meeting with Grandi, 'one can rarely make a sure move and often it is prudent to be extremely daring'.[24]

One of Cadorna's concerns was that the army could not fight a winter campaign in the mountains. He pointed out to Salandra on 13 August that, since mobilisation would take a month, it would have to be decreed at the start of September if Italy were to fight at all that year. By the end of August he faced the possibility of a winter campaign due to the delays, and pressed Grandi to equip all first-line troops for it. Grandi replied loftily on 6 September that if Italy entered the field before the end of October – which looked unlikely – he would issue orders to carry out a limited scheme, which Pollio had already established. He asked the chief of staff for detailed plans for his project, which would be presented to the cabinet at a time of Grandi's own choosing. Cadorna grew increasingly exasperated.[25]

As well as arguing with the politicians over whether to fight and therefore whether to mobilise, Cadorna also had to decide where to fight. Meeting with Salandra, Di San Giuliano and Grandi on 19 August, he learned the government's desire to possess the Trentino and Trieste by the time of the peace. However, without the necessary siege park, he regarded attacking them as impossible. Securing possession of these territories meant, he felt, defeating the Austro-Hungarian empire at its heart with the support of allies. By 1 September he had drawn up the outline of his strategy: a main attack from Friuli across the Isonzo, a defensive around the Trentino wedge and secondary offensives on Toblach and into Carinthia. He had departed from his predecessors' defensive strategies and had made the fateful decision not to seal off the Trentino before moving north-east. Whether it was within Italy's military capacity to carry out this plan never seems to have concerned the chief of staff.

After a month of fighting, the outlook of the war changed drastically.

The Germans defeated the Russians at Tannenburg on 26–30 August, easing the pressure on the Austrians and thereby closing a window of opportunity for Italy. Then, on 6 September, von Moltke's race to encircle the Anglo-French armies was checked at the battle of the Marne. Militarily, any opportunity to throw Italy's weight on to one side of the balance and win a brief war had now gone. Diplomatically, the Marne altered Salandra's estimate of the likelihood of a victory by the Central Powers and focused policy yet more firmly on diplomatic negotiation.[26] Cadorna tried to convince the king that Italy should act against Austria-Hungary while the balance was still beginning to swing in favour of the Entente:

> When it swings that way *decisively*, and our intervention appears useful to us, but not *to the others*, how will we be able to pretend that these others must compensate us?[27]

His policy was based on the political calculation that the defeat of Austria-Hungary and Germany would be advantageous for Italy. He also feared that the Central Powers might yet win, in which case Italy would suffer their revenge without hope of help.[28]

There was little chance that Cadorna's strategic arguments could affect the government's policy-line, for they ran counter to the views of the dying foreign minister. Di San Giuliano remained wedded to the necessity to secure agreements which met Italy's aspirations. He believed that these might come without the need to fight, and this view was supported by a mass of politicians and a large part of public opinion. War at this juncture was therefore out of the question, being both unpopular and unnecessary. Beyond that, the foreign minister still did not think that Italian arms would be enough to tip the balance decisively in favour of the Entente and believed that, for geographical reasons, their effect would be neither rapid nor substantial.[29]

In mid-September, under pressure from Sonnino to find out how quickly the army's deficiencies could be made up, Salandra met privately with the new head of logistical and administrative services, General Adolfo Tettoni, and learned the full extent of the shortage of artillery, officers, horses and winter clothing.[30] These revelations did no more than confirm the line of policy already agreed with Di San Giuliano. What worried the premier most was the political problem of asking the chamber for extra money at a time when neutralist sentiment was strong and after he had assured parliament in March that all deficits had been made up. In asking for more, Salandra warned Grandi on 16 September, the government would have to have a justification. The war minister replied that the document submitted by his ministry and discussed by the cabinet in March 1914 had stated that, on 1 January, mobilisation equipment had been restored to what it had been before the outbreak of the Libyan war. The premier had told parliament that the military magazines were furnished with their normal stocks. The fault was not his at all. The premier had misled the public.[31]

This letter enraged Salandra and sealed the war minister's fate. Salandra reminded Grandi that when the government statement had been read out word-for-word to the cabinet he had not given any indication that he opposed it. He demanded to know what the deficiency had been on 1 April 1914, what it would be at the end of the current month and what would be necessary to put it right.[32] Salandra's concern was not that military inefficiency forced neutrality upon Italy. He was looking to the inevitable political confrontation in the chamber of deputies, and how best to save his administration from the extremely serious and possibly fatal charge of deceiving the country.

Grandi had concealed the extent of Italy's military deficiencies for two months, but on 24 September he was forced to acknowledge to Cadorna that there were insufficient clothes and equipment to mount a winter campaign. No military action could now be taken before March 1915, as Cadorna angrily recognised.[33] At the eleventh hour, Di San Giuliano began to realise the significance of early military action. From Paris Tittoni warned that Italy must not be seen by world opinion as being for sale to the highest bidder; and from St Petersburg Carlotti urged that Italy enter the war as soon as possible, since the Entente had indicated that it would help only those powers which helped it in useful time and would reward them in proportion to their work for the common goal.

Belatedly affected by considerations that had weighed in Cadorna's mind for almost two months, the foreign minister suggested on 29 September that 'if our military conditions permit it' Italy should speed up the signing of an agreement with London and concentrate all her forces to ensure the best possible circumstances in which to gain her natural borders.[34] This policy had no future. For one thing, the army would not now be in a position to fight until the spring; and in any case London would not negotiate until Italy came off the fence.

In a letter to the king at the end of September Salandra made it plain that he did not regard Grandi as up to his job, and within a few days he was gone. As his successor Salandra selected General Vittorio Zupelli, the deputy chief of staff. The new minister could be guaranteed to work well with the chief of staff, reversing the traditional pattern of separation and ministerial predominance. He also soon struck up a harmonious relationship with the Treasury minister, Carcano. For the first time in war, minister and chief of staff worked in unison together.

On 11 October, the day he took up his new office, Zupelli laid before the premier a detailed programme by which to profit from the five-and-a-half months before the army could take the field. The training of the reservists was to be improved, administrative offices to be swept for officers to put into active units, courses at the military schools enlarged and accelerated, the militia improved and equipment expanded.[35] Zupelli's industry contrasted markedly with Grandi's lethargy. To make use of the time available to him, he was given money: 600 million lire in October and November, and a further 340 million between January and May 1915. By 1 December 1914, Zupelli expected to be able to mobilise 1 404 000 men the following spring.[36]

On 16 October Di San Giuliano died. Salandra temporarily took over the reins of the foreign ministry, unwisely coining the phrase *Sacro egoismo* (sacred egoism) in the process, before passing the foreign affairs portfolio to Sonnino. The new foreign minister was troubled by the military question:

> *Can* we enter the war at once, given our military deficiencies? Or are they so grave as to rule this out entirely for the time being, unless we are forced into war by external attack? What do the soldiers say?[37]

The soldiers said that Italy could not enter the war until the coming spring; and within days of taking office Sonnino started the process of negotiating with London, Berlin and Vienna which would last until April 1915.

On 4 December the storm Salandra had been expecting finally burst when Colajanni brought before the newly recalled chamber of deputies charges of ministerial deception over the army's readiness for war. Salandra deflected criticism of his own regime on to his predecessor, Giolitti. With enough ammunition from Zupelli to withstand the onslaught of his critics, he faced down the attack by inviting his opponents to try to topple the government on the question if they wished. A final attempt to embarrass and perhaps unseat Salandra by putting Spingardi up to speak in the senate on 15 December failed when the premier intervened to quash the debate. That same day Salandra and Sonnino were told by Cadorna and Zupelli that the army would not now be ready to take the field until the following April.

As Cadorna readied the army for war, he received an important report from Berlin setting out in detail the thoughts of Falkenhayn, his German counterpart. The chief of the German general staff intended to adopt a strategy of attrition, and likened the current battle with the Entente to a gladiatorial duel:

> decisive attacks at the beginning of the battle have no chance of succeeding because the adversary is still fresh, and therefore it is inappropriate to try them; it is necessary that the combatants first tire one another out, because only then will an all-out attack succeed.[38]

For the time being France was able to defend herself with simple barbed-wire entanglements but the moment would come when one of the two contestants felt itself stronger than the other, and then things would move rapidly to a conclusion. While Falkenhayn believed that the Germans had stronger nerves than the French, he admitted that to continue the massive frontal assaults which had been a feature of the first months of the war would be an absurd waste of human life. This dispatch should have given Cadorna pause, for if the mighty German army could not launch successful strategic strikes, then neither could the Italians. It did not.

By 21 December the chief of the Italian general staff had planned his campaign against Austria-Hungary. It rested on the assumption that the situation Falkenhayn had described was unique. Cadorna expected the first major battle to take place within a fortnight after the start of operations and two or three days' march inside the Austrian frontier, to be followed by a second great battle at twice that distance within 45 days. This would bring Italian troops to the Lubljana plain, from where they would launch a drive on Vienna.[39] Already military planning was showing signs of a dangerous narrowness of vision: cutting the wedge of the Trentino, a vital operation, was given only secondary importance and the difficulties of the terrain were not taken sufficiently into account. Also both services rejected out-of-hand the idea of an amphibious landing to support an attack on Trieste.[40]

Whether Italy would enter the war against Austria at all was still an open question. There was certainly more to be gained from intervention on the Allied side in the shape of the Trentino, the Alto Adige, the Isonzo frontier, Trieste, Istria, the Dalmatian coast, Albania, the Dodecanese and a share of the Turkish empire; and these potential gains looked the more enticing after 11 December, when the Austrian foreign minister indicated to Avarna that he was entirely unwilling to discuss the application of clause VII of the Triple Alliance, which enshrined the principle of compensation.[41] On the other hand, negotiations with Britain had stalled over Italy's refusal to commit herself to the war in advance of territorial agreements and Britain's refusal to make agreements in advance of Italian commitment. In addition, Salandra and Sonnino had to contend with the widespread feeling that Italy's aims might be achieved without her having to enter the war at all. This belief was given considerable encouragement when Prince von Bülow arrived in Rome in mid-December and began tempting Italy with half-promises of Fiume and the Trentino.[42]

The year ended with Italy facing trouble in Libya in addition to her European dilemma. In July 1914 rebellion had broken out in three areas of Tripolitania and by November general insurrection was spreading rapidly. Cadorna refused to allow North Africa to draw any forces from Europe, and the local commanders were therefore forced to withdraw to the coast. Although under considerable pressure from the colonial minister, De Martini, Cadorna stuck to his guns. By August 1915 the Italians were once more besieged in Tripoli, Homs and Zuara. It would take Graziani three years, from 1922 to 1925, to subdue Tripolitania and not until 1932 did he conquer the Senussi and pacify Cyrenaica.[43]

The New Year began with a revelation for Sonnino. At a cabinet meeting on 26 January Zupelli announced that the army would not now be ready to take the field until mid-April, and refused to advance the date despite the foreign minister's attempts to force him to accept a distinction between *pronti* ('ready') and *prontissimi* ('absolutely ready').[44] During the opening weeks of the year the timing of Italian military intervention was not a significant issue, as negotiations with Germany moved slowly forward and it became gradually apparent that Vienna would not give up the Trentino. However, by the end of February Sonnino had learned of the Allies' intention to attack the Dardanelles. If Italy joined the Entente before the Allies defeated Turkey her intervention would be perceived more favourably than if she did so afterwards. The foreign minister was now told that the date when the army would be ready had been put back to the end of April.[45] Nevertheless, with Vienna viewing the military situation as entirely favourable the Entente looked a more likely bet to assuage Italy's appetite. Accordingly on 4 March the Italian ambassador read out to Sir Edward Grey Italy's list of territorial demands.

Partnership with Italy attracted Grey, who believed it would help win over the Balkan neutrals. It became even more attractive after the Royal Navy's attempt to force the Narrows failed on 18 March. A major landing was now necessary, and the addition of Italy to the Entente would help ensure a diplomatic success; on 22 March Grey believed it would be 'the turning point of the war'.[46] By the end of the month he was prepared to push Russia to accept neutralisation of the eastern Adriatic coastline and Italian possession of the off-shore islands. At the same time Vienna, which had steadfastly refused to discuss ceding any territory to Italy until the war was over, reversed her position and indicated that she was prepared to hand over Trento and the southern Tyrol. Suddenly Sonnino was dealing with both sides at once.

Cadorna had learned from Grandi at the end of August 1914 of Italian diplomatic contacts with London, and on 10 March 1915 Salandra told him that negotiations with Austria had failed to produce adequate territorial compensation, and therefore war was approaching.[47] Making the army materially ready for war was Zupelli's task. Devising a strategy was Cadorna's. Unshakeable self-confidence and mental rigidity combined to shut his eyes to the possibility that it might be operationally impossible to carry out his planned drive to the heart of the Austro-Hungarian empire if the trench warfare of the western front were replicated in the north-eastern theatre.

Evidence existed which ought to have given the chief of staff pause. Offensive warfare in mountainous regions was extremely difficult; the pre-war staff rides had all pointed this out, and Cadorna himself had vociferously opposed Pollio's pre-war strategy of attacking across the French Alps. The Italian army badly lacked the necessary heavy artillery, and Cadorna knew it. Finally there was the evidence of the western front. Reports from the Italian military attaché in France in December 1914 and February 1915 stressed the heavy losses suffered by both sides, especially the attacker, the high rates of ammunition-consumption and the apparent impossibility of reaching a decision in current circumstances.[48] And from the military attaché in Germany Cadorna received an outstanding analysis of the new *guerra di posizione*.

Italians had had some experience of static warfare in Libya, but Colonel Bongiovanni warned Cadorna against using this as a basis for future action since it had lacked the dominant element of trench warfare – enemy artillery-fire. Also Italian trenches 'never had opposite them any enemy defensive organisation and therefore did not serve as bases for offensive action aimed at overcoming enemy resistance'.[49] After describing in detail the paraphernalia of trench warfare, Colonel Bongiovanni defined for Cadorna the central problem of static warfare:

An attack, provided that it is carefully prepared and well conducted, can carry the fire zone between the point of departure and the enemy's line without excessive losses; the really great difficulty is the barbed wire entanglement. If it is thick, deep and defended by riflemen well supplied with ammunition, it is an almost insuperable obstacle.[50]

His report recommended that the army be equipped with the right artillery if it was to perform successfully in the new environment of war and pointed out that vast quantities of munitions would be necessary. Cadorna took no notice whatever of these observations, assuming that the same conditions would not apply on the Italo-Austrian front.

In mid-April, with diplomatic negotiations failing, the German military tried a last-ditch attempt to sway Italy. Falkenhayn harrangued the Italian military attaché at some length, making it quite clear that if Italy went to war with Austria-Hungary Germany would side against her. Germany had given up the idea of a great offensive in France:

It will be more effective to resist the tenacious Anglo–French attacks, which will never succeed in dislodging us from our defensive positions, and content ourselves with the favourable situation we are now in.[51]

The war in the east would also quickly turn into a stalemate. Italian intervention could not have the decisive results its politicians expected:

Given the strength of the defensive, the modern method of war, and the nature of the terrain on the Italo–German frontier, the Italian army [will] be stuck for a long time in the mountains and in any case before it could reach Vienna or Budapest it would find German troops barring its way.[52]

Had Cadorna been as far-sighted, he would have had grounds to try to temper civilian appetites. Since he was not, sheer military practicability was never an issue in Italy's move from neutrality to intervention. In any case, Italian diplomats were receiving different signals: the Hungarian premier, Count Tisza, believed that if Italy joined the Entente she had 'a great chance of changing the result'.[53]

On 26 April, one day after the Allies had landed at Gallipoli, Italy made terms with the Entente. In return for the Brenner frontier, Trieste and Istria, the line of the Julian Alps, central Dalmatia, Valona, the Curzolari islands and the Dodecanese she bound herself to take the field in a month. The military gave every appearance of being both ready and sublimely confident. At the beginning of April Cadorna had boasted that he would be in Trieste and threatening the heart of the Austro-Hungarian Empire a month after the fighting began. On the 21st Zupelli announced that a million men could be sent to the front. And four days after the Treaty of London was signed the chief of staff told Sonnino that the army corps on the Friuli frontier would be ready to move by 12 May.[54]

The German army made a last-minute attempt to frighten Italy into preserving her neutrality. On 1 May the Italian military attaché in Berlin was deliberately allowed to catch sight of two letters written by von Hindenburg. In the first the victor of Tannenburg announced that he would command the army destined to fight Italy; and in the second he expressed Germany's utter contempt for her possible opponent – 'up to now', he wrote, 'others have had to finish their job for them'.[55] Four days later Conrad, who had always held that purchasing Italian neutrality was 'entirely impossible', changed his mind and accepted that 'war with Italy must be unconditionally avoided'.[56] A last-minute offer from von Bülow included the Trentino, but Sonnino realised that things had gone too far for it to be accepted.

Cadorna learned by chance on 5 May that Italy was pledged to enter the war by 26 May, one month after the signing of the Treaty of London. The cabinet was told two days later. Sonnino had every right to expect that, over the winter and spring, the armed forces had readied themselves. However, the final steps to war illuminated all the deficiencies of Italian military policy-making. For one thing, the army was not fully ready: stationing troops on the eastern frontier over the winter destroyed the mobilisation plan, so than when the troop-trains began to roll on 4 May it took 48 days to array the army on the front and not the 23 days the staff envisaged. The poor quality of Italian staff-work was starkly illustrated.

The concentric strategy with which Cadorna proposed to defeat the Austro-Hungarians depended upon linking up with the Russians, the Serbians and perhaps even the Rumanians, who might be tempted to join in dismembering the empire. Carefully concerted action was therefore essential, but negotiations with Russia were conducted far too slowly, and when a military convention betwen the two powers was signed on 21 May it came too late. There was no co-ordination with Serbia or Rumania at all. The Russian armies were defeated at Gorlice on 4 May and began streaming east, pursued by the Austrians. By September Russia had abandoned Galicia, Poland, Courland and Lithuania. The campaign cost her 850 000 casualties and 900 000 prisoners. It also cost Italy any chance of strategic success.

Italian strategy presupposed a successful Russia. It also relied on the psychological impact of allied success at Gallipoli. Seven days after the landing, it appeared to an Italian observer that it might succeed; after a fortnight the allies' failure was all too obvious.[57] At one level it would be easy to blame Italy's subsequent misfortunes on bad luck. But a strategy which stands or falls on the success of third parties without an intrinsic chance of success is a poor strategy. Italy did not mistime her entry into the world war – she miscalculated it. This happened in part because Cadorna did not explain his strategic presuppositions to the politicians and they never bothered to explore them.

The non-appearance of Balkan armies in the field removed one of the two preconditions upon which all prewar Italian plans for offensive war against Austria-Hungary had been based. Cadorna himself did away with the other. Instead of cutting off the Trentino wedge as a preliminary to the main offensive, he launched the Italian armies straight across the Isonzo. The half-hearted optimism of Victor Emmanuel's Order of the Day, published on 27 May, was a tacit acknowledgement of the difficulty of the task:

> Favoured by the terrain and by careful preparations, they [the Austrians] will put up a tough resistance, but your unquenchable dash will, without doubt, overcome them.[58]

Cadorna's amazing strategic vision of a march on Vienna, and his complete disregard of the realities of trench warfare, were the product of a unique personality in a position of unquestioned and unquestionable authority. No group existed to challenge his assumptions and no doctrine had been established through which to assess them. The Italian general staff, unlike its German counterpart, was a small bureaucratic secretariat whose skills and training were narrowly functional. Neither it nor the army at large had been exposed to Clausewitz's ideas; Italy would have to wait until 1942 for its first full translation of *On War*.[59] Thus the intellectual framework within which strategy was devised lacked a broad operational-political perspective. Instead, war-planning was generally conceived in defensive terms and conducted on technical and financial levels. Cadorna's scheme met no institutional or intellectual obstruction. Its boldness and daring sounded a chord which appealed to military ears. With little choice but to follow him, and little inclination not to, the army was led by its suspicious, authoritarian and brutal master into a campaign which almost broke it.

10 Conclusion

During the course of the nineteenth century the role of the Italian army underwent great changes. Prior to 1848 it was the prop of Piedmontese absolutism; its tasks were to suppress internal dissent and to defend the realm against external aggression to the best of its limited capabilities. Between 1848 and 1866 it was called upon to wage aggressive war to extend the kingdom, and in the course of the Risorgimento its complexion underwent a radical alteration. After 1866 it had a four-fold mission: to oversee external defence, fight oversea wars, foster *Italianità* and support the civil power. Three of those roles were new; the fourth, a traditional task, had to be carried out in novel social and political circumstances.

To meet all these demands successfully required of the army flexibility, open-mindedness and a wider competence than had previously sufficed. Such qualities were never evolved. Instead, by the end of the wars of the Risorgimento the army had struck a stance which thereafter remained unaltered. Politically it was the servant of the state but regarded the crown as its true master. Professionally it bore old-fashioned Piedmontese attitudes into the twentieth century. Socially it mistrusted the Italian masses as volatile and unreliable.

External defence posed great problems, both geographical and political. Vulnerability along hundreds of miles of exposed coastline was matched by land frontiers which were difficult to defend and across which attack was awkward. Most of the major cities were within easy reach of any of Italy's potential enemies. On land Italy confronted two major powers; at sea she faced three. In this situation the army chose fortification as the basis of its policy for national defence. Military analysis and military prejudice dictated its choice. Fortifications compensated for the backward state of Italy's railways. They conformed with the defensive cast of the Piedmontese military mind. They corresponded to Italy's position as the weakest of the European Great Powers. And they offered the only sure way to give Italian diplomats freedom of action. Vulnerability demanded security and masonry was deemed more reliable than manpower.

In selecting and sticking to a policy of fortification, the army neglected the problems of obsolescence and cost. Despite the artillery revolution of the late nineteenth century, which necessitated redesigning fixed defences and raised questions about their value for money, large sums

171

were spent and larger ones requested. Without the records it is impossible to say where all this money went. Pareto thought much of it was never spent on defence at all, and in 1915 he accused Giolitti of milking the military budget to win elections. However, since the majority of soldiers were such enthusiastic fortifiers, most was probably spent as earmarked.[1] And some of the extraordinary allocation was certainly hoarded against a day when the government might be less forthcoming.[2]

Overseas war was an intermittent activity for which the army was entirely unsuited. A conscript army lacked the hardihood, experience and professionalism which were necessary to tackle colonial wars. The Italian officer corps, unlike its French or British counterparts, was not trained to fight foreign wars; and skill and commitment to overseas warfare did not open up a career-path to rapid advancement or high rank. The army fought poorly overseas because it lacked expertise, flexibility and a thorough knowledge of its opponents. Instead it took abroad an exaggerated sense of European superiority, which it could maintain against Arabs and Ethiopians but not against its likely European foes.

Unlike the French army, the Italian army had no tradition of the officer as priest or schoolmaster to shape its attitude to the task of fostering *Italianità*. Nor was the task a simple one: the army was required to give conscripts military training, inculcate patriotism and remedy high rates of illiteracy. The military were ill at ease with the new conscript force. It violated their preference for quality over quantity; its record in 1866 was not such as to inspire confidence in its military worth; and it necessitated a partnership with the people at large, in whom few in authority had any confidence. As late as 1907, Victor Emmanuel III remarked that his people still had 'to be educated, to be taught habits of discipline, obedience and orderliness' and that they had yet to learn what 'patriotism, in the broad national sense, means'.[3] The army performed its task reluctantly, though with some success as far as remedying illiteracy-rates was concerned, but found another ground for dissatisfaction with the state for not using the school-system efficiently.[4]

From 1860 until the outbreak of world war, the task of supporting the civil power grew ever larger and more awkward. It increased in geographical extent and in volume; and after the 1890s it changed in character with the rise of rural and urban socialism. The need to provide local security was the reason for scattering garrisons around Italy, which hindered rapid concentration in wartime. By the turn of the century the army leadership was unhappy with this task and critical of the government for its failure to provide a civil alternative and for its unimaginative use of the *carabinieri*, as well as for pursuing policies which made confrontation inevitable.[5] Involvement in civil order affected the army in three ways: it was professionally deleterious; it increased the army's resentment towards the government; and it contributed to the unpopularity of the military in society.

All four roles had to be performed within a framework of civil–military relations which facilitated discord and discontent. The civilians were repeatedly and scathingly dismissive of their army: Giolitti remarked in May 1915 that

> the generals are worth little; they came out of the ranks at a time when families sent their most stupid sons into the army because they did not know what to do with them.[6]

Although the military record was undeniably poor, the politicians failed to acknowledge that this was not entirely the army's fault. Ministers regarded the army as merely a tool of politics without recognising that military success requires collaborative partnership. In particular, civilian politicians never saw the army as having what Huntington has termed an 'advisory function': that of reporting on the military implications of different courses of state action.[7]

The army held its political masters equally at arm's-length. Mezzacapo, Primerano and Saletta belonged to the majority of generals who saw the state as a milch-cow which ought to provide whatever they needed. Ricotti was in a distinct minority in taking the opposite view, that military policy should be based on what the country could afford. In practice the soldiers accepted what they were given, which was generally very much less than they wanted; and the gap between their desires and their allocations is another index of the distance between the army and the political world.

Betwixt army and politicians stood the crown. Outwardly the house of Savoy was uncompromisingly military. Its monarchs received a military education and generally appeared in uniform; princes of the blood occupied very senior positions in both army and navy; and the king was often closely involved in selection for the highest ranks and offices. Yet, like Nicholas II of Russia, both Umberto and Victor Emmanuel III seem mainly to have been concerned with externals, not basic issues. In September 1911 Victor Emmanuel was disinclined to travel to Naples and see his troops off to the Libyan war, but he was sufficiently worried about appearances not to want people to say that he preferred to enjoy the countryside while his soldiers set off to fight.[8] As long as the royal archives remain closed the influence and actions of the crown in military matters are difficult to trace; but the impression which remains is of style not substance, of involvement driven by the need to justify or maintain royal existence rather than by professional commitment.

The crown's powers were limited. The king could appeal to concepts of duty to prevent a war minister from resigning or asking for more money; he could not use that same authority to prevent generals from underbidding one another to get control of the war ministry. Royal support does not seem to have been a weapon of much value in the army's battles with the Treasury or the Interior Ministry. The king could have acted creatively in military affairs: the constitution made him a bridge between soldiers and politicians, and skillful use of that position might have brought the two sides together and produced habits of communication and consideration which both so conspicuously lacked. Instead he used the army as a tool to support royal conservatism.

The manipulative interest of the house of Savoy put soldiers in parliament as deputies, senators and ministers. This exposed differences and exacerbated civil-military tensions without producing any corresponding benefit. The high command was fractured as generals jockeyed for office; and the army as a whole developed a dislike and distrust of civilian politicians and a wish to retreat from the political arena. 'If you walk with a cripple, you learn to limp', proclaimed one newspaper, campaigning against putting soldiers into parliament at all.[9] The coils of parliamentary procedure irritated the soldiers, its cheeseparing exasperated them. Perhaps most annoying of all was its obstruction of internal military reform. In May 1883 a law on promotion which had wrestled its way through the chamber of deputies went to the senate for discussion and approval. Two years later there was still no sign of it. The senator charged with reporting on it, Luigi Mezzacapo, had died and with him had apparently perished all memory of it.[10]

The army planned conscientiously to defend the state to the best of its capacity. That capacity was limited not simply by Italy's geo-strategical position but also by the extent to which naval weakness impinged upon military activity: as long as the Austrian fleet lay at Pola and the Italian fleet at Taranto, the Italian navy could not prevent Austrian ships from firing on troop-trains running near the coast. Planning was also based on assumptions about the volatility of the populace, a factor which was interpreted as meaning that Italy could not afford to lose the opening battles in a war. These same assumptions, translated into manpower terms, explain why the planners chose to spend their money on forts rather than railways. They can also be seen influencing the search for a tactical doctrine.[11] The plan to send III Army to the Rhine contrasts strongly with a general strategic timorousness. How deeply the army was committed to it remains an open question.

In the last resort, the skill and success with which the officer corps handled its many tasks depended upon the depth of its professionalism. Natural weaknesses, such as the small pool of middle classes from which to draw potential officers, were exacerbated by policy choices. Commissioning from the ranks produced a layered profile like that of the Russian and French armies, with adverse effects. The army high command generally did not concern itself with improving morale and fostering cohesion and competence. The subordinate role allotted to the chief of general staff closed off another avenue to greater professionalism. No general staff *mentalité* percolated through the officer corps; instead the staff remained a small, closed corps envied for its privileges and disliked for its influence.

The professionalism of the army was further damaged by widespread suspicion that the small cohort of senior officers ran things in their own interests, manipulating pay, promotions and retirements. The army of Liberal Italy, unlike its Fascist successor, was not notably top-heavy: in 1907 there were 141 generals in an officer corps which totalled 13 703. In the same year approximately two-ninths of the ordinary budget went to pay officers' salaries. Rates of pay compared favourably with every major western European army save that of Germany; but rates of pay alone are not a very precise guide to an officer's financial standing.[12] Senior officers certainly gave the appearance of manipulating the system: the number of lieutenant-generals (the highest rank in the peacetime army) who could serve until aged 68 was originally 15, then rose to 19, and in 1911 it was proposed to increase it to 24 almost half the total number in the grade. Duelling, concerning which there was one law for very senior officers and another more draconian one for everybody else, was one of many matters in which the top levels of the officer corps expected to behave differently from those they commanded.

Finally, the sheer inertia of military bureaucracy weakened the officer corps and the army. The slow pace at which Saletta conducted the debate over fortification with Ottolenghi and his successors has already been noted. It is not an isolated case: in March 1874 a preliminary request went to all fortress-commanders asking for detailed plans for the defence of their commands in the event of a general war or a local siege. It was still unanswered fifteen months later.[13] In this respect the army certainly seems to have been a reflection of the state; but if it was bound in red tape, that was partly its own fault.

The army entered the post-Risorgimento world bedecked with attitudes appropriate to a narrower and more restricted age. In becoming the *Esercito italiano* it was forced to adapt its structure and change its role in ways which were not entirely congenial. By the eve of the First World War it was distanced from society and state alike. Exasperated by parliament, annoyed by politicians, held at arm's length by diplomats and statesmen, the target of bitter hostility from the Left, its only anchor in an uncertain world was its loyalty to the house of Piedmont. The experience of war coloured its attitude yet further, and much happened before the army high command offered its tacit support to Mussolini on the night of 27/28 October 1922. But underlying those events was a mental attitude towards both state and society, and a perception of what the army was entitled to have and ought to be asked to do, which made the choice a logical one. Giolitti's captains became Mussolini's generals. They brought with them an institutional outlook which lived on in the army of Fascist Italy.

Notes and References

ABBREVIATIONS

AA. VV. Autori Vari
ACS   Archivio Centrale di Stato
AP   Atti Parlamentari
b.   busta
DDF   Documents diplomatiques français
DDI   Documenti diplomatici italiani
Fasc.   Fascicolo
F.O.   Foreign Office
ISR   Istituto per la Storia del Risorgimento
P.R.O.   Public Record Office
racc.   raccoglitore
SME   Ufficio Storico dello State Maggiore dell'Esercito
T.   Telegramme
USM   Ufficio Storico della Marina Militare

INTRODUCTION

1. There exist only two general histories in English: Charles Martel (pseud. of C. àC. Repington), *Military Italy*, London, 1884; John Whittam, *The Politics of the Italian Army*, London, 1977.
2. For example, Giorgio Rochat, 'L'esercito italiano nell'estate 1914', *Nuova Rivista Storica*, 45, 1961, pp. 299–300.
3. Giorgio Rochat and Guilio Massobrio, *Breve storia dell'esercito italiano dal 1861 al 1943*, Turin, 1978, p. 140.
4. Ibid., pp. 167–8.
5. Carlo De Biase, *Aquila d'Oro-Storia dello Stato Maggiore Italiano (1861– 1945)*, Milan, 1969, pp. 271–3; Rochat and Massobrio, p. 166.
6. Piero Visani, 'I rapporti fra militari e politici dal 1861 ad oggi', *Politica militare*, IV, April–May 1982, p. 23; Filippo Stefani, *La storia della dottrina e degli ordinamenti dell'esercito italiano*, I, Rome, 1984, p. 313.
7. William C. Fuller, Jr, *Civil-Military Conflict in Imperial Russia 1881–1914*, Princeton, 1985, p. 3.
8. Samuel P. Huntington, *The Soldier and the State*, Harvard, 1957, p. 96.
9. The 'amoral familism' of the southern peasant is graphically described in Edward C. Banfield, *The Moral Basis of a Backward Society*, Glencoe, ILL., 1958.
10. Quo. H. Stuart Hughes, 'The Aftermath of the Risorgimento in Four Successive Interpretations', *American Historical Review*, LXI, 1955, p. 76.

1: THE ARMY AND THE RISORGIMENTO

1. Emilio de Bono, *Nell'esercito nostro prima della guerra*, Milan, 1931, p. 21.
2. Piero del Negro, *Esercito, stato, società*, Bologna, 1979, p. 63.

3. Piero Pieri, 'Il problema del reclutamento in Piemonte nel 1848–49', *Nuova Rivista Storica*, XXXII (1948), p. 269.

4. Ibid., pp. 273, 267.

5. Lucio Ceva, 'L'Alto Comando Militare (1848–1887)', *Nuova Antologia*, no. 2137 (1981), p. 220.

6. Piero Pieri, 'La guerra regia nella pianura padana', in E. Rota (ed.), *Il 1848 nella storia italiana ed europea*, Milan, 1948, vol. I, p. 169.

7. Carlo Pischedda, 'L'azione di Carlo Alberto nelle campagne del 1848–49', *Nuova Rivista Storica*, XXXI (1947), p. 134; Piero Pieri, *Storia militare del Risorgimento*, Turin, 1962, pp. 388–9.

8. Carlo Alberto to Franzini, 28 June 1848. Quo. Pischedda, p. 128.

9. Pieri, 'Il problema del reclutamento', pp. 271–2.

10. Pischedda, p. 146.

11. Giorgio Candeloro, *Storia dell'Italia moderna*, vol. III: *La rivoluzione nazionale*, Milan, 1960, p. 397.

12. Felice de Chaurand de Ste. Eustache, *Come l'esercito italiano entrò in guerra*, Milan, 1929, p. 125.

13. Paul Ginsborg, *Daniele Manin and the Venetian Revolution of 1848–49*, Cambridge, 1979, pp. 195–7.

14. Del Negro, pp. 57–8.

15. Ibid., p. 129.

16. Bernardino Farolfi, 'Dall'antropometria militare alla storia del corpo', *Quaderni storici*, XLII (1979), pp. 1067–8.

17. Only sons, first-born sons of widowed mothers and those with a brother in the service were among those exempt. Article 78 permitted the invaliding out of those with specific infirmities, physical or mental defects, or those who stood less than 1m 54 (5 feet) in height. By way of comparison, the minimum height for recruits in the British army was 5' 8" in 1861 and 5' 3" in 1900.

18. Farolfi, pp. 1070–3.

19. Raymond Grew, *A Sterner Plan for Unity: The Italian National Society in the Risorgimento*, Princeton, 1963, pp. 173–5, 178.

20. Massimo Mazzetti, 'Dagli eserciti pre-unitari all'esercito italiano', *Rassegna storica del Risorgimento*, LIX (1972), p. 565.

21. Pieri, *Storia militare del Risorgimento*, pp. 615–19.

22. Del Negro, pp. 93–4.

23. Carlo Corsi, *1844–1869: venticinque anni in Italia*, Florence, 1870, vol. II, p. 13.

24. Mazzetti, p. 570.

25. Amadeo Tosti, *Storia dell'esercito italiano (1861–1936)*, Milan, 1942, p. 46.

26. Cavour to Nigra, 24 April 1860. Quo. Francesco Bogliari and Carlo Traversi, *Manfredo Fanti*, Rome, 1980, p. 40.

27. Mazzetti, p. 572, fn. 3.

28. Ibid., pp. 571–2.

29. Piero Pieri, *Le forze armate nella età della destra*, Milan, 1962, p. 56; Giorgio Rochat and Giulio Massobrio, *Breve storia dell'esercito italiano dal 1861 al 1943*, Turin, 1978, p. 27.

30. W.R. Thayer, *The Life and Times of Cavour*, New York, 1971 (1st edition 1911), vol. II, p. 461.

31. Mazzetti, pp. 578–9.
32. Carlo De Biase, *L'Aquila d'Oro – Storia dello stato maggiore italiano (1861–1945)*, Milan, 1969, p. 36.
33. Pieri, *Le forze armate*, p. 366.
34. Garibaldi to Cavour, 18 May 1861. Quo. Thayer II, p. 482.
35. 'Il generale Govone e le condizioni sociali in Sicilia', *L'Esercito italiano*, 6 August 1902.
36. Luigi De Rosa, 'Incidenza delle spese militari sullo sviluppo economico italiano', *Atti del primo convegno nazionale di storia militare*, Rome, 1969, p. 212. For slightly different figures, see Rochat and Massobrio, p. 71.
37. Mazzetti, p. 379.
38. Rochat and Massobrio, p. 46; Del Negro, p. 190.
39. ISR. Cosenz to Giovanni Cadolini, 6 August 1897. B. 263, n. 79.
40. De Biase, p. 53.
41. Quo. John Whittam, *The Politics of the Italian Army*, London, 1977, p. 99.
42. De Bono, p. 85.
43. Mazzetti, p. 583.
44. De Biase, p. 69.
45. Massimo Mazzetti, 'Enrico Cosenz, scrittore militare', *Il pensiero di studiosi di cose militari meridionali: Atti del congresso nazionale*, Rome, 1978, pp. 101–2.
46. Caselli to Mezzacapo, 9 February 1867. Quo. Ugo Pesci, *Il generale Carlo Mezzacapo e il suo tempo*, Bologna 1908, p. 182.

2: A POLICY FOR DEFENCE

1. Federico Chabod, *Storia della politica estera italiana dal 1870 al 1896*, Bari, 1962, pp. 8, 114, 331, 336, 394–5, 568, 655.
2. De Ste. Eustache. p. 15; De Biase, pp. 102–3; Alessio Chapperon, *L'Organica militare fra le due guerre mondiali, 1814–1914*, Turin, 1920, pp. 463–4.
3. Chabod, p. 394, fn. 3.
4. Nigra to Visconti Venosta, 17 May 1875. Quo. ibid., p. 549, fn. 1.
5. 'Dello spirito militare in Italia', *Rivista militare italiana*, February 1886, p. 287.
6. Vincenzo Gallinari, 'Le riforme militare di Cesare Ricotti', *Memorie storiche militari*, 1978, p. 18.
7. AP. 17 June 1871, p. 3009.
8. AP. 30 May 1873, p. 6824.
9. PRO. Paget to Derby, 24 May 1875. F.O. 45/261.
10. AP. 16 June 1871, p. 2986; 20 June 1871, p. 3104.
11. F. Minnitti, 'Esercito e politica da Porta Pia alla Triplice Alleanza (I)', *Storia contemporanea*, III, 1972, p. 478.
12. Niccola Marselli, *Gli avvenimenti del 1870–1871*, Turin, 1873 (1st edition 1872), vol. I, p. 141.
13. Ibid., I, p. 144.
14. Del Negro, pp. 198–9, 255–7.

15. De Bono, pp. 355–6, 360–1. PRO. Herries to Derby, 4 June 1874. F.O. 45/240.
16. Minnitti (I), pp. 483–6.
17. SME. Rossi, 17 February, 16 March 1873, nos. 50, 60bis. *Addetti Militari: Parigi*, b. 1.
18. PRO. Paget to Granville, 25 March 1873. F.O. 45/217.
19. ACS. Carte Crispi-Roma. Difesa delle coste: studi della commissione mista, 1873, pp. 70, 81, 130. Fasc. 9.
20. SME. Studi sulla difesa attiva dell'Italia: Per S.E. Menabrea, Luog.te Generale: Primo studio – difesa contro la Francia, July 1873, p. 295. *Studi Tecnici G. 24*, racc. 178.
21. SME, Ipotesi di guerra prevedibili, 1874. *Comando del Corpo di Stato Maggiore G. 24*, b. 7.
22. SME. Mocenni, 9 February 1873, no. 23. *Addetti Militari: Berlino*, b. 23.
23. SME. Ricotti to Cialdini, 20 February 1874. *Comando del Corpo di Stato Maggiore G. 24*, racc. 49.
24. AP. 3 March 1874, p. 1982.
25. AP. 4 March 1874, pp. 1992–6, 1997–9, 2000–9.
26. AP. 7 March 1874, pp. 2092–6, 2098–2108.
27. Minnitti, 'Esercito e politica . . . (I)', p. 495. Army expenditure of the Great Powers in 1874, converted into lire, was as follows: Russia – 788 390 103; France – 719 929 753; Germany – 488 742 315; Great Britain – 378 418 040; Austria-Hungary – 254 983 593; Italy – 192 011 542. Chabod, p. 507, fn. 1.
28. No two sets of figures agree. For an excellent discussion of the difficulties facing the researcher wishing to sort out the ordinary and extraordinary budgets, see Rochat and Massobrio, pp. 74–5.
29. SME. Difesa Nord-Ovest Parte 1ᵃ, 18 November 1874, pp. 7, 9, 11–12. *Comando del Corpo di Stato Maggiore: Corrispondenza*, b. 48.
30. Ibid., p. 40; also p. 61.
31. SME. Difensiva Nord-Ovest Parte IIᵃ, 18 November 1874, pp. 7, 25. Ibid.
32. SME. Difensiva Nord-Ovest Parte IIIᵃ: Adunata strategica dell'esercito italiano presso Alessandria, 20 March 1875. *Comando del Corpo di Stato Maggiore: Corrispondenza*, b. 48.
33. SME. Difensiva Nord-Ovest, Parte IV G, 20 March 1875. Ibid.
34. SME. Difesa N.O. Parte VI: Difesa della zona alpina, 12 October 1875, pp. 2, 6. Ibid.
35. SME. Del Mayno, 2 August 1875, no. 43. *Addetti Militari: Berlino*, b. 27.
36. SME. Offensiva italiana contro Francia, Parte I, 6 March 1875, p. 2. *Comando del Corpo di Stato Maggiore: Corrispondenza*, b. 47.
37. SME. Promemoria circa la convenienza dell'impiego di una piuttòsto che dell'altra delle due linee Savojarde per il transito di un quinto corpo italiano d'invasione, 10 April 1875. *Comando del Corpo di Stato Maggiore: Corrispondenza*, b. 48.
38. SME. Ricotti to Segretario, Comitato di S.M.G., 18 April 1875. *Comando del Corpo di Stato Maggiore, G. 24*, racc. 49.
39. SME. Offensiva italiana contro Francia, Parte II, 9 July 1876, p. 23 (italics in original). *Comando del Corpo di Stato Maggiore: Corrispondenza*, b. 47.
40. SME. Ricotti to President, Corpo di S.M.G., 30 January 1876. *Comando del Corpo di Stato Maggiore, G. 24*, racc. 49.

41. SME. Relazione sullo studio di difesa della frontiera occidentale compilato dal Comando Generale di Torino, 17 February 1876. *Comando del Corpo di Stato Maggiore: Corrispondenza*, b. 48.

42. SME. Difensiva Nord-Est, 1875. *Comando del Corpo di Stato Maggiore*, G. 24, racc. 47.

43. F. Minnitti, 'Esercito e politica da Porta Pia alla Triplice Alleanza (II)', *Storia contemporanea*, IV, 1973, pp. 41–2.

44. PRO. Paget to Derby, 27 March 1876. F.O. 45/285; Amadeo Moscati, *I Ministri del Regno d'Italia*, vol. IV, Rome, 1964, pp. 55–7.

45. ACS. Carte Crispi-Roma. Relazione sulla nostra situazione militare, 7 July 1876. f. 24. Fasc. 10/1.

46. 'I forti di Roma', *L'Italia militare*, 3 March 1883.

47. Luigi Pelloux, *Quelques souvenirs de ma vie*, Rome, 1967, p. 99.

48. Crispi to Depretis, 3 October 1877. Quo. T. Palamenghi-Crispi, *The Memoirs of Francesco Crispi*, London, 1912, vol. II, p. 70; Carlo Mezzacapo to his wife, 19 May and 24 March (*sic* – May?) 1877. Quo. Pesci. pp. 215–6.

49. *Révue militaire de l'étranger*, 2 March 1878, pp. 113–16; 'Le nostre cose militari guidicate all'estero', *L'Italia militare*, 7 March 1878.

50. Crispi to Depretis, 27 August 1877. Quo. Chabod, p. 680.

51. Crispi to Depretis, 2 September 1877. Quo. Palamenghi-Crispi, II, p. 9.

52. ACS. Carte Crispi-Roma. Di Robilant to Ministry of Foreign Affairs, 28 February 1877; Majnoni to Comando del Corpo di Stato Maggiore, 4 March 1877. Fasc. 11/6, 7.

53. ACS. Carte Crispi-Roma. Reports by Majnoni, 6 July, 7 and 12 August 1877; Pianell to Mezzacapo, 16 August 1877. Fasc. 11/13.

54. ACS. Carte Crispi-Roma. Mezzacapo to Crispi, 24 April and 28 September 1877. Fasc. 11/9, 22.

55. SME. Difensiva Sud, 9 November 1877. *Comando del Corpo di Stato Maggiore: Corrispondenza*, b. 47.

56. SME. Difensiva Sud-difensiva contro Francia, 4 January 1878. Ibid.

57. Contra Whittam, p. 116.

58. 'Studio sulla nostra mobilitazione', *Rivista militare italiana*, August 1878, p. 227.

3: ENTERING THE TRIPLE ALLIANCE

1. Rochat and Massobrio, p. 115.

2. Nigra to Di Robilant, 9 August 1886. Quo. Chabod, p. 14.

3. C.J. Lowe and F. Marzari, *Italian Foreign Policy 1870–1940*, London, 1975, pp. 19–20; F.R. Bridge, *From Sadowa to Sarajevo: The Foreign Policy of Austria-Hungary, 1866–1914*, London, 1972, p. 93.

4. 'Italicae Res', *Revue militaire de l'étranger*, 6, 13 September, 14 October 1879.

5. 'Sulle nostre condizioni militari – I', *L'Italia militare*, 11 October 1879.

6. 'Sulle nostre condizioni militari – II' *L'Italia militare*, 18 October 1879.

7. PRO. Paget to Salisbury, 6 February 1880. F.O. 45/402.

8. SME. Lanza, 16 February, 8, 14 March 1880, nos. 18, 22, 24. *Addetti Militari: Vienna*, b. 3.

9. SME. Osio, 2 March 1880, no. 18. *Addetti Militari: Berlino*, b. 26.
10. 'Ancora sulla ferma progressiva', *L'Italia militare*, 21 February-6 March 1880; Del Negro, pp. 203–6, 258.
11. AP. 5 June 1880, pp. 142–5.
12. SME. Verbali delle sedute della Commissione per le fortificazioni alpina sulla frontiera N.E., 2 November 1880. *Ordinamenti e Mobilitazione*, b. 68.
13. SME. Relazione della Commissione per lo studio della sistemazione a difesa nel teatro della guerra Nord-Est, 28 November 1880. Ibid.
14. Ibid., 26, 27 November 1880.
15. SME. Lanza, 20 April 1880, no. 37. *Addetti Militari: Vienna*, b. 3.
16. SME. Commissione pello studio della difesa nel teatro di guerra N.O., Parte 1^1, 27 July 1881, pp. 27–8 (session of 11 July 1881). *Ordinamenti e Mobilitazione*, b. 69.
17. Ibid., pp. 80–1.
18. Ibid., pp. 93–105 (session of 14 July 1881).
19. SME. Commissione pello studio . . ., pp. 66–7. Loc.cit. As well as citing the encircling nature of the valleys on the Paduan plain, Pianell added that 'what would help to make a struggle in the mountain zone preferable for us is the fact that the particular qualities of our soldiers make them especially suited to mountain warfare'.
20. Contra Halpern, p. 178 and Whittam, p. 120.
21. SME. Conclusioni della Commissione per lo studio della difesa nel teatro di guerre nord-ovest relative alla sistemazione della frontiera dalla valle della Dora Baltea alla Piazza della Spezia, 20 December 1881, p. 44. *Carteggio Commissioni di Difesa*, b. 1.
22. 'Gli sbarchi', *L'Italia militare*, 30 April 1881.
23. SME. Bisesti, 26 May 1881, no. 46. *Addetti Militari: Berlino*, b. 26.
24. 'Le alleanze', *L'Esercito italiano*, 21 August 1881.
25. Tosti, p. 94.
26. In January 1882 Pelloux, then secretary-general at the war ministry, received a memorandum from von Moltke specifically counselling against this move. Benjamin F. Brown (ed.), *Sidney Sonnino: Diario 1866–1912*, vol. I, Bari, 1972, p. 149 (entry for 31 March 1893).
27. Del Negro, pp. 207–8.
28. 'L'ordinamento dell'esercito', *L'Esercito italiano*, 4 January 1882.
29. 'Le imprese dei falsi prussiani', *L'Esercito italiano*, 11 February 1882.
30. Quo. Minnitti, 'Esercito e politica . . . (II)', p. 38.
31. 'Dello svolgimento delle istituzioni militari nell'ultimo decennio', *Rivista militare italiana*, January 1880, p. 33.
32. 'I veri responsabili' and 'Il comitato di Stato Maggiore', *L'Esercito italiano*, 20 June, 19 July 1881; 'Del Comando Supremo', *L'Italia militare*, 14 October 1881.
33. Pianell to Carlo Mezzacapo, 7 November 1881. Quo. Pesci, pp. 231–2.
34. 'Il Comitato di Stato Maggiore Generale e i nuovi quadri organici', 'Il Ministero della Guerra e la Commissione per l'ordinamento', 'Il Comitato di Stato Maggiore Generale', *L'Esercito italiano*, 12 January, 12 March, 18 April, 10 May 1882.
35. SME. Lanza, 28 May 1882, no. 80. *Addetti Militari: Vienna*, b. 3.
36. Thayer, p. 168; Lowe and Marzari, p. 27.

37. Minnitti, 'Il secondo piano generale delle fortificazione. Studio e progetti (1880–1885)', *Memorie storiche militari*, 1980, pp. 104–6.
38. 'La fortificazione, l'artiglieria e la difesa delle coste nel loro stato attuale', *Rivista militare italiana*, November 1892, p. 1496.
39. 'Il Capo di Stato Maggiore', *L'Esercito italiano*, 15 September 1882; 'Nostre informazioni', *L'Italia militare*, 12 September 1882.
40. Minnitti, 'Esercito e politica . . . (II)', p. 40.
41. ISR Carte Cosenz. Cosenz to Lionello De Benedetti, 12 September 1898. B. 108/49².
42. 'Le combat de la division en Italie', 'L'emploi des trois armes dans le combat en Italie', *Révue militaire de l'étranger*, 15 February 1884, pp. 131–2 and 15 January 1886, p. 9. See also F. Stefani. *La Storia della dottrina e degli ordinamenti dell'esercito italiano*, vol. I, Rome, 1984, pp. 373–85.
43. 'Manoeuvres de l'armée italienne en 1882', *Revue militaire suisse*, August 1883, pp. 359–65.
44. 'L'Esercito e le elezioni', 'La quistione militare dinanzi al paese', *L'Esercito italiano*, 26 September, 29 October 1882; Minnitti, 'Esercito e politica . . . (II)', p. 35, fn. 25.
45. 'Les nouvelles lois militaires italiennes', *Revue militaire de l'étranger*, 15 May 1883, p. 515.
46. ACS. Carte Crispi-Roma. Mancini to Ferrero, 25 October 1883. Fasc. 11/27.
47. ACS. Carte Crispi-Roma. Ferrero to Mancini, 28 October 1883. Fasc, 11/27.
48. Massimo Mazzetti, *L'Esercito italiano nella triplice alleanza: Aspetti della politica estera 1870–1914*, Naples, 1974, pp. 34, 37–8.
49. 'Un opuscolo sulla difesa dello Stato', *L'Esercito italiano*, 15 January 1884.
50. Antonio Araldi, *Gli errori commessi in Italia nella difesa dello Stato*, Bologna, 1884.
51. Giuseppi Perucchetti, *La difesa dello stato*, Turin, 1884.
52. SME. Studio circa la difensiva e l'offensiva Nord-Est, April 1885, pp. 1–2. *Ordinamenti e Movimento*, b. 11.
53. Ibid., p. 10.
54. Ibid., p. 21.
55. ACS. Cosenz to Minister of War, 17 March 1885, no. 395/544, and 'Viaggio d'istruzione dell'anno 1885: Programma'. *Ministero della Guerra: Scuole militari*, b. 2.
56. AP. 31 May 1885, pp. 14239–49, 14265–7.
57. 'L'ordinamento dell'Esercito e la difesa dello Stato', *L'Esercito italiano*, 21 March 1885.
58. 'Le commissioni per l'Artiglieria e per la Cavalleria', *L'Esercito italiano*, 14 October 1886.
59. 'Il capo do Stato Maggiore', *L'Esercito italiano*, 6 January 1887.
60. 'L'Etat-major italien', *Revue militaire de l'étranger*, March 1885, p. 257.
61. ACS. Cosenz to Ricotti, 19 January, 22 August 1885. *Ministero della Guerra: Scuole militari*, b.2.
62. ACS. Corsi to Bertolè-Viale, 1 October 1888; Cosenz to Bertolè-Viale, 2 October 1888. *Ministero della Guerra: Scuole militari*, b. 24. For a description of the syllabus of the *Scuola di guerra* before Cosenz's reforms,

see 'L'Ecole de guerre italienne', *Revue militaire de l'étranger*, 15 November 1889, pp. 523–38.

63. SME. Dogliotti, 28 April/10 May 1886, 29 January/10 February and 14/26 February 1887, nos. 26, 13, 15. *Addetti Militari: Russia*, b. 2.
64. Bridge, pp. 162–6; Lowe and Marzari, pp. 41–5.
65. Giorgio Candeloro, *Storia dell'Italia moderna*, vol. VI: *Lo sviluppo del capitalismo e del movimento operaio*, Milan, 1970, p. 315.
66. AP. 18 April 1887, p. 2252.

4: CRISPI AT THE HELM

1. PRO. Kennedy to Salisbury, 26 August 1887. F.O. 45/576.
2. 'Giudizii prematuri sulle manovre miste della costa Tirrena', 'La difesa delle coste', *L'Esercito italiano*, 29 July, 7 August 1887.
3. DDI. 2nd series, vol. XXI. De Launey to Crispi, 14 September 1887. No. 144, pp. 119–20.
4. Renato Mori, *La politica estera di Francesco Crispi (1887–1891)*, Rome, 1973, p. 89.
5. Mazzetti, *L'Esercito italiano nella Triplice Alleanza*, pp. 59–63.
6. DDI. 2nd series, vol. XXI. Solms to Crispi, 27 November 1887, nos. 346, 347, pp. 297–300.
7. SME. Dogliotti, 7/19 November, 30 November/12 December, 14/26 December 1887, nos. 68,'75, 79. *Addetti Militari: Russia*, b. 2.
8. DDI. 2nd series, vol. XXI. De Launey to Crispi, 7 January 1888, no. 482, p. 409.
9. Mori, p. 94; Mazzetti, *L'Esercito italiano nella Triplice Alleanza*, pp. 77–88.
10. Mori, p. 68.
11. DDI. 2nd series, vol. XXI. Bertolè-Viale to Crispi, 24 February 1888, no. 622, pp. 518–20.
12. Ibid. Crispi to De Launey, 16 March 1888, no. 684, pp. 568–9.
13. This incident may have accelerated the decline in Italo–French relations. The Russian secret service intercepted Goiran's letters to Cosenz from Vienna and Berlin; the French may have been tipped off. Mori, p. 120, fn. 91.
14. M. Gabriele and G. Friz, *La politica navale italiana dal 1885 al 1915*, Rome, 1982, p. 42, fn. 43.
15. AP. 30 May 1888, pp. 3056–60.
16. Ibid., pp. 3069–73.
17. 'La disponibilità del generale Mattei', 'Incompatibilità militare', *L'Esercito italiano*, 3, 16 January 1889.
18. SME. Dogliotti, 14/26 February, 29 March/10 April, 14/26 July 1888, nos. 13, 32, 71. *Addetti Militari: Russia*, b. 2.
19. De Rosa, p. 198.
20. PRO. Kennedy to Salisbury, 19 October 1888. F.O. 45/603.
21. PRO. Slade to Kennedy, 25 November 1888. F.O. 45/603.
22. 'Les manoeuvres italiennes dans la Romagne', *Revue militaire de l'étranger*, 15 October 1888.

23. SME. Cosenz to Capo II° Riparto, 23 November 1888, with enclosures. *Ordinamenti e Movimenti*, b. 139.
24. Francesco Guardione, *Il generale Enrico Cosenz*, Palermo, 1900, p. 87.
25. Crispi to Bertolè-Viale, 19 April 1889. Quo. Palamenghi-Crispi, II, pp. 389–91.
26. Crispi to Bertolè-Viale, 10 July 1889. Quo. ibid., pp. 391–2.
27. R. Cohen, *Threat Perception in International Crisis*, Wisconsin, 1979, pp. 37–44; Bridge, p. 183.
28. 'Restituzione del cavallo ai Capitani di fanteria', *L'Esercito italiano*, 17 October 1900; 'L'età dei capitani di fanteria', 'Sulle condizioni degli ufficiali inferiori', *L'Italia militare e marina*, 12/13 July 1901, 2/3 October 1906.
29. Adriano Alberti, *L'Opera di S. E. il generale Pollio e l'esercito*, Rome, 1923, p. 8; De Chaurand, p. 150; De Bono, p. 122.
30. Rochat and Massobrio, p. 170; De Chaurand, pp. 137, 152; De Bono, pp. 163–4; 'Le condizioni degli ufficiali', 'La corta dei conti e l'esercito', 'L'indennità di vestiario ai sottotenenti di nuova nomina', 'Le condizioni degli ufficiali in Francia e in Italia', *L'Italia militare e marina*, 5/6 October 1896, 7/8 and 26/27 August 1897, 27/28 January 1899.
31. 'A proposito delle recenti promozioni', *L'Italia militare e marina*, 18 March 1894.
32. 'Gli ufficiali ammogliati senza permesso', 'La legge sul matrimonio degli ufficiali', *L'Esercito italiano*, 29 June 1882, 21 March 1883; 'Il disegno di legge sul matrimonio degli ufficiali', 'Pel matrimonio degli ufficiali', *L'Italia militare e marina*, 6 April, 19 August 1894.
33. PRO. Slade to Kennedy, 14 November 1888. F.O. 45/603.
34. De Bono, pp. 185, 189; 'Questioni relative alla educazione ed alla coltura militare degli ufficiali', *Rivista militare italiana*, July 1892, pp. 608–26; 'Ci vogliono ufficiali contenti', 'Gara di coltura', 'Le conferenze militari', 'Le conferenze e la coltura degli ufficiali', *L'Italia militare e marina*, 8/9 March 1898, 29/30 May, 19/20 October, 31 October/1 November 1899.
35. Eugenio de Rossi, *La vita di un ufficiale italiano sino alla guerra*, Milan, 1927, p. 66. The incident took place in 1887.
36. Niccola Marselli, *La vita del reggimento*, Rome, 1903, p. 247. The affair at Pizzofalcone can be traced in *L'Esercito italiano*, 10 April, 19, 20 May, 4 June 1884.
37. 'La mortalità nell'Esercito', *L'Esercito italiano*, 26 February 1888; 'Le disinfezioni nelle caserme', *Rivista militare italiana* 1893, pp. 1263–85.
38. Relazioni del generale Torre 1880, 1881, 1882, 1883: *L'Esercito italiano*, 7 April 1881, 21, 25 March 1882, 5 may 1883, 14 May 1884; Del Negro, pp. 208–13.
39. ACS. Commander, 38th Infantry Regiment (Carrara) to Divisional Commander (Livorno), 15 June 1885; C.-in-C. IX army corps to minister of war, 1 June 1885. *Ministero della Guerra: Gabinetto – Atti Diversi*, b. 13.
40. 'La truppa nell'ordine pubblico', *L'Esercito italiano*, 10 May 1889.
41. Domenico Farini, *Diario di fine secolo* (ed. Emilia Morelli), Rome, 1962, vol. I, p. 5 (1 February 1891).
42. SME. Zuccari, 15 February 1891, no. 23. *Addetti Militari: Berlino*, b. 122. Italics in original.
43. Mazzetti, *L'Esercito italiano nella Triplice Alleanza*, pp. 149–50.

44. SME. Brusati, 23 June 1892, no. 59. *Addetti Militari: Vienna*, b. 6.
45. SME. Zuccari, 15 July, 20 November 1891, nos. 103, 132. *Addetti Militari: Berlino*, b. 122.
46. SME. Viaggio d'sitruzione del 1891, p. 117. *Carteggio Campi, Esercitazioni, Manovre*, racc. 22.
47. SME. Brusati, 2 April 1891, no. 43. *Addetti Militari: Vienna*, b. 7.
48. Farini I, p. 71 (6 April 1892).
49. Ibid. I, p. 272 (20 May 1893).
50. 'A proposito del nuovo sistema di reclutamento e ordinamento', *L'Italia militare e marina*, 25/26 October 1895.
51. Farini I, p. 763 (9 August 1895).
52. Giorgio Rochat, 'L'esercito italiano nell'estate 1914', *Nuova Rivista Storica*, 45, 1961, pp. 300–1.
53. SME. 'Effetivi troppo ridotti, sparpagliamento delle truppe e conseguente deficienza nell'istruzione', n.d. *Ordinamento e Mobilitazione*, b. 2.
54. Farini I, pp. 76–80 (20 April 1892).
55. 'Il cavallo ai capitani di Fanteria', *L'Esercito italiano*, 11 November 1886.
56. SME. Zuccari, 19 May 1891, no. 61. *Addetti Militari: Berlino*, b. 122.
57. *I Capi di S.M. dell'Esercito: Domenico Primerano*, Rome, 1935, pp. 10–12; Farini I, p. 336 (24 November 1893).
58. SME. Panizzardi, T. 27 September 1893, no. 551. *Addetti Militari: Parigi*, b. 10.
59. 'Les grandes manoeuvres de 1892 en Italie', *Revue militaire de l'étranger*, July 1893, pp. 21–53; SME, Viaggio di stato maggiore in Sicilia, 1893. *Carteggio Campi, Esercitazioni, Manovre*, racc. 22.
60. SME. Viaggio di Stato Maggiore, 1894; Relazione, pp. 71–7. *Carteggio Campi, Esercitazioni, Manovre*, racc. 23.
61. SME. Relazione del viaggio di Stato Maggiore dell'anno 1895, pp. 71–2. *Carteggio Campi, Esercitazioni, Manovre*, racc. 24.
62. Farini I, p. 727 (8 July 1895); 'Saltiamo il fosso', *L'Italia militare e marina*, 15/16 July 1895.
63. SME. Zuccari, 16 October 1895, no. 107. *Addetti Militari: Berlino*, b. 1893–95.
64. Farini I, p. 732 (10 July 1895).
65. ACS. Carte Crispi-Reggio Emilia. Crispi to Sonnino, 25 October 1895. Scatola 12, fasc. 22, app. C/33. f. 20.
66. Ibid. Sonnino to Crispi, 25 October 1895. Scatola 12/22/C33, f. 3–5.
67. Ibid. Sonnino to Crispi, 26 October 1895. Scatola 12/22/C33, ff. 22, 9–10.
68. Ibid. Crispi to Sonnino, 27 October 1895. Scatola 12/22/C33 f. 24.
69. Ibid. Primerano to Crispi, 29 October 1895. Scatola 12/22/C33, f. 29.

5: AFRICAN ADVENTURE

1. Granville to Nigra, 15 October 1884. Quo. Candeloro VI, p. 302. Granville to Gladstone, 20 December 1884. Quo. Agatha Ramm (ed.), *The Political Correspondence of Mr. Gladstone and Lord Granville, 1876–1886*, Oxford, 1962. No. 1509, vol. 2, p. 298.
2. Candeloro VI, p. 305.
3. SME. Cosenz to Ricotti, 4 January 1885. *Volumi Eritrea*, b. 44.

4. Cosenz to Mancini, 4 January 1885. Quo. *Storia militare della Colonia Eritrea*, Rome, 1935–36, vol. I, p. 67.
5. SME. Mancini to Ricotti, 6 January 1885. *Volumi Eritrea*, b. 43.
6. SME. Ricotti to Saletta, 12 January 1885. *Volum i Eritrea*, b. 44.
7. SME. Memorie sulla prima spedizione d'Africa del Generale Tancredi Saletta, pp. 3–4. *Carteggio Eritrea*, racc. 9.
8. Mancini to Nigra, 22 January 1885. Cit. Carlo Zaghi, *P.S. Mancini, Africa e il problema del Mediterraneo*, Rome, 1956, pp. 163–6.
9. SME. Brin to Admiral Carini, 2 February 1885. *Volumi Eritrea*, b. 43.
10. SME. Ricotti to Saletta, 3 February 1885, encl. Istruzioni per il commandante superiore a Massaua. *Volumi Eritrea*, b. 43.
11. Angelo Del Boca, *Gli italiani in Africa orientale dall'unità alla marcia su Roma*, Bari, 1976, pp. 183, 187. Ricotti to Cosenz, 6 February 1885. Quo. *Storia militare della Colonia Eritrea*, I, pp. 82–3.
12. Harold G. Marcus, *The Life and Times of Menelik II: Ethiopia 1844–1913*, Oxford, 1975, p. 82.
13. SME. Mancini to Ricotti, 4 April 1885. *Volumi Eritrea*, b. 43.
14. SME. Ricotti to Saletta, 23 September 1885. *Carteggio Eritrea*, racc. 154.
15. SME. Saletta to Ricotti, 13 October 1885; Robilant to Ricotti, 7 November 1885. *Carteggio Eritrea*, racc. 154.
16. *Storia militare della Colonia Eritrea*, I, p. 103.
17. SME. Ts., Genè to Ricotti, 15, 18, 22 January 1887. *Carteggio Eritrea*, racc. 154. Di Robilant to Genè, 20 January 1887. Quo. *Storia militare della Colonia Eritrea*, I, p. 107.
18. Del Boca, pp. 221, 240–2; *Storia militare della Colonia Eritrea*, I, pp. 110–11.
19. SME. Alcune avvertenze generali intorno al modo di guerreggiare in Africa contro gli Abissini, n.d., pp. 4, 5, 8, 11, 12. *Carteggio Eritrea*, racc. 72.
20. SME. Genè to Di Robilant, 28 January 1887. *Carteggio Eritrea*, racc. 153.
21. SME. Di Robilant to Genè, 18 February 1887. *Carteggio Eritrea*, racc. 153.
22. AP. 3 February 1887, pp. 2002–14.
23. Occupazione di Uaa e di Saati, 5 August 1887; Obbiettivi di un azione contro l'Abissinia, 25 August 1887. *Storia militare della Colonia Eritrea*, I, pp. 307–10, 311–15.
24. SME. Bertolè-Viale to San Marzano, 26 October 1887. *Carteggio Eritrea*, racc. 154.
25. From 1883 weapons poured into Ethiopia through Assab and the French ports of Obock and Tajoura; by 1886 'The days of home-made gunpowder, badly-fashioned bullets and stones were . . . largely over.' Richard Pankhurst, *Economic History of Ethiopia*, Addis Ababa, 1968, p. 592.
26. L. dal Verme, 'An Italian View of the Boer War', Part III, *Journal of the Royal United Services Institution*, XLIV, 1900, p. 787; Del Boca, pp. 284–8; *Storia militare della Colonia Eritrea*, I, pp. 149–61.
27. Marcus, p, 100, fn. 3.
28. Del Boca, pp. 437–47; Rochat and Massobrio, pp. 117–18.
29. Bertolè-Viale to Crispi, 3 January 1889. Quo. Del Boca, p. 320.
30. Crispi to Bertolè-Viale, 6 January 1889. Quo. *Storia militare della Colonia Eritrea*, I, p. 190.

188 *Notes and References*

31. Del Boca, pp. 366–7.
32. Sven Rubenson, *The Survival of Ethiopian Independence*, London, 1976, pp. 389 92; Pankhurst, p. 599; Marcus, pp. 127–34.
33. G.N. Sanderson, 'England, Italy, the Nile Valley and the European Balance, 1890–91', *Historical Journal*, VII, 1964, pp. 97–109.
34. Farini I, p. 13 (19 March 1891).
35. Baratieri to Pelloux, 27 April 1892. Quo. Del Boca, p. 476.
36. Baldissera to Major Pietro Toselli, 27 April 1892. Quo. *La formazione del'impero coloniale italiano*, Milan, 1938, vol. I, pp. 110–11.
37. Salsa to his mother, 7 January 1894. Quo. E. Canevari and G. Commisso, *Il generale Tommaso Salsa e le sue campagne coloniali*, Milan, 1935, pp. 219–22.
38. Blanc to Baratieri, 3 February 1894. *Carteggio Eritrea*, racc. 2.
39. Baratieri to Mocenni, 15 February 1894. Quo. *Storia militare della Colonia Eritrea*, I, p. 255. SME. T., Mocenni to Baratieri, 6 March 1894. *Volumi Eritrea*, b. 22.
40. SME. Note by Mocenni, 2 July 1894. *Carteggio Eritrea*, racc. 12.
41. SME. Primerano to Mocenni, 14 July 1894. *Carteggio Eritrea*, racc. 2. The originals of all but two of the twelve letters Primerano is known to have written to Mocenni about the conduct of the war in Eritrea have disappeared; the content of this one is summarised on a folder.
42. Marcus, pp. 149, 153.
43. SME. Baratieri to Blanc, 14 February 1895. *Carteggio Eritrea*, racc. 155.
44. Oreste Baratieri, *Memorie d'Africa (1892–1896)*, Turin 1898, p. 98; Del Boca, p. 536 (who makes it 1 shot in 30).
45. SME. Crispi to Baratieri, 18 January 1895. *Carteggio Eritrea*, racc. 155.
46. SME. Blanc to Mocenni, 22 January 1895 (with Mocenni's hand-written answers on the back). *Carteggio Eritrea*, racc. 2.
47. Ts., Crispi to Baratieri, 5 April 1895; Baratieri to Crispi, 10 April 1895; Crispi to Baratieri, 10 April 1895; Baratieri to Crispi, 12 April 1895; Crispi to Baratieri, 13 April 1895. Quo. *La formazione del'impero coloniale italiano*, I, pp. 136–7.
48. SME. Baratieri to Mocenni, 20 May 1895. *Carteggio Eritrea*, racc. 12.
49. SME. Baratieri to Mocenni, 21 May 1895. *Carteggio Eritrea*, racc. 2. The commercial possibilities of Eritrea were consistently over-estimated.
50. Baratieri, p. 183.
51. SME. Mocenni to Nerazzini, 9 November 1895. *Carteggio Eritrea*, racc. 12.
52. Aldo Cabiati and Ettore Graselli, *Le guerre coloniali dell' Italia*, Milan, 1935, p. 90; *Storia militare della Colonia Eritrea*, II, p. 52; Del Boca, p. 591. The letter from Arimondi to Toselli dated 6 December 1895 telling him to withdraw slowly is reproduced in *Storia militare della Colonia Eritrea*, II, p. 55. Arimondi got his orders at 7 p.m. on 5 December, but admitted not despatching the letter to Toselli until 7 a.m. next day: Baratieri, p. 244.
53. SME. Mocenni to Baratieri, 9 December 1895; Baratieri to Mocenni, 9 December 1895. *Carteggio Eritrea*, racc. 155.
54. SME. Baratieri to Mocenni, 13 December 1895. *Carteggio Eritrea*, racc. 155. Baratieri to Crispi, 13 December 1895. Quo. *Storia militare della Colonia Eritrea*, II, p. 79.

55. SME. Mocenni to Baratieri, 19 December 1895. *Carteggio Eritrea*, racc. 155.
56. Del Boca, p. 607; SME. Crispi to Mocenni, 22 December 1895. *Carteggio Eritrea*, racc. 2.
57. SME. Promemoria, 12 December 1895. *Carteggio Eritrea*, racc. 2.
58. 'Les Italiens en Afrique', *Revue militaire de l'étranger*, December 1896, p. 453; *Storia militare della Colonia Eritrea*, II, p. 83; Del Boca, pp. 618–26. Of 250 000 rounds of rifle ammunition, the garrison had fired 91 000 in 11 days.
59. 'La guerra in Africa', 'I cannoni a tiro celere del Negus in confronto dei nostri', 'Cannoni a tiro celere', *L'Esercito italiano*, 14, 16, 27 January 1896 (all of which put up weak defences of the extant Italian artillery).
60. SME. Baldissera to Mocenni, 12 December 1895. *Carteggio Eritrea*, racc. 2.
61. Mocenni to Crispi, 21, 23 December 1895. *Storia militare della Colonia Eritrea*, II, p. 105.
62. Whittam, p. 135; Marcus, p. 170.
63. Farini II, p. 861 (27 February 1896).
64. Baratieri, pp. 353, 367, 369; *L'Esercito italiano*, 14 June 1896.
65. Luciano Lollio, 'La battaglia di Adua', *Rivista della guardia di finanza*, XX, 1971, p. 311, fn. 20.
66. SME. Crispi to Baratieri, 7 January 1896. *Carteggio Eritrea*, racc. 156.
67. Salsa to his mother, 17 January 1896. Quo. Canevari and Commisso, p. 282; 'Uno scritto del gen. Arimondi', *L'Italia militare e marina*, 4/5 February 1897 (Arimondi's letter is dated 31 December 1895).
68. Baratieri, pp. 303–4, 324.
69. Salsa to his mother, 6 February 1896. Quo. Canevari and Commisso, pp. 286–7; 'Un'altra lettera del Generale Dabormida', *L'Esercito italiano*, 1 April 1896 (Dabormida's letter is dated 15 February 1896); SME. Crispi to Baratieri, 9 February 1896. *Carteggio Eritrea*, racc. 156.
70. Del Boca, p. 637.
71. SME. Crispi to Baratieri, 25 February 1896. *Carteggio Eritrea*, racc. 156.
72. 'Processo Baratieri', *L'Esercito italiano*, 16 June 1896. (The witnesses were Valenzano and Ellena.)
73. 'Processo Baratieri', *L'Esercito italiano*, 12, 14 June 1896.
74. Del Boca, p. 646.
75. Sven Rubenson, 'Adwa 1896: The Resounding Protest', in R. Rotberg and A.A. Mazrui (eds), *Power and Protest in Black Africa*, New York, 1970, p. 119.
76. Baratieri, pp. 370, 372, 405; 'La battaglia di Adua dal campo abissino e da fonti russi', *Rivista militare italiana*, April 1897, p. 576.
77. SME. Relazione sul combattimento di Adua, 10 May 1896 (by Lamberti). *Volumi Eritrea*, b. 51.
78. SME. Relazione sul combattimento del 1° marzo 1896 al colle di Chidane Meret, 6 July 1896, pp. 2, 9 (by Albertone). *Volumi Eritrea*, b. 52.
79. SME. Relazione sull'azione della brigata indigeni nella giornata d'Adua fatta dal col. Cossù, già commandante del 6° batt. indigeni, 16 April 1909, p. 1. *Volumi Eritrea*, b. 52.
80. SME. Relazione Madia, 15 May 1897. *Volumi Eritrea*, b. 51.

190 *Notes and References*

81. 'La brigata Dabormida alla battaglia di Adua', *Rivista militare italiana*, July 1896, p. 1277.
82. Relazione Lamberti, op. cit.; 'La brigata Dabormida alla battaglia di Adua', op. cit., p. 1281; Lollio, p. 318; Del Boca, p. 659.
83. Del Boca suggests that Turitto rode back and told Albertone that he had gone too far forward, but was reproached for his cowardice; Del Boca, pp. 661–2. I have followed the accounts given by Cossù and Lamberti.
84. *Storia militare della Colonia Eritrea*, II, p. 126. One of the many minor puzzles connected with the battle is why all four brigade commanders left their heliographs behind that day 'almost as if they wished to avoid Baratieri's control'. Del Boca, p. 666.
85. A. Bronzuoli, *Adua*, Rome, 1935, pp. 36, 40; 'Les italiens en Afrique', *Revue militaire de l'étranger*, January 1897, p. 54; 'La battaglia di Adua dal campo abissino e da fonti russi', *Rivista militare italiana*, April 1897, p. 585. Rubenson states wrongly that Menelik's artillery 'was inferior to that of the Italians': Rubenson, *Survival*, p. 403. According to one eye-witness, the Ethiopians possessed four batteries each composed of six 55mm Hotchkiss quick-firing guns: 'Guerre de l'Erytree', *Revue militaire suisse*, April 1896, p. 249.
86. This account is drawn chiefly from Del Boca, *Storia militare della Colonia Eritrea*, II and Lamberti's *Relazione*. Baratieri had personally reduced the number of rounds per gun from the usual 130 to 90 – probably because of transport difficulties.
87. SME. Relazione Albertone, p. 43. See fn. 78.
88. SME, Relazione Cossù. See fn. 79.
89. The phrase is Madia's – an eyewitness. Relazione Madia. See fn. 80.
90. It is no longer possible to walk the ground of the battle, but according to those who have done so and have carried out experiments using detonators it is impossible to tell where the sound of firing is coming from in the labyrinth of hills. I am grateful to Professor Brian Sullivan for this information.
91. As well as the main secondary authorities and Lamberti, I follow 'La colonna Dabormida nella battaglia d'Abba-Carima', n.d. (Capt. G. Manassero), 'Rapporto di capitano Groni', 6 June 1896, and 'Relazione di capitano Menarini', 10 March 1896. SME. *Volumi Eritrea*, b. 51.
92. Del Boca, p. 691. As always, no two sets of figures agree.
93. SME. Relazione circa il combattimento del 1° Marzo, 14 March 1896 (by Brusati). *Volumi Eritrea*, b. 52. In a passage of his report which he later crossed out, Salsa said the retreat turned into disorder and flight whenever a few shots were fired or an enemy column appeared: Combattimento del 1° Marzo, 30 May 1896. *Volumi Eritrea*, b. 52.

6: 'THE MOST LIBERAL OF GENERALS'

1. Farini II, p. 1151 (4 March 1897).
2. SME. T., Di Majo, 3 July 1896. *Addetti Militari: Russia*, b. 3.
3. Arthur Marsden, 'Britain and the "Tunis Base", 1894–1899', *English Historical Review*, LXXIX, 1964, pp. 82–5, 94.

4. Salisbury to Clare Ford, 16 April 1896. Quo. ibid., p. 78.
5. SME. Promemoria circa le nostre condizioni militari giudicate all'estero, 20 November 1895. *Ordinamento e Mobilitazione*, b. 11.
6. *L'Italia militare e marina*, 1/2, 4/5 August 1896.
7. 'Dimissioni del Capo di Stato Maggiore', 'Le dimissioni del Capo di Stato Maggiore', 'Le responsibilità del Capo di Stato Maggiore', *L'Esercito italiano*, 16, 17, 19 May 1896.
8. AP. 23 May 1896, pp. 2069–70.
9. Farini II, p. 947 (27 May 1896).
10. 'Il capo di stato maggiore e le responsibilità Africane', *L'Esercito italiano*, 13 June 1896.
11. *I Capi di S.M. dell'Esercito: Domenico Primerano*, Rome, 1935, p. 15, dates Primerano's retirement from the regular army as 16 June; the actual decree was signed by Ricotti's successor, although Primerano probably knew of the war minister's intention to use the new law on limits of age against him as soon as he could legally do so.
12. Sonnino, *Diario 1866–1912*, pp. 303–4 (16 July 1896); Farini II, p. 962 (13 June 1896); Candeloro VII, pp. 23–4.
13. 'Un caso d'applicazione dei limiti d'età', 'I generali Mezzacapo e Primerano', *L'Italia militare e marina*, 5/6, 7/8 August 1896; 'L'applicazione dei limiti d'età', *L'Esercito italiano*, 6 August 1896.
14. SME. Pelloux to Valles, 18 September 1896. *Ordinamento e Mobilitazione*, b. 11.
15. AP. 20 May 1897, pp. 851–5.
16. Sonnino, *Diario 1866–1912*, p. 257 (4 March 1896).
17. 'La sentenza del processo Baratieri', *L'Esercito italiano*, 18 June 1896. Baratieri complained that the tribunal was improperly constituted: Baratieri, pp. 465–7.
18. 'La prima impressione sul progetto di ordinamento', 'Circa il progetto di ordinamento', *L'Italia militare e marina*, 1/2, 10/11 December 1896.
19. 'Le marriage des officiers en Italie', *Revue militaire de l'étranger*, March 1897, pp. 203–9. French officers had to find a marriage dowry of 1200 francs until 1 October 1900, when the practice was abolished. Pay scales in the Italian army in 1896 were as follows:

2nd lieutenant	1800 lire per annum
lieutenant	2200 lire per annum
captain	3200 lire per annum
major	4400 lire per annum
lieut-colonel	5200 lire per annum
colonel	7000 lire per annum

20. 'Il massimo e il minimo dell'età per gli ufficiali', *L'Italia militare e marina*, 2/3 June 1897.
21. 'Precisiamo meglio', *L'Esercito italiano*, 5 January 1898; De Chaurand, p. 153.
22. 'Duemila e duecento sottufficiali in attesa d'impiego', 'Sottufficiali anziani', 'I sottufficiali del regio esercito', 'I sottufficiali del R. Esercito', *L'Italia militare e marina*, 25/26 March, 16/17 November, 26/27 November, 15/16 December 1897; De Chaurand, p. 147.

23. Farini II, p. 1210 (5 December 1897); Candeloro VII, p. 50.

24. Pelloux, pp. 172–3; 'I dimissioni del generale Pelloux', *L'Italia militare e marina*, 6/7 December 1897.

25. SME. Stralcio delle relazioni sui viaggi di Stato Maggiore degli anni 1895– 1896, October 1896, pp. 87–90. *Carteggio Campi, Esercitazioni, Manovre*, racc. 25.

26. De Rossi, p. 138. SME. Prudente to (?) Saletta, 31 March 1899. *Addetti Militari: Berlino*, b. 1900. Mazzetti, *L'Esercito italiano nella triplice alleanza*, pp. 177–8.

27. SME. Verbali delle sedute della Commissione Speciale nominata col dispaccio 21 Novembre 1898–N. 7492, p. 5 (session of 18 December 1898). *Carteggio Commissioni di difesa*, b. 1.

28. Ibid., pp. 16–17 (session of 19 December 1898). Loc. cit.

29. Ibid., p. 46 (session of 23 December 1898). Loc. cit.

30. Ibid., pp. 50–57 (sessions of 7, 8 January 1899). Loc. cit.

31. SME. Istruzioni riservatissime per l'adetto militare presso la regia ambasciata di Vienna, n.d. (January or February 1897). *Addetti Militari: Vienna*, b. 10. Bridge, p. 236.

32. SME. Radunata Nord-Est, April 1897. *Ordinamento e Mobilitazioni*, b. 1.

33. SME. Relazione del viaggio di Stato maggiore, 1898. *Carteggio Campi, Esercitazioni, Manovre*, racc. 27.

34. SME. Relazione del viaggio di Stato maggiore, 1899. *Carteggio Campi, Esercitazioni, Manovre*, racc. 28.

35. SME. Commissione centrale per i trasporti militari in ferrovia, 20, 21, 22 February 1899. *Ordinamento e Mobilitazione*, b. 11.

36. 'The summer and autumn exercises of the Italian Army in the year 1899', *Journal of the Royal United Services Institution*, XLIV, 1900, pp. 420, 422.

37. Pompeo Moderni, *L'assedio di Roma nella guerra del 19** [sic]*, Milan, 1900; Eugenio Massa, *Un colpo di mano sulla Sicilia nell'anno 191*[sic]*, Rome 1901.

38. Umberto Levra, *Il colpo di stato della borghesia. La crisi politica di fine secolo in Italia 1896/1900*, Milan, 1975, pp. 80–1.

39. 'L'Esercito e l'ordine pubblico', 'Una campagna contro l'esercito', 'La truppa nei tumulti', 'Tumulti in provincia', *L'Italia militare e marina*, 31 January/1 February, 6/7 April, 4/5 May, 7/8 May 1898.

40. Levra, pp. 102–115.

41. Del Negro, p. 219. 'Statistica militare', *L'Italia militare e marina*, 10/11, 27/ 28 October 1898; 'La legge di reclutamento', 'I risultati della leva sulle classe 1877', *L'Italia militare e marina*, 30/31 August and 11/12 October 1899. Of the class of 1876, 79 000 went into category I, a short-fall of 19 000 on planned size due to stiffer physical requirements. Of the 1877 class, 104 820 went into category I – the highest figure for ten years. Exemptions on family grounds were running at some 90 000 a year.

42. 'L'esercito e la teoria del militarismo', *L'Italia militare e marina*, 26/27 July 1898; 'La risposta del prof. G. Ferrero', 'Il militarismo italiano', *L'Esercito italiano*, 24 July 1898, 20 September 1899. Girolamo Sala, *Esercito e militarismo*, Milan, 1899.

43. Bava Beccaris to Pelloux, 21 May 1898. Quo. Levra, p. 137.

44. Afan de Rivera to Pelloux, 10, 14, 18 May 1898. Quo. Levra, p. 130.

45. Sonnino, *Diario 1866–1912*, pp. 387–8 (22 June 1898); see also p. 390 (25 June 1898).
46. SME. 'Verbali delle sedute della Commissione speciale nominata col dispaccio 21 novembre 1898—N. 7492, p. 6, *'Carteggio Commissioni di difesa.*
47. 'La commission suprème de défense de l'état en Italie', *Revue militaire de l'étranger*, December 1899, p. 768; 'Per la difesa dello stato', *L'Italia militare e marina*, 7/8 November 1899.
48. SME. Commissione suprema per la difesa dello stato: verbali delle sedute tenute in Ottobre-Novembre 1899, pp. 13–15 (session of 30 October 1899). *Carteggio commissioni di difesa*, b. 1.
49. Ibid., p. 16.
50. Ibid., p. 17.
51. Ibid., p. 33 (session of 1 November 1899).
52. Ibid., p. 100 (session of 9 November 1899).
53. SME. Sotto-commissione centrale mista incaricata di definire l'assetto difensivo delle piazze marittime, verbali (sessions held on 13, 16, 30, 31 October, 10 November 1900). *Carteggio commissioni di difesa*, b. 1.
54. Sonnino, *Diario 1866–1912*, p. 432 (27 January 1900). Although Saletta told Sonnino that the Krupp guns had performed best, the press 'leaked' the story that the two Italian models were superior: *L'Italia militare e marina*, 2/3 February 1900.
55. 'Riforme ed esenzioni dal servizio militare', *L'Italia militare e marina*, 7/8 February 1900.
56. 'La disciplina a questi tempi', *L'Italia militare e marina*, 9/10 March 1900.
57. 'Le fortificazioni di Roma', 'Ancora il nostro problema militare', *L'Italia militare e marina*, 21/22 April, 13/14 June 1900.
58. The agreement stated that the German fleet would operate in northern waters, the Austrians in the Adriatic, and Italy in the western Mediterranean. The eastern Mediterranean was made common ground. Gabriele and Friz, pp. 46, 121–2; Halpern, pp. 220–1.

7: PARTNERS AND RIVALS

1. R.J.B. Bosworth, *Italy, The Least of the Great Powers: Italian Foreign Policy before the First World War*, Cambridge, 1979, p. 128. See also Carocci, p. 133.
2. PRO. Currie to Lansdowne, 1 January 1902. F.O. 45/853.
3. 'Per la difesa nazionale', 'La questione più grossa non é quella di Genoa', 'Gli sbarchi', 'Per la difesa di Genoa', *L'Italia militare e marina*, 26/27 December 1900, 15/16 February, 5/6 April, 1/2 September 1902.
4. Amadeo Tosti, *La spedizione italiana in Cina (1900–1901)*, Rome, 1926, pp. 56–61; Salsa to his mother, 30 August 1900. Quo. Canevari and Commisso, pp. 325–6.
5. 'Truppa di sbarco', 'La guerra della Cina', *L'Italia militare e marina*, 13/14 July, 23/24 July 1900.

6. Tosti, *Cina*, pp. 99–102, 83.
7. SME. Relazione del viaggio di stato maggiore dell'anno 1900, p. 166. *Carteggio Campi. Esercitazioni, Manovre*, racc. 29.
8. SME. Commissione suprema per la difesa dello stato: verbali delle sedute tenute nel dicembre 1900, pp. 7–8, 11, 14. (17 December 1900.) *Carteggio commissioni di difesa*, b. 1.
9. Ibid., pp. 17, 20 (18 December 1900).
10. Ibid., p. 31.
11. Ibid., p. 36 (20 December 1900).
12. SME. Relazione del viaggio di stato maggiore dell'anno 1900, pp. 154–5. *Carteggio Campi, Esercitazioni, Manovre*, racc. 29.
13. SME. Relazione del viaggio di Stato Maggiore dell'anno 1901, pp. 81, 137, 149–50, 160, 175–6. *Carteggio Campi, Esercitazioni, Manovre*, racc. 30.
14. Mazzetti, *L'Esercito italiano nella Triplice Alleanza*, p. 183.
15. Ibid., pp. 197–8; Luigi Albertini, *Venti anni di vita politica: Parte prima*, Bologna, 1950, vol. I, pp. 94–6. The standard work on the Schlieffen plan – Gerhard Ritter, *The Schlieffen Plan. Critique of a Myth*, London, 1958 – makes no mention of Italian participation.
16. SME. Relazione intorno al progetto di mobilitazione e radunata verso la frontiera N.E., 19 April 1902. *Ordinamento e Mobilitazione*, b. 11; Relazione sul progetto dei trasporti in vigore per mobilitazione e radunata N.E., 30 May 1910, p. 1. *Ordinamento e Mobilitazione*, b. 64.
17. Giolitti to San Martino, 30 April 1901. Quo. Giampiero Carocci (ed.), *Dalle carte di Giovanni Giolitti: Quarant'anni di politica italiana*, Milan, 1962, vol. II, pp. 39–40.
18. 'L'Esercito e gli scioperi', *L'Esercito italiano*, 7 May 1901; 'Una nuova teoria socialista', 'I socialisti e l'esercito', 'La truppa in servizio d'ordine pubblico', *L'Italia militare e marina*, 3/4 January 1903, 21/22 October 1907, 13/14 April 1908.
19. 'Gli ufficiali in Italia e fuori', 'L'esercito e l'ordine pubblico', *L'Italia militare e marina*, 9/10 January 1901, 28 February/1 March 1901.
20. 'L'esercito nella repressione dei disordine', *L'Italia militare e marina*, 11/12 March 1901; 'Perchè é necessario l'Esercito', *L'Esercito italiano*, 14 December 1902; De Bono, p. 393.
21. 'La truppa nel mantenimento dell'ordine pubblico', *L'Italia militare e marina*, 28/29 June 1906. See also 'Echi del Senato', 'La renitenza alla leva ed i partiti sovversivi', 'L'Esercito e gli scioperi', *L'Italia militare e marina*, 2/3 July 1903, 30/31 August, 29/30 September 1904.
22. 'Per le armi della Patria', 'L'educazione del soldato e la propaganda sovversiva','La salvezza dell'esercito é nell' esercito','L'antimilitarismo e la scuola', *L'Italia militare e marina*, 9/10 December 1902, 27/28 October 1904, 10/11 October, 21/22 November 1905.
23. De Chaurand, pp. 106–7. 'Gli armamenti e le alleanze', 'Le nostre alleanze', *L'Italia militare e marina*, 24/25 August, 23/24 November 1900.
24. 'La relazione Marazzi ed i materiali a tiro rapido', 'L'artigliera da campo in Europa', *L'Italia militare e marina*, 17/18 May 1902, 2/3 April 1904.
25. De Biase, p. 215; De Chaurand, p. 108. For the arguments against the quick-firing 75s, see 'Questioni di artiglieria: Sul nuovo materiale' and 'Costumanze tedesche', *L'Esercito italiano*, 15 April, 17 June 1902.
26. 'Per la migliore soluzione della questione dell'artiglieria', *L'Italia militare e*

marina, 19/20 March 1908. For a comparison of the 75/906 with other foreign guns, see 'Il nuovo materiale da campagna a deformazione', *L'Esercito italiano*, 6 May 1907.

27. On the background to the testing of a 73mm gun, 'Nuovo materiale d'artiglieria da campagna', *L'Esercito italiano*, 13 April 1906.

28. De Chaurand, pp. 111–14.

29. ACS. Carte Brusati. Dal Verme to Brusati, 27 July 1907. Scatola 9, VI–I–30/51.

30. SME. Promemoria, Ufficio Scacchiere Orientale, 6 November 1902; Barattieri, 23, 26 October 1903, nos. 152, 155. *Addetti Militari: Parigi*, b. 14.

31. SME. Viaggio di stato maggiore, 1902. *Carteggio Campi, Esercitazioni, Manovre*, racc. 31.

32. SME. Relazione del viaggio di stato maggiore dell'anno 1903, pp. 3, 13, 56–9. *Carteggio Campi, Esercitazioni, Manovre*, racc. 32.

33. SME. Sunto degli studi compiuti e dell'azione esplicata dal Comando del Corpo di Stato Maggiore per la difesa permanente dello Stato dal 1896 ad oggi, 1 January 1908, pp. 8–9. *Ordinamento e Mobilitazione*, b. 116.

34. SME. Del Mastro, 1, 17 February, 13 March, 29 April 1904, nos. 20, 28, 34, 83. *Addetti Militari: Vienna*, b. 11.

35. DDF. 2nd series, vol. V. Commandant de Saint-James to André, 13 June 1904, no. 220, pp. 259–61.

36. SME. Relazione del viaggio di Stato maggiore dell'anno 1904, pp. 17, 75–8, 95–9, 107–9, 130. *Carteggio Campi, Esercitazioni, Manovre*, racc. 33.

37. Ibid., p. 135.

38. Brusati to Giolitti, 24 February 1905. Quo. Carocci, *Dalle Carte di Giovanni Giolitti*, II, p. 372.

39. SME. Sunto degli studi compiuti . . . dal 1896 ad oggi, pp. 9–14. As fn. 33 above.

40. SME. Studi intorno alla mobilitazione N.E.: Promemoria n. 2, 30 August 1904. *Ordinamento e Mobilitazione*, b. 11.

41. SME. Relazione del viaggio di stato maggiore del 1905, p. 84. *Carteggio Campi, Esercitazioni, Manovre*, racc. 34.

42. SME. Del Mastro, 17 January 1905, no. 13. *Addetti Militari: Vienna*, b. 11.

43. SME. Saletta to Pedotti, 14 May 1905. *Addetti Militari: Vienna*, b. 11.

44. De Rossi, p. 182; 'Cronaca triste', *Il pensiero militare*, 16 January 1907.

45. 'Ricorso Ranzi', *L'Italia militare e marina*, 21/22 April 1908; 'La relazione della Commissione speciale su "Caso Ranzi"', 'Verdetta del Giurì d'onore invocato da Fabio Ranzi', *Il pensiero militare*, 10 October 1908, 6 April 1911.

46. 'La disciplina a questi tempi', 'La coltura nella carriera degli ufficiali', 'Esercito e scuole', *L'Italia militare e marina*, 9/10 March 1900, 19/20 February 1903, 25/26 July 1907.

47. PRO. Delmé-Radcliffe to Egerton, 21 March 1906. F.O. 371/82.

48. Walter Goerlitz, *The German General Staff*, New York, 1953, pp. 133–4; Mazzetti, *L'Esercito italiano nella Triplice Alleanza*, pp. 212–13; Tommasini II, pp. 259–61; Albertini, *Venti anni: Parte prima*, I, p. 258.

49. Sonnino, *Diario 1866–1912*, p. 470 (28 February 1906).

50. 'Il capo di stato maggiore dell'esercito', *L'Italia militare e marina*, 3/4 April 1906.

51.   ACS. Carte Brusati. Viganò to Brusati, 29 October 1906. Scatola 9, VI–I–30/7. (Italics in original.)

52.   SME. Relazione del viaggio di stato maggiore del 1906. *Carteggio Campi, Esercitazioni, Manovre*, racc. 51.

53.   SME. Sunto degli studi compiuti . . . dal 1906 ad oggi, pp. 19–22. As fn. 33 above.

54.   SME. Relazione intorno al progetto di mobilitazione e radunata verso la frontiera Nord Est in dato luglio 1906, 15 March 1907. *Ordinamento e Mobilitazione*, b. 64.

55.   SME. Periodo di preparazione per predisporre l'attuazione della mobilitazione generale, n.d. (Report to minister dated 7 April 1906.) *Ordinamento e Mobilitazione*, b. 2.

56.   De Rossi, pp. 186–7, 195; Mazzetti, *L'Esercito italiano nella Triplice Alleanza*, p. 230.

57.   SME. Appunti sulla conferenza tenuta in presenza di S.M. il Re il 3 luglio 1907 in merito alla difesa della piazza di VENEZIA; Verbali: Difesa del Bacino Adriatico, 5 July 1907. *Ordinamento e Mobilitazione*, b. 2.

58.   SME. Sunto degli studi compiuti . . . dal 1896 ad oggi, pp. 26–39. As fn. 33 above.

59.   Del Negro, pp. 222, 231; De Chaurand, p. 103. There was no category II between 1897 and 1907.

60.   'La ferma di due anni in Francia', 'Lo spirito militare e lo spirito dei tempi', 'La ferma sotto le armi', *L'Italia militare e marina*, 16/17 July 1902, 4/5 February 1905, 25/26 April 1905.

61.   'L'esercito dell'avvenire', 'Politica militare', *L'Italia militare e marina*, 7/8 January 1904, 19/20 October 1905.

62.   SME. Promemoria circa le condizioni di mobilitabilità in cui si trovano le nostre grande unitá, December 1906. *Ordinamento e Mobilitazione*, b. 2.

63.   'La ferma biennale e la forza dell'esercito', *L'Italia militare e marina*, 5/6 February 1907. For a list of the grounds of exemption under Vigano's law, see Del Negro, p. 223.

64.   'Il ministro della guerra borghese', *L'Italia militare e marina*, 31 December 1907/1 January 1908.

65.   'La difesa dello Stato e l'opera del ministero della guerra borghese', 'La commissione per la difesa della Stato e il consiglio dell'esercito', *L'Italia militare e marina*, 6/7 February, 20/21 February 1908; De Chaurand, pp. 72, 74. Unfortunately the records of the *Consiglio dell'esercito* for this period have disappeared.

66.   SME. San Marzano to Saletta, 25 January 1908. *Addetti Militari: Vienna*, b. 13. Tommasini III, p. 542 (19 February 1908).

67.   SME. San Marzano, 29 January, 12 February 1908, nos. 5/5, 23/35. *Addetti Militari: Vienna*, b. 13. Tittoni to Casana, 23 February 1908. Quo. Tommasini III, p. 543.

68.   D. Mack Smith, *Storia di cento anni di vita italiana – vista attraverso il Corriere della sera*, Milan, 1978, p. 143; Albertini, *Venti anni: Parte prima*, I, pp. 312–13.

69.   'L'Inchiesta sull'Esercito: relazione della Commissione', 'La nuova situazione', *L'Italia militare e marina*, 19/20, 23/4 May 1908. 'La Iᵃ Relazione della Commissione d'inchiesta sull' Esercito', *L'Esercito italiano*, 22 May 1908. De Chaurand, p. 73.

70. SME. Commissione suprema mista per la difesa dello Stato: verabli delle sedute tenute nel maggio 1908, pp. 2–5 (6 May 1908). *Carteggio commissioni di difesa*, b. 1 bis.
71. Ibid., pp. 6–12, 23–5 (6, 8 May 1908).
72. Ibid., pp. 34–8 (11 May 1908).
73. Brusati to Cadorna, 8 March 1908. Quo. L. Cadorna, *Lettere famigliari*, Milan, 1967, p. 89.
74. Cadorna to Brusati, 9 March 1908. Quo. ibid., pp. 90–1.
75. PRO. Akers Douglas to Grey, 16 June 1908. F.O. 371/469. De Chaurand, pp. 72–3, 75. Albertini, *Venti anni: Parte prima,* I, pp. 316–18.
76. SME. Relazione viaggio S.M., 1908. *Carteggio Campi, Esercitazioni*, Manovre, racc. 38.

8: REDRESSING THE BALANCE

1. Glauco Licata, 'Il Corriere della Sera e la Triplice', *Atti del VII Congresso nazionale di storia del giornalismo*, Trieste, 1972, p. 278.
2. SME. San Marzano, 14 January, 1 February 1909, nos. 6/9, 16/21. *Addetti Militari: Vienna*, b. 13.
3. PRO. Delmé-Radcliffe to Rodd, 19 February 1909. F.O. 371/683.
4. SME. San Marzano, 20 February 1909, no. 30/44. *Addetti Militari: Vienna*, b. 13.
5. USM. Formazione di una base navale passegera su territorio nemico, Allegato V: Studio in caso di conflitto fra l'Italia e L'Austria, 14 September 1907. Cartella 199/5.
6. USM. Il problema militare marittimo, 25 January 1909. Ibid.
7. USM. Progetti di imbarco per spedizioni oltremare ipotesi A, 8 July 1909; Nicastro to Pollio, 17 September 1909. Cartella 199/7.
8. Del Negro, pp. 223–4, 235–6.
9. 'Consiglio di Stato', 'Governo disciplinare – II', 'I ricorsi dell'esercito al Consiglio di Stato', 'I 1777 ricorsi degli ufficiali e sottufficiali', *L'Esercito italiano*, 23, 25 July 1902, 25 September 1908, 11 January, 10 February 1911.
10. 'La questione delle promozioni per anzianità di spalline', *L'Esercito italiano*, 11 July 1909; Tosti, p. 140; De Chaurand, pp. 245, 247–8; 'Modificazione alla legge d'avanzamento del R. Esercito', *L'Esercito italiano*, 29 March 1912.
11. 'Sull'ordinamento dell'Esercito', 'Le spese per la pubblica sicurezza in Italia', *L'Esercito italiano*, 18 December 1908, 30 May 1909. In 1907–08 army expenditure on security duties amounted to L. 7 560 848 and Carabinieri expenditure to L. 13 313 819 – a total charge on the war ministry budget of L. 20 874 667.
12. War Ministry to President of the Council of Ministers, 5 February 1910. Quo. Fiorenza Fiorentino, *Ordine pubblico nell'Italia giolittiana*, Rome, 1978, pp. 67–8.
13. 'La questione delle truppe in servizio di p.s.', *L'Esercito italiano*, 17 August 1910.
14. SME. San Marzano, 17 February, 20 May 1909, nos. 28/42, 69/102. *Addetti Militari: Vienna*, b. 13. Albricci, 16 December 1909, no. 130/184.

Addetti Militari: Vienna, b. 14. Elia, 18 February, 20 March 1909, nos. 18, 32. *Addetti Militari: Turchia*, b. 49.

15. SME. Relazione sul progetto dei trasporti di mobilitazione e radunata N.E., July 1909. *Ordinamento e Movimenti*, b. 64.

16. SME. Relazione sul viaggio di stato maggiore 1910, pp. 6–7, 12, 13, 16, 17, 120. *Carteggio Campi, Esercitazioni, Manovre*, racc. 42.

17. ACS. Carte Brusati. Spingardi to Tedesco, 30 October 1910. Scatola 10, VI–4–36/unnumbered.

18. SME. Albricci, 29 April, 30 March, 15 September, 30 December 1910, nos. 50/70, 40/53, 87/116, 113/156. *Addetti Militari: Vienna*, b. 14.

19. SME. Relazione del viaggio dei generali 1911, p. 119. *Carteggio Campi, Esercitazioni, Manovre*, racc. 44.

20. Francesco Malgeri, *La guerra Libica*, Rome, 1970, pp. 25–8.

21. Carocci, p. 139; Thayer, p. 220.

22. Bosworth, *Least of the Great Powers*, chapter 5.

23. SME. Marro, 22 April, 21 May 1911, nos. 77, 107. *Addetti Militari: Turchia*, b. 49.

24. SME. Marro, 6 July 1911, no. 146. Ibid.

25. SME. Marro to Ministry of Foreign Affairs, 8 September 1911, encl. with Marro, 11 September 1911, no. 190. *Addetti Militari*: Turchia, b. 49A.

26. SME. Marro, 11 September 1911, no. 190. Ibid.

27. Angelo del Boca, *Gli Italiani in Libia: Tripoli, bel suol d'amore 1860–1922*, Bari, 1986, p. 15.

28. D.G. Herrmann, *Italian Strategy in the Libyan War, 1911–1915*, M. Litt., Oxford, 1987, pp. 18–19, 33.

29. R.J.B. Bosworth, *Italy and the Approach of the First World War*, London, 1983, p. 75.

30. Di San Giuliano to Giolitti, 2 September 1911. *Quarant'anni*, III, pp. 59–60.

31. SME. Marro, 15 September 1911, no. 191. *Addetti Militari: Turchia*, b. 49A.

32. Memoria sulla occupazione della Tripolitania e della Cirenaica del Capo di Stato Maggiore dell'Esercito, 19 September 1911. Quo. Ministero della Guerra, *Campagna di Libia*, Rome, 1922, vol. I, p. 274.

33. Herrmann, p. 75.

34. De Gondrecourt, 10 October 1911. Quo. J.-C. Allain, 'Les débuts du conflit italo-turc, Octobre 1911–Janvier 1912', *Revue d'histoire moderne et contemporaine*, XVIII, 1971, p. 107, fn. 4.

35. ACS. Carte Brusati. Appunti relativi alla guerra italo–turca, p. 2. Scatola 10, VI–7–39/388.

36. Sergio Romano, *La quarta sponda: La guerra di Libia, 1911/1912*, Milan, 1977, pp. 72–80; *Campagna di Libia*, I, pp. 90–5; Gabriele and Friz, pp. 180–1.

37. Romano, p. 100; *Campagna di Libia*, I, p. 159, fn. 2.

38. Salvatore Bono, 'Lettere dal fronte libico', *Nuova antologia*, 2052, 1971, pp. 535–7.

39. PRO. Rodd to Grey, 27 November 1911. F.O. 371/1135. Giolitti to Vittorio Emanuelle III, 25 October 1911. *Quarant'anni*, III, p. 70.

40. Caneva to Spingardi, 10 November 1911. Quo. Romano, p. 122.

41. Caneva to Pollio, 10 November 1911. Quo. Herrmann, p. 89.

42. Romano pp. 172–3.
43. W.C. Askew, *Europe and Italy's Acquisition of Libya 1911–1912*, Durham, N.C., 1942, pp. 147–53.
44. ACS. Carte Brusati. Spingardi to Brusati, 20 November 1911. Scatola 10, VI–4–36/319.
45. Sonnino, *Diario 1866–1912*, pp. 504–5 (26 November 1911).
46. Salsa to Ines Barni Salsa, 23 November, 11 December 1911. Quo. Canevari and Commisso, pp. 361, 378–9.
47. ACS. Carte Brusati. Caneva to Brusati, 16 December 1911. Scatola 9, VI–2–34/15.
48. 'Governo del personale', 'Informazioni', 'Sistemi massonici', 'Il gen. Pecori-Giraldi e la insindicabilità dei giudizi', *L'Esercito italiano*, 15 March, 12 May 1912, 25 June, 9 July 1913.
49. PRO. Rodd to Grey, 17 January 1912. F.O. 371/1383.
50. Herrmann, pp. 113–14.
51. ACS. Carte Brusati. Promemoria, 4 May 1912. Scatola 9, VI–3–35/195.
52. ACS. Carte Brusati. Promemoria, 29 June 1912. Scatola 9, VI–3–35/214. Faravelli had made the same suggestion on 27 March 1912: Gabriele and Friz, p. 185.
53. Giolitti to Spingardi, 9 August 1912. *Quarant'anni*, III, p. 74.
54. ACS. Carte Brusati. Pollio to Brusati, 4 October 1912. Scatola 10, VI–3–43/237.
55. ACS. Carte Brusati. Spingardi to Martini, 17 April 1913. Scatola 10, VI–3–43/477.
56. SME. Baratieri to Mombelli, 21 January 1913. *Addetti Militari: Turchia*, b. 49A.
57. SME. Mombelli, 18 March, 14 April 1914, nos. 117/35, 127/50. *Addetti Militari: Turchia*, b. 49B. Caccia, 11 March 1914, no. 9/18. *Addetti Militari: Cairo*, b. 117.
58. Askew, p. 249. As always, figures differ. Romano gives a total of 4000 dead and 5000 wounded: Romano, p. 254.
59. SME. La mobilitazione e la radunata generale dell'esercito nelle condizioni attuali, n.d. (February or March 1912). *Ordinamento e Movimenti*, b. 11.
60. ACS. Carte Brusati. Spingardi to Brusati, 26 October 1912. Scatola 10, VI–5–37/361.
61. SME. Promemoria sulla organizzazione della difesa costiera, 27 May 1912, p. 3. *Ordinamenti e Mobilitazione*, b. 2; Mobilitazione ed impiego di guerra della Regia Guardia di Finanza, 14 September 1912. Ibid.
62. Adriano Alberti, *Il generale Falkenhayn. Le relazioni tra i capi di S. M. della Triplice*, Rome, 1934, pp. 67–8; Mazzetti, *L'Esercito italiano nella Triplice Alleanza*, pp. 265–7; Halpern, pp. 226–7.
63. ACS. Carte Brusati. Pollio to Brusati, 24 December 1912. Scatola 10, VII–2–42/432.
64. ACS. Carte Brusati. Pollio to Brusati, 18 January 1913. Scatola 10, VII–2–42/449.
65. SME. Pollio to Panizzardi, 21 January 1913. *Ordinamento e Movimenti*, b. 2.
66. SME. Calderari, 10 March 1913, no. 7. *Addetti Militari: Berlino*, b. 166.
67. ACS. Carte Brusati. Pollio to Brusati, 1 May 1913. Scatola 10, VII–3–43/478.

68. Pollio to Spingardi, 16 February 1913. Quo. Rochat, 'L'esercito italiano nell'estate 1914', p. 313.
69. SME. Commissione suprema mista per la difesa dello Stato, verbali delle sedute tenute nel maggio 1913, pp. 7–13 (19 May); pp. 22–3, 29 (20 May). *Carteggio Commissioni di Difesa*, b. 1 bis.
70. Ibid., p. 47 (24 May).
71. ACS. Carte Brusati. Spingardi to Brusati, 22 May 1913. Scatola 10, VII–3–43/492.
72. ACS. Carte Brusati. Cardorna to Pollio, 26 May 1913, encl. Studi sulle operazioni militari alla frontiera N-O, p. 5. Scatola 10, VII–1–41/408.
73. SME. Relazione complessiva sui progetti dei trasporti di mobilitazione e radunata N.E. e N.O., July 1913, p. 11. *Ordinamenti e Movimento*, b. 64. See also: Ordine di movimento N.1 per il Comando del XI Corpo d'Armata, 1913. *Ordinamenti e Movimenti*, b. 56.
74. Quo. Alberti, *Falkenhayn*, p. 76. Italics in original.
75. SME. Viaggi di ufficiali generali anno 1913, p. 107. *Carteggio Campi, Esercitazioni, Manovre*, racc. 51.
76. Mazzetti, *L'Esercito italiano nella Triplice Alleanza*, pp. 371–5; Alberti, *Falkenhayn*, p. 85.
77. USM. Operazioni di sbarco in Provenza, 1913–14. Cartella 295.
78. SME. Albricci to Camerana, 17 February 1914; Albricci to Pollio, 18 February 1914. *Addetti Militari: Vienna*, b. 17.
79. Pollio to von Moltke, 28 February 1914. Quo. Mazzetti, *L'Esercito italiano nella Triplice Alleanza*, p. 381.
80. Alberti, *Falkenhayn*, pp. 78–80; Rochat, 'L'esercito italiano nell'estate 1914, p. 318; Mazzetti, *L'Esercito italiano nella Triplice Alleanza*, p. 385.
81. ACS. Carte Brusati. Pollio to Brusati, 17 May 1914. Scatola 11, VIII–1–45/51.
82. De Chaurand, pp. 249–51; Rochat and Massobrio, p. 163. The 1912–13 budget was equivalent to £16 920 000 at the exchange rate then current.
83. AP. 20 December 1913, p. 653.
84. Cenni sui provvedimenti indispensabili per migliorare le attuali condizioni dell'esercito: inviato il 30 marzo 1914 al Presidente del Consiglio dal Generale Pollio, Capo di Stato Maggiore dell'Esercito, reproduced in Antonio Salandra, *La neutralità italiana [1914]: Ricordi e pensieri*, Milan, 1928, pp. 301–16.
85. AP. 2 April 1914, pp. 2144–5.
86. SME. Albricci, 9 March 1914, no. 60. *Addetti Militari: Vienna*, b. 16; Calderari, 15 April 1914, no. 70. *Addetti Militari: Berlino*, b. 166.
87. Calderari to Pollio, 29 May 1914. Quo. Alberti, *Falkenhayn*, pp. 86–7.
88. Pollio to Zuccari, 16 June 1914. Quo. ibid., p. 87.
89. SME. Promemoria N. 284, Strada e fortificazioni austriache da costuirsi alla frontiera di Val Lagarina–Batterie scomponibili di nuovo tipo a Trento–Varie, 19 April 1914. *Addetti Militari: Vienna*, b. 17.
90. Mazzetti, *L'Esercito italiano nella Triplice Alleanza*, pp. 409–12.

9: FROM NEUTRALITY TO INTERVENTION

1. Gianni Rocca, *Cadorna*, Milan, 1985, pp. 10–11.

2. DDI. 4th series, vol. XII. Di Sangiuliano to Bollati, 14 July 1914. No. 225, pp. 159–60.
3. Di Sangiuliano to Vittorio Emanuele III, 24 July 1914. Quo. Salandra, pp. 78–80.
4. Palumbo, pp. 364–5. However, the latter document is reproduced in the illustrations to *Lettere famigliari* (docs 40, 41, 42), where it bears a different date – 30 July 1914.
5. Salandra, pp. 260–1.
6. O. Malagodi, *Conversazioni della guerra*, Milan–Naples, 1960, I, p. 17 (3 August 1914).
7. Quo. W.A. Renzi, 'Italy's Neutrality and Entrance into the Great War: A Re-examination', *American Historical Review*, LXII, 1968, p. 1419.
8. Cadorna to Grandi, 29 July 1914. Quo. Rochat, 'L'esercito italiano nell'estate 1914', pp. 324–5.
9. Alberti, *Falkenhayn*, p. 87, fn. 2; Luigi Cadorna, *Altre pagine sulla grande guerra*, Milan, 1925, pp. 15–23, 26.
10. Berchtold to Merey, 31 July 1914. Quo. Segre, p. 462.
11. Conrad to Cadorna, 1 August 1914. Quo. Alberti, *Falkenhayn*, p. 82. Conrad later claimed to have received a telegram from Cadorna in answer to this letter saying that Italy would not act against Austria-Hungary if she did not take Mount Lovcen or disturb the equilibrium in the Adriatic.
12. Moltke to Conrad, 5 August 1914. Quo. Mazzetti, *L'Esercito italiano nella Triplice Alleanza*, p. 447.
13. SME. Albricci, 3 August 1914, Ts. 217, 218. *Addetti Militari: Vienna*, b. 17.
14. DDI. 5th series, vol. I. Cadorna to di Sangiuliano, 27 August 1914 and enc. No. 468 allegato, p. 256.
15. Salandra, pp. 261–3; F. Martini, *Diario 1914–1918*, Milan, 1966, pp. 22, 27 (8, 9 August 1914).
16. Mack Smith, *Storia di cento anni*, pp. 187–8, 190; Candeloro VIII, p. 33.
17. DDI. 5th series, vol. I. Di Sangiuliano to Salandra, 9, 12, 14 (2), 16 August 1914; di Sangiuliano to Imperiali, 26 August 1914; di Sangiuliano to Tittoni, 30 August 1914. Nos. 151, 219, 244, 246, 281, 453, 503, pp. 83, 127, 142 (2), 160, 245, 278.
18. See note 14.
19. *L'Esercito italiano nella grande guerra*, vol. I., pp. 67–9. The document, which is undated, is described as having been drawn up by Cadorna 'a month after he effectively took up his post'. It appears to be the same memorandum as that referred to in Rochat, 'L'esercito italiano nell'estate 1914', p. 338, where it is dated 9 August 1914; however, the figures in the two documents differ slightly. For further details of Italy's military shortages, see De Chaurand, pp. 270–1, 274–5, 309, 331–4.
20. Martini, p. 38 (15 August 1914).
21. Rochat, 'L'esercito italiano nell'estate 1914', p. 336, fn. 3.
22. Martini, pp. 50–1 (22 August 1914).
23. Rochat, 'L'esercito italiano nell'estate 1914', pp. 334–5, fn. 2.
24. Quo. Rocca, p. 56.
25. Cadorna to Grandi, 28 August 1914; Grandi to Cadorna, 6 September 1914. Quo. Rochat, 'L'esercito italiano nell'estate 1914', pp. 341–2.
26. Salandra, p. 174; see also pp. 185, 190.

27. ACS. Carte Brusati. Cadorna to Brusati, 12 September 1914. Scatola 11, VIII–4–48/120. Italics in original.
28. Cadorna to Maria Cadorna, 18 September 1914. Quo. *Lettere famigliari*, p. 102.
29. Malagodi I, p. 20 (12 September 1914).
30. Sonnino, *Diario 1914–1916*, p. 15 (16 September 1914); Salandra, pp. 270–1, 290–3.
31. Circa le deficienze nelle dotazioni di mobilitazione, 23 September 1914. Quo. Salandra, pp. 272–7.
32. Salandra to Grandi. Quo. ibid., pp. 277–81.
33. Rocca, p. 57; Sonnino, *Diario 1914–1916*, p. 19 (24 September 1914); Cadorna to Grandi, 25 September 1914, quo. Rochat 'L'esercito italiano nell'estate 1914', p. 342.
34. DDI. 5th series, vol. I. Tittoni to di Sangiuliano, 27 September 1914; Carlotti to di Sangiuliano, 28 September 1914; di Sangiuliano to Salandra, 29 September 1914. Nos. 826, 827, 842, pp. 489, 490, 501.
35. Ministero della Guerra: memoria circa provvedimenti per l'esercito, 11 October 1914. Quo. Salandra, pp. 317–28.
36. Rochat, 'L'esercito italiano nell'estate 1914', p. 339, fn. 2; Salandra, pp. 432–3.
37. Sonnino to Salandra, 30 October 1914. Quo. Sonnino, *Carteggio 1914–1916*, p. 47. Italics in original.
38. SME. Bongiovanni, 15 December 1914, no. 16. *Addetti Militari: Berlino*, b. 166. Bongiovanni was particularly well placed to receive Falkenhayn's confidences, as the two men had met as respective chiefs of staff of their national contingents during the Boxer Rebellion.
39. Rochat. 'L'esercito italiano nell'estate 1914', p. 332, fn. 2.
40. USM. Cadorna to Thaon di Revel, 29 October 1914. Cartella 323/6.
41. J. Whittam, 'War Aims and Strategy: The Italian Government and High Command, 1914–1919', in B. Hunt and A. Preston, *War Aims and Strategic Policy in the Great War*, London, 1977, p. 91; Sonnino, *Diario 1914–1916*, p. 51, fn. 183.
42. A. Monticone, 'Sonnino e Salandra verso la decisione dell' intervento', in AA. VV., *Gli italiani in uniforme*, Bari, 1972, pp. 57–87; Salandra, pp. 466–9; Sonnino, *Diario 1914–1916*, pp. 54–6 (28 December 1914).
43. Cabbiati and Grasselli, pp. 249–59; Romano, pp. 255–6; Brian R. Sullivan, *A Thirst for Glory: Mussolini, the Italian Military and the Fascist Regime, 1922–1936*, PhD, Columbia, 1984, pp. 225–57.
44. Martini, pp. 312–13 (26 January 1915).
45. Martini, p. 337 (1 March 1915).
46. Quo. Lowe, 'Britain and Italian Intervention, 1914–1915', p. 544; Martini, p. 369 (24 March 1915).
47. Rocca, pp. 55–6.
48. Giorgio Rochat, 'La preparazione dell'esercito italiano nell'inverno 1914–1915 in relazione alle informazioni disponibili sulla guerra di posizione', *Risorgimento*, vol XIII, 1961, pp. 17–22.
49. SME. Guerra di posizione, 30 March 1915, p. 9. *Addetti Militari: Berlino*, b. 166.
50. Ibid., p. 45.

51. SME. Bongiovanni to Bollati, 13 April 1915, T. 215. *Addetti Militari: Berlino*, b. 166.
52. Ibid.
53. Tisza to Avarna, 11 April 1915. Quo. Avarna di Gualtieri (1950) III, p. 392.
54. Rocca, p. 70; Martini, p. 390 (21 April 1915); Cadorna to Sonnino, 30 April 1915, quo. Sonnino, *Carteggio 1914-1916*, p. 464.
55. SME. Bongiovanni, 1 May 1915, no. 82. *Addetti Militari: Berlino*, b. 166.
56. G.E. Silberstein, 'The High Command and Diplomacy in Austria-Hungary 1914-1916', *Journal of Modern History*, vol. 42, 1970, pp. 594-6.
57. SME. Mombelli, 2, 9 May 1915, nos. 59/65, 61/68. *Addetti Militari: Turchia*, b. 49 C.
58. Martini, p. 472.
59. John Gooch, 'Clausewitz Disregarded: Italian military thought and doctrine, 1815-1943', in M.I. Handel (ed.), *Clausewitz and Modern Strategy*, London, 1986, pp. 303-24.

10: CONCLUSION

1. On occasion the army overshot its budget without authorisation. ACS. Carte Brusati. Spingardi to Pollio, 16 February 1912. Scatola 10, VI-4-36/321.
2. SME. Verbali delle sedute della Commissione speciale nominata col dispaccio 21 novembre 1898-N. 7492, p. 5. *Carteggio Commissioni di difesa*, b. 1.
3. PRO. Delmé-Radcliffe to Egerton, 14 December 1907. F.O. 371/469.
4. 'Dovere', 'Note sull'educazione morale del soldato', 'Lo spirito nazionale e l'istruzione in relazione con la ferma - I & II', 'La disciplina militari a questi tempi', *L'Italia militare*, 14 December 1878, 18 January 1879, 19, 20 August 1880, 14 May 1881.
5. One suggestion was for mobile flying columns of Carabinieri to deal with local outbreaks of disorder: 'Reparti per il mantenimento dell'ordine pubblico', *L'Esercito italiano*, 24 July 1910.
6. Malagodi, p. 58 (9 May 1915).
7. Huntington, p. 72. Bosworth's charge that Di San Giuliano made no effort to unite military and diplomatic policy during August 1914 is a particular instance of a general phenomenon: *Least of the Great Powers*, p. 402.
8. Brusati to Giolitti, 27 September 1911. *Quarant'anni*, III, p. 62.
9. 'I deputati militari', *L'Italia militare e marina*, 23/24 January 1895.
10. 'L'avanzamento nell'esercito', *L'Esercito italiano*, 10 April 1885.
11. Stefani I, pp. 259, 364.
12. In 1909 the maximum rates of pay for a captaincy were: Austria-Hungary, 4139 lire; France, 4477 lire; Italy, 4800 lire; Germany, 6241 lire. 'La crisi dei quadri', *L'Esercito italiano*, 4 June 1909.
13. SME. Memoranda by Ricotti, 1 March 1874, 3 June 1875. *Comando del Corpo di Stato Maggiore: Corrispondenza*, b. 47.

Appendix: Ministers of War, 1861–1915

Lt. Gen. Manfredo Fanti	22 January 1860 – 12 June 1861
Bettino Ricasoli (interim)	12 June 1861 – 28 September 1861
Lt. Gen. Alessandro Della Rovere	28 September 1861 – 6 March 1862
Lt. Gen. Agostino Petitti di Roreto	6 March 1862 – 8 December 1862
Lt. Gen. Alessandro Della Rovere	8 December 1862 – 28 September 1864
Lt. Gen. Agostino Petitti di Roreto	28 September 1864 – 30 December 1865
Lt. Gen. Ignazio De Genova di Pettinengo	30 December 1865 – 22 August 1866
Lt. Gen. Efisio Cugia	22 August 1866 – 4 April 1867
Lt. Gen. Genova Thaon di Revel	4 April 1867 – 27 October 1867
Maj. Gen. Ettore Bertolè-Viale	27 October 1867 – 14 December 1869
Lt. Gen. Giuseppe Govone	14 December 1869 – 7 September 1870
Lt. Gen. Cesare Ricotti Magnani	7 September 1870 – 25 March 1876
Lt. Gen. Luigi Mezzacapo	25 March 1876 – 24 March 1878
Lt. Gen. Giovanni Bruzzo	24 March 1878 – 19 October 1878
Lt. Gen. Cesare Bonelli	19 October 1878 – 19 December 1878
Lt. Gen. Gustavo Mazè de la Roche	19 December 1878 – 14 July 1879
Lt. Gen. Cesare Bonelli	14 July 1879 – 13 July 1880
Rear Adm. Ferdinando Acton (interim)	13 July 1880 – 27 July 1880
Maj. Gen. Bernardino Milon	27 July 1880 – 20 March 1881
Rear Adm. Ferdinando Acton (interim)	20 March 1881 – 4 April 1881
Lt. Gen. Emilio Ferrero	4 April 1881 – 23 October 1884
Lt. Gen. Cesare Ricotti Magnani	23 October 1884 – 4 April 1887
Lt. Gen. Ettore Bertolè-Viale	4 April 1887 – 6 February 1891
Maj. Gen. Luigi Pelloux	6 February 1891 – 15 December 1893
Lt. Gen. Stanislao Mocenni	15 December 1893 – 9 March 1896
Lt. Gen. Cesare Ricotti Magnani	9 March 1896 – 14 July 1896
Lt. Gen. Luigi Pelloux	14 July 1896 – 10 December 1897
Lt. Gen. Alessandro Asinari di San Marzano	10 December 1897 – 14 May 1899
Lt. Gen. Giuseppe Mirri	14 May 1899 – 7 January 1900

Luigi Pelloux (interim)	7 January 1900 – 7 April 1900
Lt. Gen. Coriolano Ponza di San Martino	7 April 1900 – 27 April 1902
Vice Adm. Costantino Morin (interim)	27 April 1902 – 14 May 1902
Lt. Gen. Giuseppe Ottolenghi	14 May 1902 – 3 November 1903
Lt. Gen. Ettore Pedotti	3 November 1903 – 24 December 1905
Lt. Gen. Luigi Majnoni d'Intagnano	24 December 1905 – 27 May 1906
Lt. Gen. Ettore Viganò	27 May 1906 – 29 December 1907
Senator Severino Casana	29 December 1907 – 4 April 1909
Lt. Gen. Paolo Spingardi	4 April 1909 – 24 March 1914
Lt. Gen. Domenico Grandi	24 March 1914 – 11 October 1914
Maj. Gen. Vittorio Zupelli	11 October 1914 – 4 April 1916

Source: Ufficio storico dello Stato maggiore esercito, *L'esercito italiano dal 1° tricolore al 1° centenario*, Rome, 1961, pp. 287–8.

Bibliography

1. UNPUBLISHED SOURCES

Archivio Centrale di Stato

Carte Brusati
Carte Crispi-Roma
Carte Crispi-Reggio Emilia

Minstero della Guerra: Scuole militari
Ministero della Guerra: Gabinetto-Atti Diversi

Istituto per la Storia del Risorgimento

Carte Consenz

Public Record Office

F.O. 45 General Correspondence: Italy, 1870–1906
F.O. 371 General Correspondence: Italy, 1906–1915

Ufficio Storico dello Stato Maggiore dell'Esercito

Addetti Militari: Berlino
Addetti Militari: Cairo
Addetti Militari: Parigi
Addetti Militari: Russia
Addetti Militari: Turchia
Addetti Militari: Vienna

Carteggio Campi, Esercitazioni, Manovre
Carteggio Commissioni di Difesa
Comando del Corpo di Stato Maggiore, G. 24
Comando del Corpo di Stato Maggiore: Corrispondenza
Ordinamento e Mobilitazione
Ordinamenti e Movimenti

Carteggio Eritrea
Volumi Eritrea

Ufficio Storico della Marina Militare

Cartella 199
Cartella 295
Cartella 323

2. NEWSPAPERS AND JOURNALS

Il pensiero militare, 1906–1911
Journal of the Royal United Services Institution, 1880–1914
L'Esercito italiano, 1881–1914
L'Italia militare, 1878–1894
L'Italia militare e marina, 1895–1908
Revue militaire de l'étranger, 1883–1900
Revue militaire suisse, 1878–1898
Rivista militare italiana, 1878–1914

3. PARLIAMENTARY RECORDS

Atti Parlamentari: Camera dei Deputati, 1870–1914
Atti Parlamentari: Senato, 1870–1914

4. BOOKS AND ARTICLES

Alberti, Adriano, *L'opera di S.E. il generale Pollio e l'esercito*, Rome, 1923.
——, *Il generale Falkenhayn. Le relazioni tra i capi di S.M. della Triplice*, Rome, 1934.
Albertini, Luigi. *Venti anni di vita politica Parte Prima*, Bologna, 1950, 1951.
——, *Epistolario I: Dalla guerra di Libia alla Grande Guerra* (O. Bariè, ed.), Milan, 1968.
Allain, J.C., 'Les débuts du conflit italo–turc; Octobre 1911–Janvier 1912', *Revue d'histoire moderne et contemporaine*, XVII 1971, pp. 106–15.
Araldi, Antonio, *Gli errori commessi in Italia nella difesa dello Stato*, Bologna, 1884.
Askew, William C., *Europe and Italy's Acquisition of Libya 1911–1912*, Durham, N.C., 1942.
Avarna Di Gualtieri, C., 'Il Carteggio Avarna-Bollati, luglio 1914–maggio 1915', Parts 1, 2, 3. *Rivista storica italiana,*, LXI, 1949, pp. 248–74; *Rivista storica italiana*, LXII, 1950, pp. 66–87; *Rivista storica italiana*, LXII, 1950, pp. 375–94.
Baratieri, Oreste, *Memorie d'Africa (1892–1896)*, Turin, 1898.
Battaglia, Roberto, *La prima guerra d'Africa*, Turin, 1959.
Bertoldi, Silvio, *Vittorio Emanuele III*, Turin, 1970.
Bogliari, Francesco and Carlo Traversi, *Manfredo Fanti*, Rome, 1980.
Bompiani, Giorgio, *Scritti storici e militari*, Milan, 1937.
Bono, Salvatore, 'Lettere dal fronte libico', *Nuova antologia*, no. 2052, 1971, pp. 528–40.
Bonomi, Ivanoe, *La politica italiana da Porta Pia a Vittorio Veneto (1870–1918)*, Turin, 1944.
Bosworth, R., *Italy, the Least of the Great Powers. Italian Foreign Policy before the First World War*, Cambridge, 1979.
——, *Italy and the Approach of the First World War*, London, 1983.
Bovio, Oreste, 'I primi 15 anni dell'esercito italiano', *Rivista militare*, IC, 1976, pp. 13–19.

Bridge, F.R., *From Sadowa to Sarajevo. The Foreign Policy of Austria-Hungary 1866–1914*, London, 1972.

Bronzuoli, A., *Adua*, Rome, 1935.

Cabiati, Aldo and Ettore Grasselli, *Le guerre coloniali dell'Italia*, Milan, 1935.

Cadorna, Luigi, *Lettere famigliari*, Verona, 1967.

——, *Altre pagine sulla grande guerra*, Milan, 1925.

Candeloro, Giorgio, *Storia dell'Italia moderna*, vol. III, *La rivoluzione nazionale*, Milan, 1960.

——, *Storia dell'Italiana moderna*, vol. IV, *Dalla Rivoluzione nazionale all'Unità*, Milan, 1964.

——, *Storia dell'Italia moderna*, vol. V, *La costruzione dello Stato unitario*, Milan, 1968.

——, *Storia dell'Italia moderna*, vol. VI, *Lo sviluppo del capitalismo e del movimento operaio*, Milan, 1970.

——, *Storia dell'Italia moderna*, vol. VII, *La crisi di fine secolo e l'età giolittiana*, Milan, 1974.

——, *Storia dell'Italia moderna*, vol. VIII, *La prima guerra mondiale, il dopoguerra, l'avvento del fascismo*, Milan, 1978.

Canevari, E. and G. Comisso, *Il generale Tommaso Salsa e le sue campagne coloniali*, Milan, 1935.

Carocci, Giampiero, *Giolitti e l'età Giolittiana*, Turin, 1961.

Caulk, R.A., 'Firearms and princely power in Ethiopia in the nineteenth century', *Journal of African History*, XIII, 1972, pp. 609–30.

Ceva, Lucio, 'L'Alto Comando Militare (1848–1887)' *Nuova Antologia*, 2137, 1981.

——, *Le forze armate*, Turin, 1981.

Chabod, Federico, *Storia della politica estera italiana dal 1870 al 1896*, Bari, 1951/1962.

Chapperon, Alessio, *L'organica militare fra le due guerre mondiali 1814–1914*, Rome, 1921.

Cohen, R., *Threat Perception in International Crisis*, Wisonsin, 1979.

Comando del Corpo di Stato Maggiore Italiano, I Capi di S.M. dell'Esercito: Enrico Cosenz, Rome, 1935.

——, *Domenico Primerano*, Rome, 1935.

——, *Tancredi Saletta*, Rome, 1935.

——, *Alberto Pollio*, Rome, 1935.

Corsi, Carlo, *1844–1869: venticinque anni in Italia*, Florence 1870.

——, *Italia 1870–1895*, Turin, 1896.

Dabormida, V., *La difesa della nostra frontiera occidentale in relazione agli ordinamenti militari odierni*, Turin, 1878.

D'Angiolini, Piero, Giampiero Carocci and Claudio Pavone, eds, *Dalle carte di Giovanni Giolitti: Quarant'anni di politica italiana*, 3 vols, Milan, 1962.

De Angeli, Felice, *Storia di Casa Savoia*, Milan, 1906.

De Biase, Carlo, *Aquila d'Oro-Storia dello Stato Maggiore Italiano (1861–1945)*, Milan, 1969.

De Bono, Emilio, *Nell'esercito nostro prima della guerra*, Milan, 1931.

De Chaurand de Saint Eustache, Felice, *Come l'esercito italiano entrò in guerra*, Milan, Mondadori, 1929.

Decleva, E., *Da Adua a Sarajevo. La politica estera italiana e la Francia 1896–1914*, Bari, 1971.

Della Rocca, E., *Autobiography of a Veteran 1807–1893*, London, 1899.

De Rosa, Luigi, 'Incidenze delle spese militari sullo sviluppo economico italiano', *Atti del primo Convegno Nazionale di Storia Militare*, Rome, 1969.

De Rossi, Eugenio, *La vita di un ufficiale italiano sino alla guerra*, Milan, 1927.

Del Boca, Angelo, *Gli italiani in Africa orientale dall'unità alla marcia su Roma*, Bari, 1976.

——, *Gli italiani in Libia: Tripoli, bel suol d'amore, 1860–1922*, Bari, 1986.

Del Negro, Piero, *Esercito, stato, società*, Bologna, 1979.

Documents diplomatiques français, 1st series IX, Paris, 1939; 1st series X, Paris, 1945; 1st series XI, Paris, 1947; 2nd series V, Paris, 1934; 3rd Series II, Paris, 1931.

Farini, Domenico, *Diario di fine secolo*, ed. Emilia Morelli, Rome, 1962.

Farolfi, Bernardino, 'Dall'antropometria militare alla storia del corpo', *Quaderni storici*, XLII, 1979, pp. 1056–91.

Fiorentino, Fiorenza, *Ordine pubblico nell'Italia giolittiana*, Rome, 1978.

Gabriele, M. and A. Friz, *La politica navale italiana dal 1885 al 1915*, Rome, 1982.

Gallinari, Vincenzo, 'Le riforme militari di Cesare Ricotti, *Memorie storiche militari*, 1978, pp. 11–33.

Ginsborg, Paul, *Daniele Manin and the Venetian Revolution of 1848–49*, Cambridge, 1979.

Giolitti, Giovanni, *Memoirs of my Life*, London, 1923.

Gooch, John, 'L'Italia contro la Francia: I piani di guerra difensivi ed offensivi 1870–1914', *Memorie storiche militari*, 1980, pp. 153–67.

——, 'Italy before 1915: The Quandary of the Vulnerable', in E.R. May (ed.), *Knowing One's Enemies: Intelligence Assessment before the Two World Wars*, Princeton, N.J., 1984, pp. 205–33.

——, 'Clausewitz Disregarded: Italian military thought and doctrine, 1815–1943', in M.I. Handel (ed.), *Clausewitz and Modern Strategy*, London, 1986, pp. 303–24.

Grew, Raymond, *A Sterner Plan for Unity: The Italian National Society in the Risorgimento*, Princeton, N.J., 1963.

Guardione, Francesco, *Il generale Enrico Cosenz*, Palermo, 1900.

Halpern, Paul, G., *The Mediterranean Naval Situation 1908–1914*, Harvard, 1971.

Herrman, D.G., *Italian Strategy in the Libyan War, 1911–1915*, M. Litt., Oxford, 1987.

Hill, Richard, *Egypt in the Sudan 1829–1881*, London, 1959.

Holt, P.M., *The Mahdist State in the Sudan, 1881–1898. A Study of Its Origins, Development and Overthrow*, Oxford, 1958.

——, *A Modern History of the Sudan*, London, 1961.

I Documenti Diplomatici Italiani, 1870–1939. Ministero degli Affari Esteri, Rome, 1952–.

Labanca, Nicola, *Il generale Cesare Ricotti e la politica militare italiana dal 1884 al 1887*, Rome, 1986.

Levra, Umberto, *Il colpo di stato della borghesia. La crisi Politica di fine secolo in Italia 1898/1900*, Milan, 1975.

Licata, Glauco, 'Il Corriere della sera e la Triplice', *Atti del VII Congresso nazionale di storia del giornalismo*, Trieste, 1972, pp. 277–85.

Lollio, Luciano, 'La battaglia d'Adua' *Rivista della guardia di finanza*, XX, 1971, pp. 303–28.

Lowe, C.J., 'Anglo–Italian Differences over East Africa, 1892–1895', *English Historical Review*, LXXXI, 1966, pp. 315–36.

———, 'Britain and Italian Intervention, 1914–1915', *Historical Journal*, XII, 1969, pp. 533–48.

———, and F. Marzari, *Italian Foreign Policy 1870–1940*, London, 1975.

Mack Smith, Denis, *Victor Emanuel, Cavour and the Risorgimento*, Oxford, 1971.

———, *Storia di cento anni di vita italiana – visto attraverso il Corriere della sera*, Milan, 1978.

Malagodi, Olindo, *Conversazioni della guerra* I: *Da Sarajevo a Caporetto*, ed. Brunello Vigezzi, Milan–Naples, 1960.

Malgeri, Franceso, *La guerra libica*, Rome, 1970.

Maravigna, Pietro (ed.), *Un Secolo di Progresso Italiano nelle Scienze militari 1839–1939*, Rome, 1940.

Marcus, Harold, G., *The Life and Times of Menelik II. Ethiopia 1844–1913*, Oxford, 1975.

Marsden, Arthur, 'Britain and the "Tunis Base", 1894–1899', *English Historical Review*, LXXIX, 1964, pp. 67–96.

———, 'Salisbury and the Italians in 1896', *Journal of Modern History*, 40, 1968, pp. 91–117.

Marselli, Niccola, *La guerra e la sua storia*, Milan, 1881.

———, *Gli avvenimenti del 1870–71*, Turin, 1893.

———, *La vita del reggimento*, Rome, 1903.

Martel, Charles (pseud. of C.àC. Repington), *Military Italy*, London, 1884.

Martini, Ferdinando, *Diario 1914–1918*, ed. Gabriele De Rosa, Milan, 1966.

Mazzetti, Massimo, 'Dagli Eserciti pre-unitari all'esercito italiano', *Rassegna storica del Risorgimento*, LIX, 1972, pp. 563–92.

Mazzetti, Massimo, *L'esercito italiano nella triplice alleanza: Aspetti della politica estera 1870–1914*, Naples, 1974.

———, 'Enrico Cosenz, scrittore militare', *Il pensiero di studiosi di cose militari meridionali: Atti del Congresso Nazionale*, Rome, 1978.

Melograni, Piero, *Storia politica della Grande Guerra, 1915/1918*, Bari, 1969.

Mezzacapo, Luigi, *Armi e politica*, Rome, 1881.

Ministero della guerra, *Campagna di Libia*, I, Rome, 1922, 1938.

———, *L'Esercito italiano nella grande guerra (1915–1918)*, I, Rome, 1927/1974.

———, *Storia militare della Colonia Eritrea*, Rome, 1935, 1936.

Minnitti, Fortunato, 'Esercito e politica da Porta Pia alla Triplice Allenza (I)', *Storia contemporanea*, III, 1972, pp. 465–502.

———, 'Esercito e politica da Porta Pia alla Triplice Alleanza (II)' *Storia contemporanea*, IV, 1973.

———, 'Il secondo piano generale delle fortificazione: Studio e progetti (1880–1885)', *Memorie Storiche Militari*, 1980, pp. 91–119.

Molfese, F., *Storia del brigantaggio dopo l'unità*, Milan, 1964.

Montanelli, Indro and Nozza, Marco, *Garibaldi*, Milan, 1962.

Monticone, Alberto, *La Germania e la neutralità italiana 1914–1915*, Bologna, 1971.

———, 'Sonnino e Salandra verso la decione dell' intervento' in 'AA.VV.', *Gli italiani in uniforme*, Bari, 1972.

Mori, Renato, *La politica estera di Francesco Crispi (1887–1891)*, Rome, 1973.

Moscati, Amadeo, *I Ministri del Regno d'Italia*, III, Rome, 1960; IV, Rome, 1964.

Nellisen, Niek, 'Le"corrierre della Sera" et la campagne de presse á propos de la Libye (1910–1911)' *Risorgimento*, 1980, pp. 295–316.

Palamenghi-Crispi, T., *The Memoirs of Francesco Crispi*, London, 1912.

Palumbo, Michael, 'German–Italian Military Relations on the Eve of World War I', *Central European History*, XII, 1979, pp. 343–71.

Pankhurst, Richard, *Economic History of Ethiopia*, Addis Ababa, 1968.

Pedotti, Ettore, *Enrico Cosenz*, Rome, 1898.

Pelloux, Luigi, *Quelques souvenirs de ma vie*, ed. Gastone Manacorda, Rome, 1967.

Perucchetti, G., *Teatro di guerra Italo-Svizzera*, Turin, 1878.

——, *La difesa dello stato*, Turin, 1884.

Pesci, Ugo, *Il generale Carlo Mezzacapo e il suo tempo*, Bologna, 1908.

Pieri, Piero, 'Il problema del reclutamento in Piemonte nel 1848–49', *Nuova Rivista Storica*, XXXII, 1948, pp. 263–78.

——, *Guerra e politica negli scrittori italiani*, Milan-Naples, 1955.

——, *Le forze armate nella età della Destra*, Milan, 1962.

——, *Storia militare del Risorgimento*, Turin, 1962.

——, 'Orientamento per lo studio di una storia delle dottrine militari in Italia', *Atti del primo convegno nazionale di storia militare', Rome, 1969, pp. 123–62*.

Pischedda, Carlo, 'L'azione di Carlo Alberto nelle campagne del 1848–49', *Nuova Rivista Storica*, XXXI, 1947, pp. 125–54.

Radziwill, *Lettres de la princesse Radziwill au General de Robilant (1889–1914)*, 4 vols, Bologna, 1933.

Ragionieri, E., *Risorgimento e Risistenza*, Rome, 1964.

Ramm, Agatha, 'Great Britain and the Planting of Italian Power in the Red Sea, 1868–1885', *English Historical Review*, LIX, 1944, pp. 211–36.

——, (ed.), *The Political Correspondence of Mr. Gladstone and Lord Granville 1876–1886*, Oxford, 1962.

Renzi, W.A., 'Italy's Neutrality and Entrance into the Great War: A Re-examination', *American Historical Review*, LXXIII, 1968, pp. 1414–32.

Repaci, A., *La finanza pubblica italiana nel secolo 1861–1960*, Bologna, 1962.

Ricci, A., *Appunti sulla difesa d'Italia in generale e della frontiera nordovest in particolare*, Turin, 1872.

Roberts, L.E., 'Italy and the Egyptian Question, 1878–1882', *Journal of Modern History*, 18, 1946, pp. 314–32.

Robinson, Ronald and John Gallagher with Alice Denny, *Africa and the Victorians: The Official Mind of Imperialism*, London, 1967.

Rocca, Gianni, *Cadorna*, Milan, 1985.

Rochat, Giorgio, 'La preparazione dell'esercito italiano nell'inverno 1914–1915 in relazione alle informazioni disponibili sulla guerra di posizione', *Risorgimento*, XIII, 1961, pp. 10–32.

——, 'L'esercito italiano nell'estate 1914', *Nuova Rivista Storica*, 45, 1961, pp. 295–348.

——, and Giulio Massobrio, *Breva storia dell'esercito italiano dal 1861 al 1943*, Turin, 1978.

Rodd, James Rennell, *Social and Diplomatic Memories 1909–1919*, London, 1925.

Romandini, Massimo, 'La "Gazetta di Adua"' *Africa*, 36, 1981, pp. 306–14.
Romano, Sergio, *La quarta sponda. La guerra di Libia, 1911/1912*, Milan, 1977.
Roncati, Michele, *Brevi Commenti ai quattro discorsi del generale Alfonso La Marmora*, Turin, 1871.
Rota, E., *Il 1848 nella storia italiana ed europea*, Milan, 1948.
Rotberg, R. and A.A. Mazrui (eds), *Power and Protest in Black Africa*, New York, 1970.
Rubenson, Sven, *The Survival of Ethiopian Independence*, London, Addis Ababa, 1976.
Russi, Luciano, *Carlo Pisacane: Vita e pensiero di un rivoluzionario*, Milan, 1982.
Sala, Gerolamo, *Esercito e Militarismo*, Milan, 1899.
Salandra, Antonio, *La neutralità italiana [1914]: Ricordi e pensieri*, Milan, 1928.
Sanderson, G.N., 'England, Italy, the Nile Valley and the European Balance, 1890–91' *Historical Journal*, VII, 1964, pp. 94–118.
Segre, Roberto, *Vienna e Belgrado 1876–1914*, Milan, 1935.
Seton Watson, Christopher, *Italy from Liberalism to Fascism*, London, 1967.
Silberstein, G.E., 'The High Command the Diplomacy in Austria-Hungary 1914–1916', *Journal of Modern History*, 42, 1970, pp. 586–605.
Sonnino, Sidney, *Diario 1866–1912*, ed. Benjamin F. Brown, Bari, 1972.
——, *Diario 1914–1916*, ed. Pietro Pastorelli, Bari, 1972.
——, *Carteggio 1914–1916*, ed. Pietro Pastorelli, Bari, 1974.
Stearns, Peter N., *The Revolutions of 1848*, London, 1974.
Stefani, Filippo, *La storia della dottrina e degli ordinamenti dell'esercito italiano*, I, Rome, 1984.
Stella, Sabino, *La pace perpetua e l'esercito*, Turin, 1891.
Stone, Norman, 'Moltke and Conrad: Relations between the Austro-Hungarian and German General Staffs, 1909–1914', in P. Kennedy, ed., *The War Plans of the Great Powers*, London, 1979, pp. 222–51.
Thayer, John A., *Italy and the Great War. Politics and Culture, 1870–1915*, Madison and Milwaukee, 1964.
Thayer, W.R., *The Life and Times of Cavour*, II, New York, 1971, (1st edn 1911).
Theobald, A.B., *The Mahdiya. A History of the Anglo-Egyptian Sudan, 1881–1899*, London 1951.
Tommasini, Francesco, *L'Italia alla vigilia della Guerra: la politica estera di Tommaso Tittoni*, Bologna, 1934–41.
Tosti, Amadeo, *La spedizione italiana in Cina (1900–1901)*, Rome, 1926.
——, *Storia dell'esercito italiano (1861–1936)*, Milan, 1942.
Traniello, Vincenze, *Il tenente generale Alberto Pollio*, Bologna, 1919.
Treves, Fratelli, *La formazione de l'impero coloniale italiano*, I, Milan, 1938.
Varanini, Varo, *L'Abissina attuale*, Turin, 1935.
Varanini, Varo, *Storia della guerra italiana*, vol. XIV, *I Capi, le armi, i combattenti*, Milan, 1935.
Visani, Piero, '"Guerra di Popolo" e "Guerra regia" nel Risorgimento', *Politica militare*, IV, 1982, pp. 59–67.
Whittam, John, *The Politics of the Italian Army*, London, 1977.
——, 'War Aims and Strategy: The Italian Government and High Command 1914–1919', in B. Hunt and A. Preston, *War Aims and Strategy in the Great War 1914–1918*, 1977, pp. 85–104.
Zaghi, Carlo, *P.S. Mancini, l'Africa e il problema del Mediterraneo*, Rome, 1956.
——, *L'Europa davanti all'Africa. La via del Nilo*, Naples, 1971.

Index

Index